Konoe Fumimaro and the Failure
of Peace in Japan, 1937–1941

Konoe Fumimaro and the Failure of Peace in Japan, 1937–1941

A Critical Appraisal of the Three-Time Prime Minister

KAZUO YAGAMI

McFarland & Company, Inc., Publishers

Jefferson, North Carolina, and London

LIBRARY OF CONGRESS CATALOGUING-IN-PUBLICATION DATA

Yagami, Kazuo.
   Konoe Fumimaro and the failure of peace in Japan, 1937–1941 :
a critical appraisal of the three-time prime minister / Yagami Kazuo.
    p.   cm.
   Includes bibliographical references and index.

   ISBN 0-7864-2242-4 (softcover : 50# alkaline paper)

   1. Konoe, Fumimaro, 1891–1945.   2. Prime ministers—
Japan—Biography.   3. Japan—Politics and government—
1926–1945.   I. Title.
DS885.5.K6Y34   2006
952.03'3092—dc22   2005034167

British Library cataloguing data are available

On the cover: Konoe Fumimaro *(Mainichi Photo Bank)*

Manufactured in the United States of America

McFarland & Company, Inc., Publishers
  Box 611, Jefferson, North Carolina 28640
   www.mcfarlandpub.com

To my wife, Frances, and two children,
Michelle and Michael.
They are the heart of my life.

Contents

Preface

Prince Konoe Fumimaro served as Prime Minister three times during the period of the most turbulent era of the history of modern Japan from the China Incident in July 1937 to Japan's Pearl Harbor assault in December 1941. Despite his tenacious effort to save Japan from taking its tragic path, Konoe was destined to fail and face the fate of the nation — the ultimate defeat and national humiliation of foreign occupation — and the tragic finale of his own life on December 16, 1945, four months after Japan's fall.

This book attempts to portray in a fair fashion this tumultuous experience of Konoe as Japan's most decorated court noble and politician and yet a grossly misunderstood individual. It consists of six chapters.

The first chapter is a brief sketch of Konoe's upbringing, educational background, and political training. It is highlighted by the publication of Konoe's sensational and controversial article "Reject the Anglo-American–Centered Peace," Konoe's first meeting with his political "mentor," Prince Saionji Kinmochi, Konoe's disappointing experience at the Paris Peace Conference, and his effort to reform the House of Peers.

The second chapter describes the tumultuous 1930s and the rise of Konoe as a "Messier"-like figure who would save the deeply troubled nation, characterized by rapidly emerging right-wing militarism, the decline of party politics, and the development of political conflict between Saionji and Konoe over the issue of determining the course Japan should pursue.

The third chapter talks about Konoe's first cabinet. The focus of this chapter is the China Incident, which took place only a month after Konoe's inauguration as Prime Minister in June 1937, and Konoe's endeavor to achieve a diplomatic settlement of the incident with the nationalist government of China in order to stop the deterioration of Japan's relationship with the Western powers subsequent to the incident. The chapter ends with the illustration of Konoe's frustration and disappointment when he had to step down from premiership, and was replaced by a contrasting figure, Hiranuma Kiichiro, known to be laconic and cautious.

The fourth and fifth chapters deal with Konoe's return to the premiership, his continuous effort to achieve a settlement of the China Incident, his engagement in U.S.-Japan diplomatic talks. These chapters provide detailed accounts of a series of policies Konoe undertook, starting with national mobilization, the creation of the National Service Association (Taisei Yokusankai), the Wang Ching-wei maneuver, the Tripartite Pact, and Konoe's proposed summit with Franklin Roosevelt. As discussed in the fifth chapter, the readers of this book should find the most shining moment of Konoe's political life in his attempt to achieve a diplomatic settlement with the United States. Contrary to Konoe's general reputation as a weak and indecisive politician, he was tenacious and firmly committed to the cause.

The last chapter describes Konoe's war experience and the twilight of his life from the end of the war to his death on December 16, 1945. It also talks about Konoe's effort to achieve an early termination of the war, his reaction to Japan's defeat, his expectations of and involvement in the aftermath of the defeat, and the irony of his fate that led to Konoe's suicide.

My overall aim with this book is to provide not only a fair account of Konoe and his role as a politician but also a concisely written description of the turbulent era of Japanese politics from the 1920s to the end of 1945.

Such success as I have achieved would have never been possible without the assistance I have received from various institutions and individuals. First of all, a word of appreciation goes to Florida State University and the Association for the Asian Studies, Inc. Both institutions provided me with monetary assistance. Their generosity made it possible for me to conduct productive research at the Library of Congress and elsewhere.

I am also thankful to Dr. Winston W. Lo, Dr. Neil T. Jumonville, and Dr. Peter P. Garretson of Florida State University, Professor Kondo Masaomi of Daito Bunka University in Tokyo, and the staff of the Asian Reading Center at the Library of Congress for the various suggestions, encouragement, and assistance I have received from them. I owe them a great deal for making it possible for me to complete this project.

My special thanks also go to my former schoolmates Dr. Roy Campbell and Dr. James Maynor, Jr., who spent many hours on proofreading and editing my entire manuscript. I would like to express my gratitude also to Mr. Yang Jun-gin, doctoral candidate at Florida State University, who kindly helped me to have proper pronunciation of Chinese names and words. Thanks to these individuals, many errors that I would have made otherwise, have been avoided. The errors that remain are of course mine alone.

Lastly, my greatest appreciation goes to my wife, Frances. Without the cooperation and sacrifices she made to support me in many ways, my manuscript would have never been completed.

In the text that follows, all Japanese and Chinese personal names are written in an Oriental style — a surname first followed by a given name.

Introduction

At dawn on December 16, 1945, just a few hours before he was to appear at Sugamo Prison in Tokyo as a war criminal, Konoe Fumimaro, the former Prime Minister of Japan, was found dead. He had killed himself by taking potassium cyanide. He was 54.

For Japan, the death of Konoe was far more than a tragic finale of his life. It also symbolized the end of the most turbulent and critical epoch Japan had ever witnessed. It was the time in which Japan, along with Germany and Italy, had challenged the world's existing political, economic, and ideological structures. Democracy and capitalism were put on trial by two newly rising ideologies: Fascism and Nazism.

Parallel to this turbulent and dynamic epoch-making struggle were the equally tumultuous challenges Japan faced internally. The right-wing nationalists, the driving force for Japan's challenge to the existing world order, attempted to dismantle Japan's adopted western political and economic systems, seeing them as insufficient, outmoded for carrying out their mission, and, more importantly, the root cause of destruction of the indigenous national character. They challenged the status quo of pro-western authority, parliamentary government, party politics, and capitalism. It was an attempt to undo what had been established through the Meiji Restoration and the subsequent modernization, and to restart Japan's quest by creating a new system that would be more applicable to national spirit than the existing system. Japan found itself on the verge of a stormy political and economic reform movement that was later called the Showa Restoration. It divided Japanese society intricately and critically over the direction the nation should take. The rapid rise of militarism and political instability was further intensified by factionalism in the military and politics in the late 1920s and early 1930s.

The background of this rise of militarism and right-wing nationalism is traced to major international occurrences, particularly Japan's involvement in China. It began when Japan emerged as a victor first in the Sino-Japanese War in 1895 and again a decade later in the Russo-Japanese

War in 1905. These victories brought Japan onto the world stage of politics, consequently creating tension between Japan and the other major powers, first with the Soviet Union and later with the Anglo-Saxon powers.

Despite the military clash in 1895, at the beginning of the twentieth century the Sino-Japanese relationship was not necessarily characterized by animosity only. For instance, convinced that China had to follow Japan's success in modernization, a considerable number of Chinese students came to Japan to study. By 1906, the number of Chinese students studying in Japan had reached 1,300.[1] The most prominent of these students was Sun Yat-sen, who lived in Japan from 1897 to 1903, using it as the base for his revolutionary activities. These students, including Sun, established a good relationship with the Japanese leaders who were sympathetic to their revolutionary cause. Among those Japanese leaders were ultranationalist Toyama Mitsuru, future Prime Minister Inukai Tsuyoshi, and radical socialists Kotoku Shusui and Kita Ikki.

Many Japanese also went to China, motivated by various reasons. Some went there out of a sense of altruism, some for the spirit of adventure, and some for the cause of Japanese imperialism. Among them, most memorable is Kita Ikki. As a strong advocate of socialism, Kita went to China twice in 1911 and 1916 to support the Chinese Revolution.[2]

It took little time, however, before the Sino-Japanese relationship turned sour as Japan began to exploit China's political instability. After the fall of the Manchu dynasty in 1911, Yuan Shih-k'ai established a republic, along with Sun Yat-sen. China later became divided, however, when Yuan arbitrarily tried to establish his own dynasty. Then, after the death of Yuan in 1916, China entered the era of warlords. Despite Sun Yat-sen's effort to unify the nation under his three principles— nationalism, democracy, and people's livelihood — China's political instability was worsened, creating an opportunity for Japan to take advantage of the situation for political and economic exploitation.

The most notorious action taken by Japan was the submission of the Twenty-one Demands to China in 1915. With other major powers unable to intervene on behalf of China because of their preoccupation with World War I, Yuan Shih-k'ai had no choice but to accept the Japanese demands. Naturally this acceptance raised enormous outrage among the Chinese nationals. Such outrage was further intensified with the 1919 Versailles Peace Settlement, which accepted the Japanese demand to legalize Japan's control over both Shantung and the Pacific islands that were formerly owned by Germany. This outrage resulted in a nationwide anti-Japanese movement known as the May Fourth Movement, led by students and intellectuals.

Despite this continuous turmoil in China, the following decade of the 1920s was considered a period of international cooperation. It began with the Washington Conference in 1921–22 at which a series of agreements were made. First, in 1921, in the Four Power Pacific Treaty, the United States, Great Britain, France, and Japan agreed to maintain the status quo of each nation in terms of their possessions in the Pacific. This was followed in 1922 by the Five Power Naval Treaty (the above four nations plus Italy), which was meant to achieve naval arms reduction, and the Nine Power Treaty (the nations in the Five Power Naval Treaty plus the Netherlands, Belgium, Portugal, and China), which dealt with the principles and policies regarding Chinese issues. Along with the other major powers, Japan signed these treaties. Shidehara Kijuro, one of the Japanese delegates to the conference, became Foreign Minister shortly after the conference and promoted harmonious foreign policy, so-called Shidehara Diplomacy. Then, in 1925, the Treaty of Locarno was signed by France, Germany, and Great Britain as a mechanism to establish a mutual security. Under this treaty, Germany became a member of the League of Nations and pledged to settle any future problems in a peaceful fashion. The 1928 Kellogg-Briand Pact followed the Treaty of Locarno. All major powers but Russia signed it. The pact denounced all wars except those for self-defense. Seemingly, Wilsonian democracy was indeed on the way to becoming reality.

As it turned out, however, the era of peace had little substance. In the Nine Power Treaty, the signatory nations made a pledge to respect the sovereignty, independence, and territorial integrity of China. They also agreed to respect the principle of the Open Door policy — equal opportunity in commerce in China for all nations. No nation, however, actually had any intention of following up on these principles, refusing to renounce the unequal treaties imposed on China during the nineteenth century.

Thus, it was rather inevitable that this decade-long period of international cooperation would come to a halt when the U.S. stock market crashed in 1929, followed by worldwide and unprecedented economic depression. Japan was one of the nations most severely hit by this economic collapse. Boosted by the war economy associated with World War I, Japan had been in good shape economically until the end of the 1910s. Shortly after the war was over, however, the Japanese economy began to decline. After the catastrophic earthquake on September 1, 1923, Japan was already facing an economic crisis by the eve of the 1929 stock market crash in the United States.[3] Hence, the impact of the stock market crash on Japan and the following depression was enormous. As will be discussed later, along with this economic problem, by the late 1920s Japan became politically and socially unstable as shown in the decline of party politics and the rapid rise of militarism and right-wing nationalism.

The Manchurian Incident in 1931 was one ramification of such political, social, and economic turmoil, and this was followed by a series of political assassinations and coups d'etat in the 1930s. Then the Marco Polo Bridge Incident took place in 1937. Although initially considered to be a minor incident, it quickly escalated into a major war between Japan and China, causing apprehension in the West about Japan's aggression as a growing threat to their interests in the Far East and Southeast Asia. It was the beginning of a shift in the nature of the Sino-Japanese conflict, from regional to global. The West began to put economic pressure on Japan through sanctions. In order to deal with such increasing menaces, Japan took a series of countermeasures: national mobilization, the creation of the new political structure, the Wang Ching-wei maneuver, the Tripartite Pact, and then, as the last resort, seeking a diplomatic settlement of the Sino-Japanese conflict through intensive negotiations with the United States. None, however, bore fruit, resulting in Japan's Pearl Harbor assault at the end of 1941.

It was during this critical period in Japan's prewar era, 1937–1941, that Konoe took the center stage of Japanese politics. Becoming Prime Minister three times during this short period, he took far greater responsibility than any politician could ever imagine in Japan's effort to find a diplomatic solution to the crisis. As history has witnessed, however, Konoe failed. This failure resulted in not only his personal tragedy but also in great national tragedy. It brought Japan into a "doomed" conflict with the United States and ended in devastating defeat, followed by the humiliating experience of submitting to the occupation of foreign powers.

Not surprisingly, the robust popularity Konoe received in the prewar era plummeted. Along with Tojo, he became a prime target of the public in their quest to find someone who ought to be responsible for Japan's defeat. Similarly, before the war, journalists and academicians had treated Konoe as a rising star. They praised Konoe as someone who could save Japan from national crisis. These same people, however, became critical in their postwar assessment of Konoe. Most of the postwar writings on Konoe have one thing in common: an assertion that it was his character flaws (a weak mind and indecisiveness) that ultimately caused Konoe's failure, making him frequently bungle at crucial moments.

One may find this assertion plausible because Konoe was fundamentally irresolute, and he himself was aware of it. It was indeed this awareness that partially made him reluctant to lead the nation. In 1936, when the Okada cabinet fell after the February Twenty-six Incident, Prince

Saionji (1849–1940), as a Genro, recommended Konoe to the Emperor as Okada's successor, but Konoe turned down the recommendation.[4] Clearly, Konoe's own doubt about himself with regard to his suitability for leadership was one factor in his decision.

No matter how plausible it seems, however, the above assertion is difficult to sustain. Konoe's reign came at the time when Japan was going through its most difficult time internally and externally. Internally Japan was intricately divided, particularly with regard to coordination between the civilian government and the military. With the rapid decline of the political parties in the early 1930s and the simultaneously rising military power, the civilian government and the military became too estranged to make a coordinated effort to deal with many pressing issues. The military began to function as if it were an autonomous institution, making it extremely hard for the civilian government to enact any effective policies. When Konoe took office in 1937, with the recently re-instituted requirement of selecting an Army Minister from among the active generals, the military had almost reached the point of having absolute autonomy, keeping the government often unaware of ongoing military actions. Konoe took various efforts to alter the situation; however, none succeeded.

Externally as well, Konoe had little capacity to have any control over unfolding international events, as indicated in the following examples. In 1937, Japan concluded the Anti-Comintern Alliance with Germany and Italy. The initial reason for Japan to join this alliance was to check Communist expansion and the Soviet threat to Japanese interests in Manchuria and northern China. It was, however, abruptly shattered by the German-Soviet Non-Aggression Pact in August 1939. Then, in late 1940, the Konoe government leaned toward the Tripartite Pact. This time, Konoe hoped that the Soviet Union would be on the side of the Axis in order to keep the United States out of the European conflict. Konoe's hope, however, was once again shattered by the German decision to invade the Soviet Union in June 1941. To Konoe, this made the pact meaningless. One has to wonder how relevant Konoe's personality would have been with regard to these two German decisions. After this debacle over the Tripartite Pact, Konoe realized that the only option left for him to save Japan from a fatal confrontation with the Allied powers was to reach a diplomatic settlement with the United States to solve the China Incident. Once again Konoe faced a situation that was too much for him to cope with. Neither Japan nor the United States was able to compromise over the U.S. key demand for reaching a diplomatic settlement with Japan — a total withdrawal of the Japanese troops from China and Indo-China. Although Konoe displayed unusual tenacity and assertiveness in his effort, he was destined to fail from the outset.

Thus, internally and externally, Konoe had little control over the unfolding events, making the assertion that he ultimately failed because of his character flaws superficial at best. Taking into consideration this perfunctory and stereotyped assertion, this study attempts to produce a more fair and balanced account of Konoe and his era. Accordingly, it focuses little on Konoe's character but instead makes a close examination of how the external and internal circumstances of Japanese politics and economy shaped Konoe's policy making.

The sources used for this study are both secondary and primary. While some secondary sources such as *Konoe Fumimaro* by Yabe Teiji, *The Road to the Pacific War* (eight volumes by the Academy of Japan International Politics— Study Group on the Cause of Pacific War), *Konoe Fumimaro: Emperor, Military, and Nation* by Okada Takeo, and numerous contemporary articles, mostly written in the 1930s and early 1940s, provide good background, the bulk of this study relies on primary sources.[5] The most significant and useful are the two writings by Konoe himself, *Seidanroku* and *Ushinawareshi Seiji (Lost Politics)*, and the diary of Harada Kumao.[6]

Seidanroku, consisting of various essays by Konoe, is an excellent source for understanding his personality and the roots of his ideological and political thoughts. *Ushinawareshi Seiji* is a memoir covering the period from Konoe's first cabinet to the end of the Pacific war. It provides in great detail an account of Konoe's political involvements over the major issues. *Diary of Harada Kumao* is a set of nine volumes. Throughout his diary, Harada, a personal secretary of Prince Saionji with wide-ranging personal associations with those who shaped the most turbulent era of Japanese modern history, provides the inside stories of contemporary Japanese politics. It is a great source in helping us to understand the complex and divided nature of Japanese politics. In addition, the documents Kido Koichi, the diaries of Kido Koichi, Ugaki, and Yabe, the memoirs of Cordell Hull and Joseph C. Grew, and Konoe's numerous public speeches and statements also provide important information that gives added depth to this study. Incidentally, except for very few materials, most of the sources used for this study are written in Japanese. Accordingly, most of the quotes in this study are translations from Japanese to English. Little work on Konoe has been done by non-Japanese scholars. *The Search for a New Political Order: Konoe Fumimaro, the Political Parties, and Japanese Politics During the Early Showa Era* by Gordon M. Berger is the only significant work done by a non-Japanese scholar.

Considering the scarcity of work on Konoe in English, although this study is not particularly addressed to a non-Japanese audience, it will make a significant contribution by providing a rare account of Konoe in English for non-Japanese readers. It is rather strange to find that, despite Konoe's stature and the crucial role he played — in many ways greater than Tojo's— Western scholars have paid little attention to Konoe. While that alone makes this study significant, as stated earlier, the primary significance of this study comes from the establishment of a better understanding of one of the most unfairly assessed political figures, Konoe Fumimaro, and his role in modern Japanese history. It has been six decades since the end of World War II. Yet the ramifications of that war are still relevant to our lives, making historians continuously reengage in writing on the war in order to better understand it. In such engagement, it is a firm belief of the author of this study that a proper understanding of Konoe and his role is indispensable.

1

Konoe's Background and Upbringing

On October 12, 1891, Konoe Fumimaro was born in Tokyo as an heir of the Prince Konoe family, the head of the five regency families.[1] His mythological ancestry goes back even to the prehistoric age of the gods in close association with the Imperial family. According to legend, the founder of the Konoe family, Amemokoyane no Mikoto, ranked highest among the gods who greeted Ninigino Mikoto, grandson of the goddess Amaterasu, on his descent to Japanese soil, and from him sprang the Fujiwara family.[2] The Fujiwara family for centuries had conducted ceremonial affairs of the Imperial Court and played an important role in national development. It is well known historically that Fujiwara Kamatari, one of the most powerful figures of the Fujiwara family, played a significant role in the success of the AD 645 *Taika* Reforms (Great Political Reforms). During the Fujiwara Period (894–c. 1200), Japan made enormous cultural growth, and generation after generation the Fujiwara family played the role of regent giving political assistance to the Emperor. Konoe was a direct descendant of this extremely distinguished noble court family, Fujiwara.

One of the descendants of the Fujiwara family, Motomichi, took the name of Konoe. He resigned from the post of regent in 1202 when he was unable to get along with Minamoto Yoritomo, who ended the rule of the long-lasting aristocracy by establishing a feudal government in Kamakura in 1183. Then Yoritomo took the policy of separation of the regency, creating five regent families, including the Konoe family as head regent.[3] Meanwhile, the seventeenth generation of the Fujiwara family, Nobutada, did not have any sons. The fourth son of the Emperor, Goyosei, became his heir. This was the direct infusion of imperial blood into the Konoe family.

With this impressive noble birth, Konoe was destined to have a prestigious future. Indeed, he had prestige in his public life except during the brief period of the post–World War II era. In his private life, however, he was not so fortunate. Literally from the moment of his birth, Konoe's life was struck by tragedy. His mother Sawako died from the complications of childbirth, only eight days after Konoe's birth. She was only twenty-three years old. A year later, Konoe's father, Atsumaro, married Sawako's sister, Motoko, giving Konoe one half brother and three half sisters. Konoe was not told that Motoko was not his birth mother. When the truth was finally revealed to him, he was already a young adult. Having kept believing that Motoko was his real mother, he was deeply shocked and greatly affected emotionally by this news. In his later years, Konoe had repeatedly said, "Until I reached adult age, I had been made to believe that my stepmother Motoko was my real mother. After the truth was revealed to me, I could not help thinking that the world was full of lies."[4]

The second tragedy struck Konoe when he was fourteen years old — the death of his father, Atsumaro, at the age of forty-two. Born with a diligent and rather aggressive nature, Atsumaro had excelled in his life, particularly at school. In April 1885, when Prince Saionji Kinmochi (1849–1940) left Japan for Europe as a minister to Austria, Atsumaro followed Saionji across the ocean to study abroad. He spent more than five years in Germany.[5] In September 1890, he returned to Japan and began to get involved in politics. Despite his youth, Atsumaro became remarkably successful in a short time. In 1895 he became the head of Gakushuin (an academic institution for court nobles), and in the following year became the president of the House of Peers. He was only thirty-two years old.

Atsumaro was a supporter of constitutionalism in internal politics, and in foreign affairs he was a strong advocate of nationalism.[6] This aspect was particularly prominent in his view on East Asia. After Japan's victory in the Sino-Japanese War of 1894–95, sensing an increasing tension between Western imperial powers in East Asia and Japan as a newly emerging Asian power, Atsumaro became an initiatory figure in advocating a policy of East Asian security — defending East Asia from Western imperialism. To enhance his cause, he set up the East Asian Study Club in 1898 and also the National Club of Comrades in 1900. He began to distance himself from Prince Saionji Kinmochi and Ito Hirobumi, the founder and president of Seiyukai, who were inclined to take a conciliatory policy toward the West.

It is interesting to note that Konoe Fumimaro was destined to share his father's thoughts about East Asia. There is no indication in Konoe's writing, however, that he was directly influenced by his father's political thoughts. He was only fourteen years old when Atsumaro died. Also, Konoe did not take any serious interest in politics until he was nearing graduation from college. It is not difficult to speculate, however, that as

Konoe got involved in politics, his particular interest in Chinese affairs was influenced by his father's strong concern for China.

So, undoubtedly Atsumaro made a great success in the political arena. At the same time, however, his politically vigorous and unorthodox activities created adversaries and exhausted the family fortune, throwing the family into considerable debt. When Atsumaro died, the Konoe family was by no means well off.

Recalling the unpleasant experience he had shortly after his father's death, Konoe wrote, "When my father was alive, various people came to see us from morning to night. I was constantly flattered even though I was only a small child. After his death, all this suddenly ceased. Those who had been taken care of by my father now completely changed their attitudes toward us and urged us to pay back money my father allegedly borrowed from them. Because we did not have much money, we used our valuable possessions to clear our debts. One wealthy fellow refused to accept our offer and kept returning what we gave him."[7] Embittered by the experience, Konoe became rebellious toward the world around him. During his junior high and high school years, Konoe confined himself almost entirely to reading. As Konoe himself pointed out, he became a gloomy young man.[8]

In 1909 Konoe entered high school, and he initially took an interest in philosophy. Strongly influenced by his German and philosophy teacher, Iwamoto Tei, he began to think of choosing a profession in philosophy. When he was a senior, however, social studies became more attractive to him. Konoe first studied philosophy at Tokyo Imperial University. Then, shortly after, he transferred to Kyoto Imperial University and enrolled in the Department of Law. He spent most of his time, however, studying sociology under the well-known Marxist scholar Kawakami Hajime.

While at Kyoto Imperial University, Konoe translated Oscar Wilde's *The Soul of Man Under Socialism* into Japanese. It appeared in the May and June 1914 issues of the third series of the journal *Shin Shicho*. Because of the book's radical content, however, these issues were banned.[9] Although it is not clear why Konoe translated Oscar Wilde's book, this translation demonstrates Konoe's ideological inclination at that time.[10] What should be noted here is that it was during this particular period of his life when the ideological foundation of Konoe's political thought was being shaped.

Another memorable event during Konoe's university period was his first meeting with Saionji Kinmochi. In 1912, Saionji's second cabinet fell when it faced the dispute with the army regarding establishing two additional divisions. Home Minister Katsura Taro replaced Saionji and formed his third cabinet. This triggered a rising concern about the tyrannical

Konoe Fumimaro (left) in his youth with his younger brothers and sisters (©
Mainichi Photo Bank).

power of military cliques and a growing bureaucracy, which developed
into a nationwide movement to protect constitutional government.
Through this movement, Konoe began to be interested in politics and also
to develop a favorable image of Saionji.[11]

As mentioned above, however, because of the political tensions
between his father and Saionji and also because of the absence of a close
relationship between the Konoe family and the Saionji family, Konoe had
never seen Saionji. Nonetheless, one day Konoe felt like seeing Saionji and
went to see him without even a letter of introduction. According to Konoe,
this meeting left him with quite a bad impression. The Konoe family had
a higher noble status than Saionji's, and Saionji addressed Konoe accordingly, calling him "Your Excellency." Being a university student and still
wearing the school uniform, Konoe thought that Saionji was making fun
of him. Offended, Konoe did not see Saionji again until he had graduated
from Kyoto Imperial University in 1917.

On November 11, 1918, a year after his graduation, the First World
War came to an end with the Allied victory. Shortly before, on the night
of November 6, Konoe wrote an essay, "Eibeihoni no Heiwashugi o Haisu
(Reject the Anglo-American–Centered Peace)."[12] It was published in the
December 15, 1918, issue of the journal *Nihon oyobi Nihonjin* (*Japan and*

Japanese). It is difficult to overemphasize the significance of this essay. It represents the essence of Konoe's ideological views. It is the foundation and key to understanding his later policy making. Throughout his entire political career, Konoe never wavered from these views.[13] He wrote:

> Democracy and humanitarianism will be the dominant ideologies in the coming postwar era, and this will have a grave impact on Japan as a member of the world community. One has to remember, however, the essence of democracy and humanitarianism is the equality of all human beings. Nationally, it means civil rights and international recognition of equal right of existence and opportunity for each nation, forbidding any special rights and monopolies. Such rights are eternal and a fundamental rule of human morality, and it is nonsense to say that this rule is not applicable to the Japanese constitution.
>
> What is regrettable, however, is that, today, Japanese leaders tend to follow blindly an Anglo-American version of democracy and humanitarianism, and, therefore, fail to see its true nature. In Bernard Shaw's book, *Fate and Man*, Napoleon says the following: "The English are good at using moral and religious feeling to express their own desire. Furthermore, once one makes his or her ambition holy and makes it public, it takes determination to accomplish his or her goal. While daring to commit robbery and plunder, the English always have a moral excuse, and while advocating freedom and independence, they divide up the world under the name of colony and squeeze profit from them."
>
> The Anglo-Americans all conclude that it is German despotism and militarism that have brought such a major disturbance to world peace. Germany is an enemy of humanity. Therefore, Germany has to be punished in order to preserve justice and humanity. Accordingly, this war is a fight for democracy and humanitarianism against despotism and militarism, for justice against violence, and for virtue against evil.
>
> One cannot help feeling deeply hateful toward the German disregard for justice and humanity and the atrocities they committed. Also, it is natural that the Anglo-Americans condemn such atrocities. It is, however, a shrewd and unacceptable argument by the Anglo-Americans to say that a man has to be an enemy against justice and humanity because he has disturbed the peace. Such an argument becomes possible only when one assumes that the prewar situation of Europe was the best from the standpoint of justice and humanity. One has to wonder who has assumed that the prewar situation in Europe had been the best for justice and humanity, therefore, anyone who disturbs it ought to be punished as an enemy of humankind!
>
> The European conflict is a fight between the accomplished nations and the unaccomplished nations and between those who find the preservation of the status quo beneficial and those who find the destruction of the status quo beneficial. The former demands peace, and the latter demands war. Therefore, peace does not necessarily always bring justice and humanity, and militarism is not necessarily always against justice and humanity.
>
> The Anglo-American peace is only based on a principle of "safety first" by those who find the preservation of the status quo beneficial, and it has nothing to do with justice and humanity. It is servile that, when Japan, consider-

ing its international standing, should be advocating the destruction of the status quo along with Germany and Italy, our leaders, intoxicated by the "beautiful words" of the Anglo-Americans and influenced by an Anglo-American–centered peace, consider peace equal to humanity and long for the League of Nations as a God-given device. One should not oppose the League of Nations but congratulate it if it is organized truly around the idea of justice and humanity. There is, however, the possibility that the League of Nations might create a situation where the established nations confine the non-established nations politically and economically, and, therefore, the latter have to get behind the former permanently. In short, it is the Anglo-Americans who get the most benefit from the League of Nations. The others, although they joined the League under the pretense of justice and humanity, get almost no benefits. On the contrary, they are obliged to get weaker politically and economically. This is an intolerable situation not only with regard to Japan's position but also with regard to justice and humanity in general. As for Japan's entering the League of Nations at the upcoming Peace Conference, therefore, the central questions Japan cannot fail to address are the end of economic imperialism and nondiscriminatory treatment of the Asians by the Caucasians. The threat to justice and humanity is not just militarism alone. Although the world has been saved from the hail of bullets with the defeat of Germany, what threatens the equal right of existence for each nation is not arms alone. In essence, economic imperialism is equal to military imperialism, and it also should be resisted. [14]

This essay was written only a year after Konoe's graduation from Kyoto Imperial University, indicating that he was not just a literary and noble young man but also someone with potential to be a fine politician.[15] It is indeed significant when one considers that the essay was written not only by such a young man but also at the time when Germany had just been defeated and the victorious Anglo-American powers were proclaiming themselves the champion of justice and humanity.

Konoe's essay was, therefore, in a sense untimely, but it was insightful. What followed after the Peace Conference proves that the questions Konoe raised were on target. It can be quickly recalled here that the failure to resolve the questions of colonialism, racism, and economic unfairness was one key factor, if not the only factor, that led to another worldwide conflict only two decades later.

A month after the publication of Konoe's essay, on January 18, 1919, the Paris Peace Conference began, and Saionji Kinmochi was chosen to head the delegation from Japan. Working at the Home Ministry but still having no clear direction in terms of his career plans, Konoe seized this opportunity to shape up his future life. Konoe asked Saionji to allow him to accompany him to the conference. As Konoe himself wrote, it was a rather strange fate that he took his first journey overseas as a member of the delegation under Saionji just like his father, Atsumaro, did thirty-four years before.[16]

Saionji's party left Japan for Paris on January 14, 1919. On the way, when they stopped at Shanghai, two unexpected incidents took place. One was Konoe's encounter with the translation of his essay "Reject the Anglo-American–Centered Peace" and a rebuttal against it in the journal *Millard's Review*.[17] It was the work of Thomas F. Millard, an anti-Japanese American journalist and a chief editor of the journal. In it, Millard warned that close attention had to be paid to the fact that the Japanese delegation included Konoe, who wrote such an anti–Anglo-American and anti-establishment essay. Learning about Millard's warning, Saionji censured Konoe. Other than that, there is no evidence that Konoe's accompanying Saionji created any obstacle for Japan's participation in the Peace Conference. The other unexpected event was Konoe's meeting with Sun Yat-sen, who happened to be in Shanghai as a refugee. Sun read Konoe's essay in the *Millard Review*. He found so much to share in Konoe's essay that he took the initiative to meet him. According to Konoe, it was an uplifting meeting. He was particularly impressed by Sun Yat-sen's passionate view on the national awakening in the Far East.[18]

These two incidents at Shanghai reinforced Konoe's expectation regarding the Paris Peace Conference. To Konoe, the conference was the finest opportunity to emend the world situation for an establishment of real peace.[19] It turned out, however, to be disappointing to Konoe. Even before the Japanese delegation reached Paris, the news they were receiving from there was discouraging. Konoe increasingly felt betrayed. Hence, after he reached Paris, he titled his first report to Japan "Power Still Rules the World." According to Konoe, nothing was mentioned at the conference about the removal of the barrier of economic unfairness, one of the main components of Wilson's Fourteen Points. Also not mentioned was the issue concerning freedom from racial discrimination with regard to immigration. When the draft of the League of Nations was about to be adopted at the fifth convention of the Peace Conference held at the French Foreign Ministry on April 28, 1919, the Japanese delegation asserted a ban of racial discrimination as a condition for Japan's agreement to the League of Nations. The representatives of the other powers, however, took no consideration of Japan's assertion.[20] To Konoe, as he wrote in his article, "Impression of Peace Conference at Paris," in June 1919, these disappointing outcomes from the conference were clear proof of the persistence of power as an iron rule.[21]

Though far from satisfactory, Konoe did not necessarily see the conference as a total failure. He argued, "Although it suffered from the severe infringement by European and American self-interests, the principle of Wilson's Fourteen Points, particularly with regard to national sovereignty, at least became the core spirit of the Peace Conference and has brought new hope to the small nations that have long suffered from oppression. In this sense, it is indeed Wilson's great achievement that the League of Nations has been set up. It is a result of his passion and effort. His name, Wilson, will gloriously and eternally shine in the history of humankind. It would be premature to declare the ruin of idealism from the disappointing result of the conference."[22]

Having completed the mission at the Peace Conference, Saionji Kinmochi and his party left Paris for Japan on July 17, 1919. Konoe did not accompany them but traveled to France and Germany to visit various places, including the University of Bonn where his father had studied more than three decades earlier. Then he went on to visit England and the United States. While having an emotional experience in Bonn tracing his father's past, Konoe also closely observed the European and American social structures. It helped Konoe to see Japan and its social structure objectively and comparatively, making him critical of some of the traditional aspects of Japanese society.[23] In November 1919, Konoe finally returned to Japan.

During the following decade, until the arrival of the turbulent era of the 1930s, as a member of the House of Peers, Konoe steadily built up his political career by becoming involved in many issues. The most significant was the issue of reforming the House of Peers. He became a member of the House of Peers when he was still a university student. With his noble court family background, a seat at the House of Peers was hereditary to him. As a member, he developed his concern for the role of the House of Peers. In his short essay "Attitude Japanese House of Peers Should Take," Konoe elaborated on how the House of Peers as the Upper House should function in its relation with the Lower House. According to Konoe, if both houses always agreed with each other, the two-house system was meaningless, but at the same time, if they disagreed constantly, it had no merit and became harmful. How should the Japanese House of Peers deal with this dilemma? In a comparison with the two-house system of England, Konoe argued that the best way to deal with this problem was through the self-restriction of the House of Peers. The House of Peers was designed to be the opposition power set against the political party–oriented Lower House. Unlike that of England, it was constitutionally far freer from any restriction by any outside force than the Lower House. For example, the government had no right to dissolve the House of Peers. In that sense, it was possible for the House of Peers to abuse its constitutionally protected position. Unless the constitution was amended, there was no law to prevent it. Consequently, self-restriction was the only way to have any control of the House of Peers. Konoe believed it could be feasible and effective since the House of Peers was not party-oriented.[24]

In 1921 he set up the Club of Constitutional Study with Mori Kaku, an influential member of the Diet from the Seiyukai Party. The promotion of reform of the House of Peers was the main aim for the club. Then, in 1922, Konoe joined Kenkyukai, which created a little controversy. Kenkyukai, the most powerful faction of the Upper House, opposed Konoe's effort to reform the House of Peers. It made little sense, therefore, that Konoe, while pushing for the reform of the House of Peers, joined Kenkyukai. As Yabe Teiji points out, this was perhaps the result of political maneuvering by then Prime Minister Hara Satoshi from Seiyukai and Mori Kaku to strengthen their party position by having Konoe as a member of Kenkyukai.[25]

In January 1924, succeeding the second Yamamoto cabinet, Kiyoura Keigo formed his cabinet, which predominantly consisted of the members of the House of Peers, particularly from Kenkyukai. When it triggered the movement of protection of the constitutional government, despite his membership in Kenkyukai, Konoe supported the movement pushed by the political parties Kenseikai, Seiyukai, and Kakushin Club, and contributed to the fall of the Kiyoura Keigo cabinet. The new cabinet was formed under the premiership of Kato Takaaki in June 1924. It was a coalition cabinet of the above three parties.

In November 1928, Konoe Fumimaro in kimono giving a radio broadcast (© Mainichi Photo Bank).

In November 1927, Konoe ended his polemical membership in Kenkyukai. Then, in the following month, he set up Kayokai (Tuesday Club). It was a club only for the heirs of princes and marquises. The most memorable involvement of Kayokai in politics came in February 1928 when Home Minister Suzuki Kizaburo was forced to resign because of his questionable interference in the general election. Prime Minister Tanaka Giichi attempted to appoint his close personal friend, Hisahara Fusanosuke, as a successor. Strongly opposing Tanaka's action, Minister of Education Mizuno Rentaro submitted his resignation in protest. Pretending that he accepted Mizuno's resignation, Tanaka fabricated the Emperor's wish for having Mizuno continue to serve as Minister of Education to force Mizuno to take back his resignation. Although Mizuno did so, when Tanaka's action was criticized, he was obliged to turn in his second resignation. It was the House of Peers that became a driving force for the accusation against Tanaka. Konoe led Kayokai to support the House of Peers. The Prime Minister was forced to resign in July 1929, and his successor was Hamaguchi Osachi of the Minseito.

One upshot of Konoe's strong involvement in the reform of the House of Peers was a selection of Konoe Fumimaro as the Vice Chairman of the House of Peers in 1929. Four years later, in June 1933, Konoe, succeeding Tokugawa Iesato, became the fifth Chairman of the House of Peers.[26] Again he was "destined" to follow in his father's footsteps.

2

Konoe and Turbulence of the 1930s

The Japanese economy already had been unstable since the end of the First World War due to the overextension of capital investment and production and also the end of Japan's economic advantage as a supplier to meet the strong demand for war goods. Japan's economy deteriorated further from the severe destruction caused by the great earthquake and the subsequent major conflagration in September 1923. With no administration able to take any effective measure to cope with the problem, this economic difficulty was the continuous trend throughout the 1920s. Succeeding Tanaka Giichi as Prime Minister in July 1929, Hamaguchi Osachi took a couple of radical measures to turn around this economic stagnation. One was the policy to enhance economic efficiency, meaning heavier work conditions (fewer workers and lower wages for the same production) and the concentration of capital to fewer hands. The other was lifting the embargo on gold and returning to the gold standard in order to buttress the value of the yen and halt inflation. Unfortunately, however, the stock market crash in the United States and the following worldwide economic depression did not give these measures a chance to be fully tested.

What followed for Japan was unprecedented economic turmoil. The prices of goods steeply declined because of deflation, and international trade also dropped sharply while the unemployment rate skyrocketed. Naturally, in this situation, the industrial corporations and the agricultural industry had an extremely difficult time in running their businesses. The lives of the farmers and the industrial workers became almost unbearable.

Along with the internal and external political turmoil, these economic hardships fomented social and political discontent. The nation was losing its trust and confidence in the politicians who were not only unable to cope with the problems but were also frequently involved in political corruption and rivalry. The parliamentary government and party politics came under attack. Growing militarism and the rise of the right-wing nationalism were a natural consequence of these trends. The arrest of Socialists and Communists and the counterattacks by the anarchists became daily occurrences.[1]

It was in the midst of these circumstances that the London Naval Arms Reduction Conference took place in January 1930. Despite the desire of the Japanese navy to obtain a ratio of 10:10:7 for the United States, Great Britain, and Japan, respectively, in cruisers and other warships, Wakatsuki Reijiro, the head of the Japanese delegation, accepted the ratio of 10:10:6.

Finding it unacceptable, the naval officers led by Admiral Kato Kanji launched an attack against the Hamaguchi government. They were joined by the Seiyukai Party leaders such as Inukai Tsuyoshi and Hatoyama Ichiro. Their argument was that the supreme command was independent, and, therefore, the government had no authority to make any decision with regard to national defense.

Admiral Kato resigned after he appealed directly to the Emperor. Despite Kato's effort to oppose the government, Prime Minister Hamaguchi, with the support of Saionji and the political party Minseito, succeeded in pushing through the ratification of the agreement. This brought dire political consequences. Although the Seiyukai leaders' making use of the military discontent for political goals may have had a short-term gain, in the long run it weakened the position of party politics and brought grave consequences for the future of the parliamentary government. Outraged by the ratification of the agreement, the right-wing militarists and the civilian radicals began to target those who supported the agreement, thus triggering series of political assassinations and coups d'etat in the 1930s.

The first victim was Prime Minister Hamaguchi, who was shot and seriously injured by the right-wing radical Sakyoya Tameo at the Tokyo railroad station on November 14, 1930. Hamaguchi survived the initial attack, but died a few months later. The assassin was sentenced to death, but later his sentence was reduced, and he was eventually released in 1940. He resumed his right-wing political activities.[2]

Following this assassination was the so-called March Incident. The plotters were the military officers Koiso Kuniaki, Nagata Tetsuzan, and Hashimoto Kingoro, and one of the top leaders of the civilian right-wing radicals, Okawa Shumei. Seeing no hope in the existing political system, in March 1931 they attempted to have "national reform" by establishing a new cabinet under the leadership of the Minister of the Army, Ugaki Kazushige, as Prime Minister. Despite the elaborate plan, this coup d'etat never took place, allegedly because at the very last minute Ugaki changed his mind, withdrawing his support for the coup attempt.[3]

As these two incidents symbolize, the politically stormy era of the

1930s had already begun by early 1931. Strangely enough, however, around that time Konoe Fumimaro, who only a year after his graduation from college wrote the sensational article "Reject the Anglo-American–Centered Peace" and had been passionately involved in the Upper House reform movement a decade earlier, was showing little interest incurrent affairs.

According to Konoe, this changed when he again encountered Mori Kaku in May 1931. It was a reunion after a decade, since they had established together the Club of Constitutional Study in 1921. Konoe recalled what Mori said to him during their meeting: "Time is changing drastically. Dealing with such issues as party politics and the House of Peers is becoming trivial. We have to keep up with this change. Otherwise we face serious consequences."[4] Seeing Mori Kaku as a politician with a strong belief in party politics, Konoe was surprised at this remark. Konoe even sensed a tone of fascism in it.

After this meeting, Konoe began to see Mori regularly and, through him, he became closer to the right-wing nationalists. Konoe began to pay close attention to the swiftly moving current affairs such as the Manchurian problem, the rise of militarism, and the increasingly expanding social instability. It was like the second eye opening for him.

Meanwhile, the turbulence of the 1930s continued. On September 18, 1931, the Manchurian Incident took place. By this time, with a weakening economy and a rapidly growing population, much was at stake in Manchuria for Japan. Things were not going well for Japan, however. There were strong and growing anti-Japanese elements in Manchuria. In addition, there had been threats from the head of the Kuomintang Party, Chiang Kai-shek, who was determined to unify the whole of China.

Chiang launched the so-called Northern Expedition to remove all the warlords in north China. He began to move his troops to the north in April 1928. Alarmed by this, the Kwantung Army officers wanted to replace Chang Tso-lin's army with their own troops and send them into key areas in Manchuria in order to have all of Manchuria under their control. Their plan, however, was opposed by Prime Minister Tanaka. Then the Kwantung Army assassinated Chang Tso-lin, hoping that his death would cause some local disturbances, thus giving them an excuse to move troops to the key areas in Manchuria. However, no major outbreaks took place. On the contrary, Chang Hsueh-liang, son of Chang Tso-lin, came to power and promised his loyalty to Chiang Kai-shek. These circumstances became alarming enough for the Kwantung officers to take a drastic action.

On September 18, 1931, the small section of the Southern Manchurian Railroad in Mukden was blown up. The Kwantung Army promptly issued a communiqué stating that it was the Chinese troops that were responsible for that incident and the following attack on Japanese guards. What really took place was that a small group of the Kwantung Army was ordered to blow up the section of the railroad to create an excuse to bring down Chang Hsueh-liang from power.

With only a vague idea of what really happened, the Wakatsugi cabinet adopted the policy of keeping the incident as a local matter and tried to settle it promptly. Contrary to their desire, the Kwantung Army rapidly moved their troops and put all of southern Manchuria under their control. Even the Korean troops led by Army General Hayashi Senjuro were sent to Manchuria. Hayashi did so without first obtaining an imperial sanction, thus violating the core principle of the military code.

To make matters worse for the government, the Kwantung Army's action in Manchuria was welcomed and enthusiastically supported by the public, and there was a growing criticism of the government effort led by Foreign Minister Shidehara Kijuro to achieve a conciliatory settlement of the Manchurian issue.[5] Having almost literally no support with regard to its Manchurian policy, the Wakatsugi cabinet fell in December 1931. Inukai Tsuyoshi replaced Wakatsugi.[6]

In September 1932, the Lytton Committee that conducted an investigation of the Manchuria Incident submitted a report to the League of Nations.[7] It recommended the creation of an autonomous regime under Chinese sovereignty for province and a withdrawal of all Chinese and Japanese forces. This was unacceptable to the Japanese army. Then Japan withdrew its membership from the League of Nations in 1933 when the League of Nations Security Council Assembly voted 42 to 1 against Japan.

Not surprisingly, Konoe did not share the assessment of the Lytton Committee over the Manchurian Incident. In the beginning of his article published in 1936 in Tokyo, "Improve the Present Situation of the World," Konoe states, "Since the Manchurian Incident took place, Japan has been in a very

Portrait of Konoe Fumimaro (© Mainichi Photo Bank).

difficult position internationally. Japan's activities in Manchuria have already been questioned many times at the League of Nations. Japan is like a defendant to be judged in the world court in the name of world peace. Facing this situation, in order to get the consideration of Japan's position from the so-called Western Peace Advocates, I think we not only ought to explain that Japan's action in Manchuria is indispensable for Japan's existence but also openly express to them our belief of how to achieve a true world peace."[8] This article clearly expresses Konoe's position, stating that the Manchurian Incident was justifiable and the result of the unfairly structured world political and economic systems. Therefore, it was not only inevitable and indispensable for Japan but also should be commended as a positive action for the sake of changing the current world structure to achieve true peace. Although it may sound naive and like self-justification, Konoe truly believed that in order to rectify the world's unfair structure, expelling Western imperialism from China and Asia as a whole was a first and essential step. Japan's involvement in Manchuria, therefore, was not an act of aggression but a necessary step, and should be considered an action designed to benefit both China and Japan.

This is the same argument Konoe made as a young college graduate in 1918 in his article "Reject the Anglo-American–Centered Peace." This sympathetic and supportive remark to the plotters of the Manchurian Incident helped Konoe strengthen his popularity and support not only from the right-wing radicals, but also from the public in general.[9]

A month later, the Manchurian Incident was followed by another coup d'etat, the so called October Incident. It was caused by about 120 young military officers led by Hashimoto Kingoro, a lieutenant and influential member of the extremely radical right-wing organization, the Cherry Blossom Club.[10] Realizing that contemporary party politics and a conciliatory foreign policy were not sufficient to settle the Manchurian issue, they plotted the uprising in order to have national reforms by setting up a cabinet under Lieutenant Colonel Araki Sadao. Unlike the March Incident, this time they tried to achieve their goal by themselves without relying on any support from the civilians.[11] It was abortive, however, because the top leaders of the military became aware of the plot beforehand.

Then, in the following year, on May 15, 1932, the incident that altered the nature of Japanese politics at a very critical juncture of modern Japanese history took place. It had grave consequences for the course Japan would take in the next decade or so, up to the end of the Pacific war in 1945.

This incident, known as the May Fifteenth Incident, was carried out by the naval officers and the army cadets led by a naval lieutenant, Koga

Kiyoshi, and a radical agrarian reformer, Tachibana Kosabro. It was designed to kill Prime Minister Inukai and the Lord Keeper of the Privy Seal, Makino Nobuaki, who pledged to fulfill the Emperor's wish to suppress the Kwantung Army in order to achieve a prompt and peaceful solution to the Manchurian Incident.

In addition to the assassination of Inukai and Makino, the plotters planned to attack the Seiyukai headquarters, the Mitsubishi Bank, the police headquarters, and various electrical power plants. They failed in all but one of their goals— the assassination of Inukai. When the assassins broke into the Prime Minister's official residence, Inukai attempted to talk to them, believing he would be able to dissuade them. His attempt ended in vain. He was killed on the spot.

What made the May Fifteenth Incident so significant is that, with this incident, the age of party politics came to an end. Until the incident, Japanese politics had been characterized by party politics. Particularly, from June 1924 to May 1932, the president of one of the two major parties had always led the Japanese government. That ended with the assassination of Inukai and did not resume until the arrival of the post–World War II era. From May 1932 to August 1945, eleven men led the government. Four of them were admirals, four were generals, and only three were civilians.[12]

Hence, the May Fifteenth Incident was clearly a turning point of prewar Japanese politics. It was a transition of power from political parties to the military. After the incident, the military became increasingly autonomous and assertive in policy making. Accordingly, the Kwantung Army in Manchuria almost got a free hand to do whatever they desired to do.

Shortly after the May Fifteenth Incident, Konoe met Saionji and gave him his thoughts about future political prospects. Konoe told Saionji that to let the military coup d'etat destroy the party cabinet was sheer nonsense. Its establishment took ten years effort. So, maintaining parliamentary politics and party cabinet were absolutely essential. To do so, the Seiyukai party had to form a cabinet even if it might lead to a further confrontation with the military.[13] If that was not possible, Konoe continued to say that letting the military be in charge was the other choice to take and, even though risky, it might be the best. Konoe explained to Harada why it might be the better approach. To Konoe, putting the military in position to govern would likely restrain them from any devious action and also likely lead them to stumble in their governing, causing them loss of their political muscle. So, to Konoe, despite risks, the above two options were worthwhile to take, and perhaps, the only choices.[14]

To Saionji, however, neither option was acceptable. Taking into consideration the Emperor's wish to have the next Prime Minister be neither supportive of the radical nationalists nor abusive to the constitution, Saionji recommended an admiral, Saito Makoto. Saionji thought Saito, the former governor-general of Korea who was known to be moderate in his political views, could be acceptable to both the military and the civilians.

Then Konoe, with regard to Saionji's recommendation, wrote the following:

> In the end, Saionji prevailed. It was Saito Makoto who became Prime Minister, creating neither party nor military but a "compromise" cabinet. Saionji actually wanted to see a continuation of the party cabinet. He realized, however, the political party did not have any support but resentment from the military and had also became completely untrustworthy in the eyes of the nation. To Saionji, therefore, the creation of a party cabinet at this juncture was counter-effective, only causing the government further friction with the military. So was the creation of military cabinet. Saionji knew that the government take-over by the military would likely lead a new cabinet into extreme radicalism. So, to Saionji, the best choice the nation could make was a compromise cabinet.
>
> How did this compromise cabinet actually function? Under a compromise cabinet, although the military had a clear edge in terms of power, a political party was still able to have some control over excessive use of power by the military. There might be a situation in which the army's use of power was absolutely uncontrollable, and there was no way to suppress it but to let the army go their way. Under the compromise cabinet, even in this situation, a political party was not totally powerless. By letting the army have its way, the political party was still able to delay the outcome of the army's action from becoming effective. Consequently the political party was able to minimize the potential risks that might result from the army's action. According to Konoe, this was the essence of the compromise cabinet Saigon suggested.[15]

Clearly the ideological difference between Konoe and Saionji played a role here in terms of what a cabinet should be like after the May Fifteenth Incident. Saionji argued that the military officers were being carried away by their passion. As long as this was so, one had to avoid stimulating them and instead wait for them to cool down. Once they restored their calmness, diplomacy would be back on the right track and the cooperative nature of Shidehara Diplomacy would return.[16] As Saionji's remark indicates, he did not see the necessity of having any fundamental change both internally and externally. What was the best for Japan was to keep the status quo.

Sharply disagreeing with Saionji, Konoe responded to Saionji's "do-nothing approach." He argued that the direction Japan was undertaking then was molded by the world situation. Regardless of whether or not the military rose or the Manchurian Incident took place, it was fate that Japan had to face. With regard to waiting for the military to cool down, it would never happen as long as politicians failed to recognize this fate of the nation. The military would continue to be a driving force, and Japan would increasingly speed up a move in fateful direction. It was, however, very dangerous to let the military lead the nation. In order to retake politics from the hand of the military, the politicians had to recognize this fate of the nation, take the lead (not the other way around), and enact various reforms in order to find a way out of this fateful situation. Without realizing this fate of the nation, if the politicians did nothing but try to oppress the military, they would never be able to take politics back into their hands.[17]

According to Konoe, Saionji was amused by his remarks and said, "Again, Konoe's argument of taking a lead."[18] Whether or not this is amusing, the ideological difference between Konoe and Saionji at this critical juncture of Japanese politics was very significant in determining the fate of Japan. In the end, Saionji's approach prevailed, and the trend of compromise politics continued until the end of World War II. As the aftermath of the February Twenty-six Incident in 1936 proved, however, what Saionji expected to see never took place. Instead of cooling down, the passion of the right-wing nationalists sharply escalated, causing them to stage continuous uprisings. The first of these was the Shinpeitai Incident in July 1933,[19] followed by the October Fascist Incident in August 1933,[20] the November Incident in November 1934,[21] and the assassination of Nagata Tetsuzan in August 1935.[22] All but the assassination of Nagata ended in failure.

In the midst of this political turmoil, Konoe went to the United States in May 1934.[23] By this time, there was a growing expectation for Konoe to form a cabinet. Facing serious issues such as Japan's international isolation and the increasingly intensified right-wing actions at home, and despite being a moderate, Prime Minister Saito was worn out from governing. He was eager to step down and let Konoe be his successor. Considering that it would be a better option for Konoe to go abroad to see Japan from outside, however, Saionji persuaded Saito to remain in office and recommended Konoe to take the trip.

Publicly, it was a trip to attend the high school graduation of his older son, Fumitaka. As Konoe wrote in his memoirs, however, the main purposes were to promote U.S. understanding of Japanese diplomacy after the Manchurian Incident and to examine the U.S. view on the upcoming Naval Arms Reduction Conference.[24]

It was a rather short but quite busy trip. Visiting the major cities of the United States, Konoe had meetings with various dignitaries such as President Franklin Roosevelt, former President Herbert Hoover, Secretary of State Cordell Hull, Wall Street tycoon Thomas W. Lamont, Colonel Edward House, and many others. Through these meetings and the speeches he delivered, Konoe, while listening to the U.S. views, made his best effort to convey the important task of the revolutionary changes taking place in Japan and Japan's position on major issues such as Manchuria or the ratio of naval arms reduction.

Konoe found some Americans with solid knowledge about Japan who were supportive of Japan's position and role in the international arena. He realized, however, that in general the U.S. public's knowledge of Japan was almost zero creating fundamental obstacles for promoting mutual understanding between the two nations. So there was a need for Japan to make an effort to remedy the situation. According to Konoe, such an effort could be in the form of setting up Japanese cultural centers in major U.S. cities or creating student exchange programs. Konoe realized, however, the most immediate need for Japan was an improvement political propaganda. To Konoe, China was doing far better than Japan when it came to political propaganda, leading the U.S. public's mood toward being more sympathetic to China than to Japan. For example, Konoe was quite disappointed to find out that Colonel Edward House, who he thought understood better than anyone else Japan's position as a have-not nation, was actually critical toward Japan. House told Konoe that the Japanese political situation was similar to that of prewar Germany, and so Japan was destined to share the fate of Germany. House's view, Konoe believed, was to a great extent the outcome of ineffective Japanese propaganda.

Besides these rather unsatisfactory experiences, there was one unexpected outcome from Konoe's trip that might have been one of the causes of the future failure of his diplomacy. As stated earlier, Konoe met with various dignitaries during his stay in the United States, and among them was Thomas W. Lamont, one of the most influential figures of Wall Street and known to be pro-Japanese. He made a great contribution in promoting U.S. investment in Japan.

After his return to Japan, Konoe wrote an article about his trip to the United States. In it, he made a remark about what Lamont had told him: "When I saw Lamont in New York, he said that President Roosevelt did not know anything about diplomacy, and Hull was an economist who knew nothing about diplomacy and had very little knowledge about the Far East."[25]

When Konoe's article was translated and published in a U.S. journal, *The Daily Worker*, Lamont read Konoe's remarks and was infuriated by them. Lamont stated that Konoe's remarks were far from the truth and were a pure distortion of what he had told him. Whether it was the truth or a distortion, what really infuriated Lamont was Konoe's insensitivity and disregard for the potential trouble Lamont might have with Roosevelt or Hull because of these publicized remarks by Konoe.

So infuriated was Lamont that on September 24, 1934, he wrote a letter to Joseph C. Grew, the U.S. Ambassador to Japan.[25] In it, he says, "I would like to draw your attention to the most mean-spirited treatment I have received from Prince Konoe. I have always met well-behaved Japanese gentlemen. Seeing this man's behavior, I cannot help, however, but be convinced that Konoe is the worst bounder. I hate seeing this type of man coming to the United States and dealing with the improvement of the U.S.-Japanese relationship."[26]

Realizing the seriousness of this matter, Konoe wrote a letter to Lamont to express his regret. In the letter, Konoe defended himself by saying that it was the Japanese press that publicized his conversation with Lamont without getting his consent. Sympathetic to Konoe, Grew also sent a letter to Lamont to speak for Konoe. Their effort, however, did little to minimize the damage done to Konoe's image.

In his article "Nichibei Gaiko ni Okeru Fushin no Tanjo" ("Birth of Distrust in U.S.-Japan Diplomacy"), Professor Hosoya Chihiro of Hitotsubashi University points out that it is likely that the image the U.S. leaders had of Konoe through the above episode, and the image Konoe had of the U.S. leaders through his trip to the United States, had a subtle influence on the issue of the summit meeting in 1941.[27]

Konoe returned to Japan in mid-summer of 1934. Japan was still in the midst of political turbulence. A year and a half after Konoe's return, the incident that put the whole nation into a state of shock took place on February 26, 1936. This so-called February Twenty-Six Incident shared a similar background with the preceding incidents, such as the anti-capitalism and anti-democracy movements caused by economic and social problems particularly in the rural areas, the lack of trust of the government brought on by corruption and the rivalry of party politics, discontent toward the trend of arms reduction, and repugnance toward pro-Western diplomacy, particularly Shidehara Diplomacy. This incident, however, significantly differs from the others in one respect, factionalism in the army. It is indeed this factionalism that became the immediate cause of the incident.

Traditionally, the army, since the establishment of Japan's modern military, had been dominated by the officers from the Choshu clan until the death in 1922 of Yamagata Aritomo, who was the founder of the Japanese army and served as one of the most influential Genros.[28] After the death of Yamagata, the domination of the army by the Choshu officers began to diminish and thus created a chance for the non-Choshu officers to rise up. Yamagata was succeeded by Tanaka Giichi. Then, with Tanaka's demise, there was no appropriate leader to succeed him, thereby further weakening the Choshu officers' domination. By this time, the army was clearly divided into two factions: the Choshu faction and the non-Choshu faction.

The leading officers of the Choshu faction, such as Nagata Tetsuzan, Tojo Hideki, and Yamashita Tomoyuki, were mostly coming from well-off families and were the graduates of the Military Academy. Exposed to modern thinking in terms of how the army should be in order to deal with future wars, they placed a great emphasis on two things: (1) Modernization of the army by equipping it with modern machinery such as tanks and airplanes and placing less reliance on human resources (meaning the reduction of the size of the army), and (2) A comprehensive approach (total mobilization) to military affairs by coordinating the military, politics, and economy. Because of these approaches, they were called the Tosei-ha (the Control faction).

The non–Choshu officers, led by Mazaki Jinsabro and Araki Sadao, often called the Kodo-ha (the Imperial Way faction), strongly believed that what was essential for Japan to win future wars was not machinery but "spirit of Yamato."[29] Already resentful about the long domination of the army by the Choshu officers, they were further infuriated by the approach taken by the Tosei faction. The assassination of Nagata Tetsuzan was one result of such infuriation.

In the midst of this army factionalism in the mid-1930s, one academic theory, first made public almost three decades ago and making a great contribution to the promotion of parliamentary government and party politics, became the focus of controversy. It further intensified the military factionalism by strengthening the movement of the right-wing radicals. This so-called Organ Theory came from a prominent constitutional law scholar, Minobe Tatsukichi. According to his theory, the Emperor was an organ of the state. He was not above the state but contained within it.

Making an argument for the Emperor as a national polity by the right-wing nationalists groundless, Minobe's Organ Theory caused a strong reactionary attack on Minobe by not only the radical militarists but also the nationalist scholars and politicians. The initial attack came from a member of the House of Peers and a director of Kokuhonsha, Kikuchi Takeo, in February 1935. He denounced Minobe as a traitor, a rebel, and an academic bandit. Then Hiranuma Kiichiro and the members of Seiyukai, seeing a political opportunity to overthrow the Okada cabinet, joined the attack. This intensified attack against the Organ Theory eventually obliged Minobe to resign his seat in the House of Peers and give up his teaching position at Tokyo Imperial University. His books were banned, and he was almost killed by a fanatical right-wing nationalist.

As this reactionary movement against the Organ Theory indicates, in the mid-1930s, an ultranationalistic ideology became increasingly dominant. The ideological control was intensified, and liberalism and democracy were almost completely eradicated. Two years later, in March 1937, under pressure from the army and ultranationalists, the government issued *Cardinal Principles of the National Entity of Japan (Kokutai no Hongi)*. Thus, infuriated and threatened by the long domination of the army by the Tosei-ha and its policy orientation, the Kodo-ha saw an opportunity for them to take action to turn the situation around and have their cause prevail.

On the snowy morning of February 26, 1936, by mobilizing more than 14,000 men of the infantry regiments of the First Division and the Imperial Guards Division, the rebels attacked and occupied the key government buildings, killing a number of senior statesmen. Their mission was to establish a military government under General Mazaki as Prime Minister by eradicating the destructive elements to the nation such as Genro, elder statesmen, financial and military cliques, bureaucrats, and political parties. Some of the major targets were Prime Minister Okada Keisuke, former Prime Minister Saito Makoto, Minister of Finance Takahashi Korekiyo, General Watanabe Jotaro, who had replaced Mazaki as an inspector general of military education, the Grand Chamberlain Suzuki Kantaro, and former Lord Keeper of the Privy Seal Makino Nobuaki.[30] Saionji Kinmochi was also on the list. His name was taken off, however, at the last minute because of the disagreement among the rebels about whether or not Saionji should be spared.

Saito, Takahashi, and Watanabe were killed. It was initially believed that Prime Minister Okada was also killed, but in fact Okada's brother-in-law had been mistaken for Okada and killed by the assassins. The rebels occupied the Ministry of the Army, the Diet, and the Prime Minister's residence and demanded national reforms.

What resulted was not acceptance of their demands, however. Without having any clear idea about what would follow after the rebellion, the rebels put their hopes in their expectation that the army leaders and, most importantly, the Emperor would support their cause. Their expected outcome did not come to fruition.

Initially, War Minister Kawashima showed his sympathy toward the rebels. Also, General Araki and General Mazaki naturally did not want the government to take any military action to suppress the rebellion. They urged Kawashima to persuade the Emperor to accept the demands of the rebels. All this changed, however, when the Emperor showed his determination to subdue the rebels. Even General Mazaki became hesitant to fully support the rebels, so the rebellion was doomed.

All together nineteen men were sentenced to death, including Captain Isobe, officer Muranaka Koji, an influential intellectual and nationalist, Kita Ikki, and his follower, Nishida Mitsugu.[31] General Mazaki was arrested as a supreme leader of the rebellion but was later released because of insufficient evidence.

The failure of the Kodo-ha in their quest for Showa Restoration had two significant outcomes. One was the decisive loss of power of the Kodo-ha, ending factionalism in the military. The other was the restoration of the practice of choosing the Minister of the Army from among the active army generals.

With regard to the latter, as Konoe points out in his postwar writing, *Ushinawareshi Seiji* (*The Lost Politics*), with the re-enforcement of this practice, the military greatly enhanced its political power, putting the cabinet almost completely under military control.[32] Perhaps Konoe, more than anyone else, knew how difficult it was to run the government under this situation. As will be discussed later, during his reign, Konoe was unbearably frustrated about having no control of his own cabinet to carry out his policies, often at the most critical moments.

Concerning the fiasco of the Kodo-ha, Konoe made an insightful argument.[33] He stated that the Kodo-ha policy orientation was rooted in an observation of the Russian Revolution by two Japanese militarists, General Araki and Lieutenant General Kobata, who happened to be in Russia as military attachés during the revolution. They were strongly concerned with the fate of Russia, particularly the rise of Communism. Their observation eventually developed into the policy guideline for the Kodo-ha in the 1930s.

Internally, their aim was to maintain and protect national polity by restoring Japan to a society based on Japanese traditions and spirit. In order to achieve that aim, it became essential to prevent a Communist intrusion into Japan. Rather naturally, therefore, the Kodo-ha focused on the policy of moving northward, dealing with the Soviet Union. To them, it was out of the question to become militarily involved in China and support the policy of moving southward. Consequently, they opposed the Manchurian Incident and the China Incident, and also they strongly opposed the advancement of Japanese troops into French Indo-China and the confrontational approach toward the United States.

Hence, with regard to policy making, internally and externally, there was a strong disagreement between the Kodo-ha and the Tosei-ha. Konoe argued that the February Twenty-six Incident ended this rivalry, opening up a way for the Tosei-ha to satisfy the desire of moving southward. Konoe saw, therefore, the beginning of Japan's tragic end in the fiasco of the Kodo-ha.[34] He argued that, prior to the February Twenty-six Incident, Japanese politics and society in general were inundated with "Japanism." It was the general perception that it was the Kodo-ha, led by Generals Araki and Mazaki, who placed the military and the entire nation on the wrong path. So, by clearing away the Kodo-ha after the February Twenty-six Incident, the Tosei-ha was applauded by the nation as well as the foreign powers. To Konoe, this applause made little sense, however. As already mentioned above, what really took place was that, through the February Twenty-six Incident and the triumph of the Tosei-ha over the Kodo-ha, the army greatly enhanced its political power and gained almost a free hand in leading the nation in any way they wished, thus bringing Japan to its fatal destiny.

An implication Konoe was seemingly making from the above argument is important. It would have been possible to avoid the war in the Pacific. As we generally understand today, it was not right-wing nationalist thought that directly caused the military confrontation between Japan and the United States, but the power struggle among the imperial nations over the economic and political interests in China and the southern Pacific. So, it is possible to make a convincing argument that if somehow the Kodo-ha had been able to maintain their stronghold in the military and to check the Tosei-ha's southward movement, Japan would have taken a different path, altering history drastically.

After the February Twenty-six Incident, the Okada cabinet came to an end, and Okada was succeeded by Hirota Koki. Before Hirota was chosen, however, Saionji actually recommended the appointment of Konoe to be Prime Minister. On March 4, 1936, Saionji met with Konoe. During the meeting, which lasted nearly two hours, Saionji gave the reason why Konoe ought to be the next Prime Minister. He stated that Konoe was the most suitable candidate because of his popularity in almost every segment of society, whether it was the military, the political parties, or the House of Peers.[35]

At first, Saionji had been rather reluctant to recommend Konoe. He knew the enormity of the hardship Konoe would face. Saionji wanted Konoe to be in charge when the time was calm, not at this most unstable and unpredictable moment. Saionji came to the realization, however, as many people did, that Konoe was perhaps the only political figure who might be able to put Japan on the right track.

In December 1936, Konoe Fumimaro on the platform of the National Diet (© Mainichi Photo Bank).

Contrary to Saionji's wish, Konoe turned down the recommendation, claiming poor health. Konoe also responded to Saionji's argument of why he should be recommended.[36] Konoe argued that a person who enjoyed popularity from all sides would be restricted in his governing because those who supported him would naturally expect to be pleased, and if not, would turn antagonistic.[37]

Saionji, however, did not accept Konoe's reasoning in turning down his recommendation, and was determined to make Konoe form his cabinet. He told Konoe that, at the current juncture, a matter of being healthy or not was secondary. He also said that he had authority and was determined to recommend anyone he hoped to be Prime Minister to the Emperor. Saionji urged Konoe to free himself from any trivial matters and accept his recommendation.[38]

Despite Saionji's strong recommendationto the Emperor and the Emperor's personal request for Konoe's acceptance, Konoe was as solid as a rock and showed no sign of wavering. His poor health and also his awareness of the unsuitability of his personality for the job were surely reasons for Konoe's stubbornness. As Konoe said in his writing, however, the essential reason for his rejection was his realization that he would not be effective in his governing because of the great gap existing between him and Saionji in their views, particularly in terms of the military after the debacle of the Kodo-ha.[39]

Saionji then selected Foreign Minister Hirota Koki. Facing two imminent tasks, the formulation of a clearly defined national policy and the settlement of the North China problem, Hirota's cabinet came up with the
policy called "The Fundamental Principles of the National Policy." It
specified Japan's goals in Asia, including the establishment of security in
Japan's leadership status in East Asia and Japan's advancement into the
South China Sea. It provided a basic guideline of how to achieve these
goals as characterized by such policies as the expansion of the military,
administrative reform, a new economic plan, and the reorganization of the
Japanese way of life. As Mikiso Hane points out in his book, *Modern Japan:
A Historical Survey*, this policy became a blueprint for the Japanese Empire
in terms of Japan's policy orientation, pursued by Hirota's successors, and
it eventually led Japan into the war in the Pacific.[40]

Though significant because of the specification of Japan's direction,
Hirota's cabinet suffered from the very beginning of his premiership. In
forming his cabinet, Hirota selected a few party politicians: Kawasaki
Takukichi, Yoshida Shigeru, and Shimomura Hiroshi. Then, led by General Terauchi Yoshikazu, the army bluntly interfered with this selection
by arguing that those selected were too liberal.

Facing such blunt political interference by the military, Hamada Kuni-
matsu, a member of the Seiyukai, retaliated. In January 1937, at the Sev-
entieth Parliamentary Session, Hamada bitterly criticized the military,
saying that the political ideology of the military was oriented toward a
dictatorship. Infuriated by Hamada's speech, General Terauchi accused
Hamada of insulting the military. Hamada responded by saying, "General
Terauchi claims that, in my speech, there are some remarks that are insulting to the military. As a representative of the nation, I cannot keep myself
quiet over the charge that I have insulted the nationally honored military.
General Terauchi, I would like you to point out which of my remarks actually insulted the military. If there is indeed such a remark, I would like to
apologize by committing '*hara-kiri.*' If not, however, I would like you to
do the same."[41] This so-called *Hara-kiri Monto* (dialogue) brought the fall
of the Hirota cabinet. Enraged, Terauchi urged Hirota to step down. When
Hirota refused, Terauchi resigned, causing the resignation of Hirota's entire
cabinet.

Saionji recommended General Ugaki Kazushige as Hirota's successor.
Ugaki's cabinet was never organized, however. The army found Ugaki
unacceptable for the following reasons: first, he was engaged in arms reduction as War Minister under Kato Takaaki; second, he equivocated in the
March Incident of 1931; and third, he was considered too close to party
politicians.[42] Facing the army's refusal to provide any general as a possi-

ble candidate, Ugaki was unable to appoint anyone as Minister of the Army. He was a clear victim of the revived practice that an appointee for Army Minister had to be made from among active army generals. As a last resort, Ugaki asked the Lord Keeper of the Privy Seal, Yuasa Kurahei, to issue an Imperial Order compelling the army to provide an army general.[43] Finding Yuasa unfavorable to his proposals, Ugaki felt it useless to pursue it further.

Already apprehensive about the fall of Hirota, Konoe was outraged by Ugaki's failure to form his cabinet because of the army's interference. Unable to remain indifferent, he wrote a letter of reproach to General Terauchi. In his letter, Konoe argued that while it made sense to debate a policy in terms of "right and wrong," rejecting a person who had been given an Imperial Order to be Prime Minister made no sense and raised a serious concern with regard to justice. Konoe emphasized that it was neither his being for or against formation of Ugaki cabinet nor correctness of a choice of Ugaki that made him speak up but his desire to preserve justice and respect the national polity. Clearly, to Konoe, nothing was more important than national justice and he was deeply worried that Ugaki's debacle would cause great disorder. When some associates of Konoe, afraid that the letter might result in something fatal to him, attempted to restrain him, Konoe told them that he had no regret to die for right cause.[44]

After Ugaki's fiasco, Army General Hayashi Senjuro, who was favorable to the army, was selected to be the successor to the Hirota cabinet. When Hayashi carried out the surprised dissolution of the Diet without any specific reason, however, the opposition parties, Seiyukai and Minseito, gained a majority and launched a movement to overthrow the Hayashi cabinet. Losing support even from the army, in May 1937 Hayashi resigned after serving for only four months.

Hayashi wanted Konoe to be his successor. On May 29, Hayashi sounded out Konoe regarding his interest in the job. Just like his refusal in the aftermath of the February Twenty-six Incident, Konoe told Hayashi that because of his poor health and inexperience, he should not be the one to be selected.[45] Then, Hayashi chose Army Minister Sugiyama under the consideration that a choice of any civilian would be taken as concession by the military to the political party and, therefore, would have negative repercussions for the military situation, particularly in China.[46]

Agreeing with Hayashi, Konoe and the Lord Keeper of the Privy Seal, Yuasa, supported the choice of Sugiyama Gen. Despite their support, the Sugiyama cabinet was never formed because of the strong opposition from Saionji against selecting an active Army Minister as Prime Minister.

Then Saionji, seeing no other appropriate candidate, once again recommended Konoe. He told his personal secretary, Harada Kumao, "It is absolutely bad to select the active Army Minister as Prime Minister. In this situation, I think, Konoe should be the one. I have always hesitated to choose Konoe and in fact wanted to avoid selecting him. If I am consulted, however, I cannot agree to choose someone in whom I have no faith. A choice has to be made in a reasonable manner. Although, considering the situation, it is quite pitiful that there is no other appropriate person but Konoe after all."[47]

Under Saionji's recommendation, the Imperial Order came to Konoe once again. Even to Konoe, it was out of the question to turn it down this time. In June 1937, rather reluctantly, Konoe accepted the Imperial Order. Thus, at the age of forty-six he embarked on his quest for the salvation of a deeply divided and troubled nation.

3

Konoe's First Cabinet

When Konoe accepted the Imperial Order to become Prime Minister, he was at the prime of his life. He enjoyed popularity and support from literally every segment of society. Tired and apprehensive about the endless political turmoil and the uncertainty of the direction in which Japan was heading, the nation was anxious to have a new leader, someone different and fresh who might be able to pull the nation together. In the eyes of the nation, Konoe was ideally fitted to fulfill such a national need. His status as one of the most distinguished court nobles, his well-acknowledged high intelligence, even his physical appearance (he was unusually tall for an Asian, over six feet), and most significantly, his indifference to any political ambition and fame made Konoe so unconventional, fresh, and attractive as a politician. In short, Japan found a desperately needed sense of security and hope in having Konoe as a leader.

It was Konoe, however, who, more than anyone else, knew that such high expectations placed on him were closer to an illusion than reality. As discussed in the previous chapter, although Konoe had an insightful grasp of the internal and external state of the nation, considering the enormity of the task and also the self-acknowledged unfitness of his character for politics, he himself knew that he fell short in terms of the capacity to fulfill the obligations of being Prime Minister.[1]

Facing an Imperial Order for the second time, however, it was his fate to accept it. He began to select the members of his cabinet. The Minister of the Army, Sugiyama Gen, and the Minister of the Navy, Yonai Mitsimasa, remained in office as Konoe desired. Konoe also wanted the Minister of Finance, Yuijo Toyotaro, to do the same. Facing the strong request of the army to appoint Baba Eiichi as Minister of Finance, Konoe reluctantly allowed Baba to be a member of the cabinet, not as Minister of Finance but as Home Minister. Yuijo protested against Baba's membership in the cabinet and resigned. In the end, a Vice Minister of Finance, Kaya Okinori, became Finance Minister.[2] With regard to selecting a Foreign Minister, Konoe strongly desired to have former Prime Minister

Hirota for the position. Konoe believed that Hirota, possessing characteristics to be a fine politician, such as tenacity, ambition, and shrewdness,
could play the role of making up for his weaknesses and could also serve
as his successor in case of his unexpected resignation.[3] At first, Hirota hesitated to take the position. In the end, he gave in to the resoluteness of
Konoe and Saionji. Another notable appointee, Kazami Akira, became the
chief secretary of the cabinet. He was quite appealing to the public because
of his personality and unorthodox political style.

Overall, the forming of Konoe's cabinet went smoothly. The only
exception was his decision to have Baba as Home Minister. Considering
Baba's pro-army style of financing and his unpopularity over his notorious financial policy under Hirota's cabinet, Konoe avoided selecting Baba
as Finance Minister. Nonetheless, by having Baba as Home Minister,
Konoe's cabinet still faced the army utilizing Baba as a source of influence
on Konoe's governing. In fact, in selecting the head of the Planning Board,
a position almost equivalent to Vice Premier, Konoe encountered the
army's challenge to having Home Minister Baba hold concurrently the
position of the head of the Planning Board.[4] It was fortunate for Konoe's
cabinet that Hirota agreed to take the position while serving as Foreign
Minister. Thus, Konoe managed to avoid some potentially dire consequences. Still, over this episode of the Baba controversy, Konoe could not
escape a minor setback. The national enthusiasm over having Konoe as a
Premier was somewhat diminished.

On June 4, 1937, four days after Konoe's reception of the Imperial
Order, his newly appointed cabinet was inaugurated. Right after the inauguration ceremony, Konoe announced his basic plan of governing. In it,
he stated, "If we continue to be in discord domestically, the international
community will see us worthy of contempt. I would like to mitigate the
discord as much as possible. It is desired that, by restraining ourselves, each
one of us tries to reduce conflict over interests, favoritism, and factionalism. To some extent, it is unavoidable to have conflict because of differ-
ences in the perception of our time. If we, however, without being
self-centered, seriously and deeply examine both international and
national circumstances we face today and keep talking to one another, we
will be able to avoid any drastic conflict. I would not say that you should
minimize conflict by totally being selfless. Considering today's situation,
I think the cabinet has to take appropriate leadership. My broad and extensive visions are, externally, to establish true peace based on international
justice and, internally, to carry out policies and set up institutions based
on socialist ideas."[5]

As this statement indicates, Konoe believed that his ultimate task as

The ministers of Konoe's first cabinet. In front and from right, Army Minister Sugiyama, Navy Minister Yonai, Prime Minister Konoe, and Foreign Minister Hirota. Konoe's first cabinet was inaugurated in June 1937 (© Mainichi Photo Bank).

a premier was to achieve an elimination of the discord between the government and the military. It was upon the consideration that only such an achievement would make it possible for Japan to establish what he advocated in his article "Reject the Anglo-American–Centered Peace," a creation of world peace truly based on international justice.

It was a formidable task. As Konoe recalled in his postwar memoir, *Ushinawareshi Seiji,* by the time Konoe announced the basic policy of his first cabinet, the army's political interference had markedly increased.[6] There was no longer Kodo-ha as a factional rival to Tosei-ha in the Army, and, if any attempt to appoint a member of Kodo-ha as Army Minister was made, it went nowhere because of the revived practice of choosing the Army Minister from among active army generals. Accordingly, the Army Minister was someone above the authority of the cabinet. He existed only to announce army policy as national policy and, hence, literally controlled the matter of life or death for the cabinet. Konoe was obliged to realize that, not being able to know where the army policy was coming from, his cabinet was destined to be manipulated by the shadow of the Supreme Command.

Understandably, Konoe was eager to obtain a national pardon for the convicted plotters of the February Twenty-six Incident. Despite his effort, Konoe's attempt to restore the Kodo-ha caused nothing but political commotion. The most significant factor in the restoration of the Kodo-ha was the fate of Mazaki Junzaburo. Almost one and a half years had passes since the February Twenty-six Incident, yet the trial of Mazaki was going nowhere. Considering Mazaki's position as one of the central figures of the Kodo-ha, the direction of Mazaki's fate was potentially explosive. Contention rose over the concern for the unfair treatment of Mazaki in comparison with that of General Ugaki after the March Incident in 1931. Just like Mazaki, Ugaki was not involved directly in the incident. Therefore, he was not put on trial and was later even given the Imperial Order to form his cabinet (although it was never organized). To many radical right-wing nationalists, including Konoe, what happened to Mazaki was harsh and unjust in comparison to the treatment Ugaki received.

In this setting, Konoe apprehended that if Mazaki happened to be given a guilty verdict, there would most likely be another rebellion. Also, even in the case of an innocent verdict, although unlikely, there would be political backlash by the Tosei-ha. So Konoe, taking into consideration the need to maintain internal peace, stop the unfair treatment of Mazaki, and, most importantly, restore national unity by bringing the Kodo-ha back to power, came to the conclusion that it would be best for the nation to seek a political settlement of Mazaki's case, a national pardon, rather than waiting for the settlement of a seemingly insoluble trial.[7]

Konoe's effort went nowhere. Even though he was not completely lacking support, in general, the thought prevailed that a national pardon would do more harm to the nation than good. Naturally, the army showed no sign of support for the pardon. Taking into consideration the constitutionality of a pardon, the navy also opposed it. There had been no precedent for a pardon since the enforcement of the constitution in 1889. Even Kido Koichi, who was Konoe's closest friend in the political arena and was sympathetic to his situation, also basically opposed the pardon. The strongest opposition came from Saionji. When he learned of Konoe's idea of a national pardon, Saionji was outraged: "If Konoe is to carry out something so unreasonable, it would be better for Konoe to step down. The Prime Minister doesn't have to be him."[8] Saionji's outrage was a result of his multiple apprehensions over the pardon: its constitutional ramifications; the negative impact on Konoe's political future; and potentially emotional harm to the Emperor because of his feelings toward Konoe. In his diary, Harada recalled how the Emperor reacted when Konoe formed his first cabinet. According to Harada, the Emperor believed that Konoe, unlike his predecessors, would strictly defend the constitution and was thus pleased with Konoe's first cabinet. He even said to the newly selected

Home Minister, Baba, "Under Konoe's administration, now I do not have to talk about the constitution."[9]

Facing opposition from a wide range of social arenas, and despite Konoe's tenacious effort, the national pardon did not take place. It was ironic, however, that Mazaki was released in the end because of insufficient evidence to convict him. For all others, however, the sentences were carried out. Konoe was deeply disappointed.

Then, only a month after Konoe formed his cabinet, an incident took place that was destined to lead not only Konoe's political life but also the nation down their tragic path. This was what is known as the Marco Polo Bridge Incident. Konoe stated in his postwar writing that he as well as many government officials, even the army officers on the domestic front, did not know that by the time Konoe accepted the Imperial Order, the army's actions in China since the Manchurian Incident had already created a tense situation. In fact, the situation was tense enough to bring armed conflict at any moment.[10] Hence, the incident was rather unexpected to Konoe and the nation as well. Only the Kwantung Army was not surprised. Unlike the Manchurian Incident, this incident was not a plot. It was rather accidental but not unexpected by the Kwantung Army, creating an opportunity for them to further advance their political and military quest in China.

The incident itself began as a skirmish. On the night of July 7, 1937, Japanese troops were conducting night maneuvers near the Marco Polo Bridge located in the city of Beijing. After the maneuvers, one Japanese soldier was found missing, and a request to search the area was made by Japanese troops. The Chinese unit, led by General Sung Che-yuan, also joined the search. Although the man in question shortly rejoined his unit (he had left it for a short while only to take care of a physiological need), unfortunately several gunshots were fired. By the next morning, more troops from both sides came to the scene. Fortunately, however, it did not go any further. The local authorities from both sides somehow managed to get the situation under control. On July 11, four days after the incident, a cease-fire was concluded. It was never found out how the shooting started and who shot first. This remains a mystery even today.

As soon as he learned about the Marco Polo Bridge Incident, Konoe promptly expressed his basic policy toward it: a policy of non-expansion.[11] Ishihara Kanji, chief of the operations division of the general staff, shared the same policy.[12] Both Konoe and Ishihara were convinced that Japan was not ready to engage in a major war militarily and economically. They were afraid that any major military confrontation with China would surely develop into a war of attrition, consequently making Japan vulnerable to the Soviet threat from the north.

On June 4, 1937, Konoe Fumimaro and the members of his first cabinet posing for a photograph (© Mainichi Photo Bank).

Then, in his consideration of how to achieve a successful non-expansion policy, Konoe recalled his meeting with the Chinese ambassador to Japan, Chiang Tso-pin, in 1932. Konoe was living in the city of Kamakura, Kanagawa Prefecture, at that time, and Chiang Tso-pin also happened to be staying there. In the summer of 1932, Chiang visited Konoe with his secretary, Ting Shao-jeng, who was Konoe's high school classmate.

In the meeting, Ambassador Chiang, who was an immediate subordinate to Chiang Kai-shek, told Konoe his thoughts on the Sino-Japanese relationship.[13] According to him, if the present Sino-Japanese relationship continued, not only would a major clash between Japan and China be inevitable but also the United States, Great Britain, and the Soviet Union would become part of it. In the end, what would most likely follow would be another world war. Japan should note that Chiang Kai-shek and his Nationalist Party were the central forces of China. Although there were some other leaders such as Wu P'ei-fu, they were only marginal powers. It would be impossible to solve the Sino-Japanese problems as long as Japan kept engaging in them. Although the Japanese military, by making the small factions of the Chinese military cliques confront each other, was trying to obstruct the Chinese unification effort, the Chinese interest in unification was steadily growing under the central leadership of Chiang Kai-shek and the Nationalist Party. Therefore, the goal of the Japanese military, to overthrow the Nationalist Party, had almost no prospect of being accomplished. If the current situation continued, China would become more and more desperate in their resistance. Konoe absolutely had no reason to disagree with Ambassador Chiang.[14]

Then in 1935, in order to make a definite plan for improving the Sino-Japanese relationship, Ambassador Chiang went back to China to have a talk with Chiang Kai-shek, who was leading the punitive force against the Communists in the Sian area. In the summer of that year, Ambassador Chiang sent Ting Shao-jeng back to Konoe with the completed plan. The summary of the plan follows:

1. China would not question the Manchurian issue for the time being.
2. All unequal treaties would be abolished, except those regarding Manchuria, thereby putting China and Japan on equal standing. It was to be done, however, with two conditions: one was China's self-restraint from anti-Japanese education, and the other, Japan's halting its propaganda of Japanese superiority over the Chinese.
3. A treaty of economic partnership between the two nations would be discussed once the principle of equality in the Sino-Japanese relationship was established.
4. A military alliance would be formed based on the establishment of a treaty of economic partnership.

Konoe generally agreed with this plan and strongly suggested the Okada cabinet make the effort to accept it. The army, however, found the plan unacceptable. Hoping for China's early recognition of Manchurian sovereignty, the army was particularly dissatisfied with China's decision not to question the Manchurian issue.

Recalling these past memories, Konoe did not hesitate to have a direct talk with Chiang Kai-shek. This explains why, shortly after the Marco Polo Bridge Incident broke out, Konoe did not agree to Army Minister Sugiyama's request to send three home divisions to support about five thousand troops already in China. First of all, Konoe was afraid that such a dispatch would put Japan in a more difficult position in the international community. Secondly, Konoe did not want such a dispatch to become an obstacle to his effort to have direct engagement with Chiang Kai-shek.

Sugiyama was not, however, about to give up his plan to send the troops. At the Five Minister Conference held on July 11, Sugiyama again suggested sending troops. Although there was opposition from Navy Minister Yonai Mitsumasa, the plan was adopted with one condition: that the dispatch of troops would immediately be canceled if any situational change made it unnecessary. It was only a few hours before the cease-fire treaty was concluded.[15]

Thus, although reluctant, Konoe agreed to the decision to dispatch the troops with one condition: that the policy of non-expansion be maintained. Konoe told Harada that disapproving of the dispatch of troops did not make much difference because, if that happened, the Minister of the Army would have to resign, consequently causing the fall of his cabinet, and whoever replaced him would not be able to control the military. Konoe thought that it would be more reasonable for him to agree to the dispatch and take responsibility for whatever would follow.[16] Sugiyama accepted Konoe's condition, and the dispatch of the troops was made.

As feared by Konoe, the dispatch did nothing but escalate deterioration of the Sino-Japanese relationship. While the Japanese public was excited about and strongly supportive of the government's tough stand against China, the Chinese responded to the deployment of Japanese troops by further strengthening their resistance. The Chinese army, withdrawing toward the Paoting area as had been agreed by General Sung and the Japanese army in North China, halted their withdrawal and began to reenter Beijing, thus setting the stage for further military clashes.[17] On July 28, the Chinese militia in Tungchow attacked, killing 260 Japanese solders and civilians in retaliation for an accidental bombing of the Chinese barracks by a Kwantung Army plane.[18]

Alerted and wishing to prevent further deterioration, Konoe decided to send Miyazaki Ryusuke to Nanjing to sound out the Nanjing government for a possible summit between Konoe and Chiang Kai-shek.[19] Although Sugiyama agreed to send Miyazaki, when Miyazaki was about to board at Port Kobe, he was arrested by the local military police. Puzzled, Konoe tried to get an explanation from Sugiyama. Such an explanation, however, never came.

Meanwhile, contrary to Konoe's wish for non-expansion, the escalation of the incident continued, showing no sign of abating. Worried that a continuation of this trend would make Japan's advocacy for non-expansionism increasingly harder to sell to other powers and would also make it less feasible for Japan to establish foreign and financial policies if there was nothing but distrust between the government and the military, Konoe attempted to find out how far the army thought the military zone would expand.[20]

At July's special parliamentary session, Konoe made an arrangement to have the Minister of Overseas Development, Otani Sonyu, ask Sugiyama about how far the army intended to go. Sugiyama ignored the question by keeping silent. Then the Minister of the Navy, Yonai Mitsumasa, unable to stand by, said, "It has been decided that the military advancement is to halt somewhere between Yung-ting ho and Paoting." Infuriated, Sugiyama shouted at Yonai, "It is very foolish for you to say such a thing here."[21] Frustrated, Konoe was compelled to appeal to the Emperor.[22] Konoe told him that if this situation continued, it would be fairly difficult for the government to carry out foreign, financial, and other governing affairs, bringing the nation and its people immeasurable misfortune. Konoe asked the Emperor to tell him in advance of any essential matters concerning the Supreme Command. The Emperor responded by saying, "Your appeal is quite reasonable."[23]

A few days later, the Emperor told Konoe that he had conveyed Konoe's concern to the Minister of the Army and the Minister's remark that the army was not able to say anything about military operations at a cabinet conference, at which ministers of the political parties were usually present.[24] The Emperor promised that he would directly inform Konoe and the Minister of Foreign Affairs about any matters regarding supreme command.

Through these episodes, Konoe was convinced that there was an even wider gap between the cabinet and the military, and he fell far short of having sufficient power to control the military. He also realized that, to make the situation worse, the executive military officers themselves on the domestic front lacked the power to control their overseas subordinates.

Meanwhile the military escalation continued. On August 9, 1937, in Shanghai, two members of the Japanese marine troops were killed by the Chinese Peace Preservation Corps. Upon the request of Army Minister Sugiyama, the Konoe cabinet sent two home divisions to Shanghai.[25] It was followed by the military clash between Japanese and Chinese forces. With this so-called Shanghai Incident, the military conflict between Japan and China expanded from North China to Central China.

Captain Matsui Sekon was appointed as the commander-in-chief of the Japanese expeditionary army in Central China.[26] On the day of his departure, he said to Sugiyama, "I would like to go as far as Nanjing. So, I would like you to prepare the army for it." Also to Konoe, he said, "Prime Minister, please approve my intention to go as far as Nanjing." Konoe, who understood that the primary purpose of sending troops was to protect the Japanese residents in central China, was somewhat puzzled and asked Sugiyama whether the army really intended to go as far as Nanjing. Sugiyama responded, "At most, to Wu-hu." Contrary to Sugiyama's prediction, however, the Japanese troops advanced to Paoting in northern China and far beyond Wu-hu in Central China, spreading the chaos of war to a wider area.

The minor incident that began at the Marco Polo Bridge was no longer minor. It was at this time that the Konoe government began to refer to the incident as the China Incident. Although Konoe still wanted to settle the incident as a local matter, the situation simply did not allow him to sustain his wish. Accordingly, Konoe realized that merely mitigating the discord between his government and the military was hardly enough. The Konoe government began its structural change in order to enhance its political power and prepare the nation for the rapidly expanding military conflict with China.

The first thing Konoe did was to set up a cabinet counselor system. It was adopted on October 15, 1937, after the Seventy-second Diet adjourned.[27] Ugaki Kazushige and Araki Sadao from the army, Abo Kiyokazu and Suetsugu Nobumasa from the navy, Machida Chuji (Minseito president), Maeda Yonezo (Seiyukai), and Akita Kiyoshi (the Association of the First Bank) from the political parties, Go Seinosuke and Ikeda Seihin from the business world, and Matsuoka Yosuke (South Manchuria Railway president) from the diplomatic field were selected as members. The system was designed to assist Konoe's cabinet in policy making with regard to the Sino-Japanese Incident. It did not meet Konoe's expectation, however, but became a mere pool organization to fill vacancies in the event that any cabinet member resigned.[28]

Shortly after setting up this counselor system, the Minister of Education, Yasui Eiji, resigned, and upon request from Konoe, Kido Koichi accepted the position. At the Far East Trial in 1946, Kido testified that he accepted Konoe's request because, as a close friend, he became very sympathetic to Konoe, who was rather isolated in his own government, and also, he shared Konoe's desire to end the Sino-Japanese Incident by the end of 1937.[29] Knowing that Kido had all the qualities of a shrewd politician, while Konoe did not have any practical experience in administration and, as a politician, lacked executive ability, Saionji was very pleased by Kido's decision to join Konoe's cabinet.

Then, in November 1937, as further structural change, the Imperial Headquarters was set up. Konoe wanted to join the Imperial Headquarters in order to have a coordinated policy between the government decision making and the military operation and also to prevent an inclination that the Headquarters, as a mere military organization, would become detached from the governing body.[30] Considering that accepting Konoe's request would violate the right of the supreme command to be independent, both the army and navy turned down Konoe's request. The Imperial Headquarters became exactly what Konoe had feared. To make matters worse, the army and navy could not even coordinate with each other.

In addition, there was a protest from Sugiyama about the leaking of confidential matters through Konoe's close associates. Thinking that a great number of ministers may be sources of the leaks, Sugiyama suggested that Konoe downsize the cabinet by lowering the number of ministers.[31]

Having already been frustrated by the constant interference of the army, and seeing no sign of narrowing the gap between national affairs and military operations, Konoe started thinking about his resignation. Konoe met Kido and told him about his intent to resign and asked him to convey it to Saionji and Home Minister Baba. Konoe told Kido that he was not able to make a decision regarding Sugiyama's request, but something had to be done to make some changes to the current situation. Konoe continued to say that it might be most appropriate for him to step down. The timing was right, since having established the Imperial Headquarters, his government was entering the second phase of its plan.[32]

Strongly opposing Konoe's decision, Kido said to him,

> To think like that itself is very disturbing. People might think it would be the same as your dying as a beggar. It will be a great shock to the nation. Above all, we'll be very sorry for the Emperor. The Emperor as well as the nation has great confidence and expectations on you. Knowing that you are in charge gives them hope and a sense of security. Therefore, if you resign now, internally it might cause further social and economic chaos, and externally, it might result in a sharp decline in the value of our currency, thus making it hard for Japan to buy goods from foreign nations. Diplomatically and politically it is also absolutely unwise. Our overseas troops were fighting as hard as they could and achieving victory after victory. If the central government shows any sign of weakness because of your resignation, it would make China contemptuous of Japan, and Japan would lose its dignity to the other nations. Nonetheless, if you dare to resign, Saionji would ask the Emperor to reissue the Imperial Order. If you say that you will have no intention to accept it when that happens, I would like to decline to be an intermediary between you and Saionji.[33]

Agreeing with Kido, Harada conveyed Konoe's intention to resign to Saionji. Saionji was outraged. He thought Konoe was impossible. To him, Konoe had been always a discerning individual. Now, suddenly, he seemed to be a man with no brain.[34] Then Harada told Saionji that Konoe was actually a thoughtful individual, but his timidity often made him shy away under criticism; that was why he sometimes acted like a man with no opinion.[35] Understanding that Konoe's resignation was out of the question, Saionji asked Kido and Harada to encourage Konoe to remain in office. In the end, such encouragement paid off. Konoe agreed to stay in power, at least for the time being.

Meanwhile, after the Shanghai Incident, the Japanese army showed no sign of slowing down. By the end of October, the fall of Nanjing became almost certain. Corresponding to such development, there was a new attitude in Japan's response to Chinese resistance. There was a growing thought that it would be better off for Japan to wait for the fall of Nanjing before it further pursued a peace settlement with China. Accordingly, Japan did not show much enthusiasm when Germany, with an apprehension that the continuous conflict between Japan and China would become an obstacle for its own interests and advancement in China, offered to mediate between the governments of China and Japan through Herbert von Dirksen, German ambassador to Japan, and Oskar P. Trutmann, German ambassador to China.[36]

On December 13, Nanjing fell into the hands of the Japanese army. The Nationalist government fled to Chungking and, declaring it the capital, continued their resistance. The Japanese government held the Imperial Headquarters—Cabinet Liaison Conference to discuss how a fundamental policy toward China and a peace settlement ought to be sought in this new setting. On December 22, 1937, the Konoe government offered China four basic conditions for peace through Ambassador von Dirksen and expected to have China's response by early January of the following year. Those four conditions were the following:

1. China should abandon its pro-Communist anti–Japan and Manchuria policies and cooperate with Japan and Manchuria in a joint anti–Communist policy.
2. A non-military zone would be created in each required area with a special organization set up there.
3. An economic agreement would be reached among Japan, Manchuria, and China.
4. China would be required to pay an indemnity to imperial Japan.

The day before, December 21, Konoe's cabinet had also made the following statement as an outline for dealing with the China issues: "The Nanjing government, indicating their readiness for long resistance, is showing no sign of regret. Also, as our military expansion goes on, our occupied area has been getting larger. It is becoming urgent to deal with such an expanded area. In order to cope with these developments, from now on, we do not necessarily expect to have a settlement with the Nanjing government itself, but will find another route to do so. That is the way we have to deal with the long resistance of the Nanjing government."[37]

As one can see from the four conditions Japan offered to China and the above statement, some government and military officials overvalued the fall of Nanjing as an advantage in dealing with the Nationalist government. They began to see that it was no longer necessary to deal with the Nationalist government, which, in their eyes, had become equivalent only to one of the provincial governments. Japan, therefore, should wait for the birth of a new central government in China. Significantly, Konoe and Kido were inclined to share this thought.

On the other hand, while the nation in general was supportive of such a tough stand against China, the General Staff Office had apprehensions about such a change of tone and continuously sought an early settlement of the conflict with China. To them, the war against China was the wrong war at the wrong time. The real threat to Japan was the Soviet Union. Therefore, in order to prepare for a war against the Soviet Union, it was vital to Japan to settle the war with China as early as possible.

In response to such apprehensions, Konoe told Kido that, although he understood that the General Staff Office was eager to achieve peace, since Japan had already expanded so much into China, Japan could not act like a defeated nation and seek a halfway mutual peace by giving in to enemy's demands. If that happened, to Konoe, the other nations might start thinking that Japan was now vulnerable to foreign pressure. This sort of development might even cause an economic setback for Japan, such as sharp decline in value of its currency, putting Japan into a dire situation in international business. In the worst case, Japan might get into a panic. Therefore, Konoe emphasized that the nation had to stand firm and act strictly and responsibly to the circumstantial conditions it was confronting.[38]

Kido shared Konoe's opinion. Like Konoe, he was apprehensive about the General Staff Office's haste manner to achieve a peace settlement, believing that such hastiness would only result in revealing Japan's plan to achieve peace without actually producing any peace settlement. To Kido, Japan would gain nothing from the General Staff Office's plan; it would actually help the enemy. So, he argued, instead of hastiness, what Japan needed was to have more deliberations and form a comprehensive peace plan to cover everything. Kido also stated that Japan should not have Germany as a mediator for a peace settlement. Kido believed that Germany would take advantage.[39]

While these high-handed rhetorical talks were widely spreading in Japan, the response from the Nationalist government was not forthcoming. Then, at the Imperial Conference held on January 11, 1938, Konoe's government adopted its basic policy in settling the China Incident. It stated that it was Japan's unwavering policy to establish the foundation for peace in the Orient in cooperation with China and Manchuria and, by utilizing that foundation as a core force, to make a contribution to world peace. With regard to the disposition of the China Incident, both China and Japan should clear away all past discords between them and re-establish a new relationship based on a broader point of view. Both nations would mutually respect their sovereignty and territorial rights, and make it their ultimate goal to establish an unshakable unity between them. In order to achieve all of these aims, the two nations would make a definite promise to meet the following conditions: (1) Japan, Manchuria, and China were to abolish any political, educational, and commercial propaganda that would destroy the goodness of their relationships; (2) Japan, Manchuria, and China were to have mutual cooperation in realizing cultural affiliations and anti-Communist policy; and (3) Japan, Manchuria, and China were to conclude a treaty of mutual assistance for an industrialized economy.[40]

Konoe specified that if the Nationalist government of China sincerely reflected on their position and sought peace according to the above conditions, Japan would be ready to negotiate. If not, Japan would cease to deal with the Nationalist government, promote the establishment of a new

Chinese government, and, in cooperation with it, rearrange its relationship with China and ultimately build a new China.

Then, on January 13, 1938, the Nationalist government finally responded to Japan's offer for peace conditions—not with acceptance, however, but instead with a further inquiry. According to the response from Chiang Kai-shek, the Japanese peace conditions were too vague. China needed elaboration. To the Konoe government, this was enough to conclude that Chiang had no sincere wish to have peace.

Three days later, on January 16, Konoe's famous statement of "No deal with the Nationalist government" came. It stated,

Since the fall of Nanjing until today, the imperial government of Japan has been patient to give the last chance to the Chinese Nationalist government for their reflection. The Nationalist government, however, unable to understand Japan's sincere intention and

In October 1937, Prime Minister Konoe swinging a golf club (© Mainichi Photo Bank).

also failing to see the unbearable suffering of their own people, continues to take a policy of resistance and take no consideration for the comprehensive peace of the Far East. Imperial Japan, therefore, no longer dealing with the Nationalist government of China, expects an establishment and development of a new Chinese government that can truly be in cooperation with Japan. By adjusting diplomatic relations with China, Japan is ready to cooperate for the establishment of such a newborn China. From the beginning, Japan has kept a policy of respecting China's territorial right and sovereignty and also the right of other nations to protect their interests in China. Japan has no intention to alter that policy. Japan's responsibility toward the peace of the Far East is becoming increasingly greater. The Japanese government sincerely hopes that our people will take their further share in carrying out this grave task.[41]

With this statement, diplomatic relations between China and Japan were cut off. It did not take long, however, for Konoe to realize that the above statement was a mistake. Konoe himself stated that it was deeply regrettable.[42] For the next ten months or so, Konoe took various steps to achieve the restoration of diplomacy. It was not successful, however, until November 3, 1938, when Konoe made another statement that Japan would not necessarily reject a deal with the Nationalist government if it abandoned its anti-Japanese policy and made an effort to establish a new order in the Far East. With this statement, the diplomatic channel was somewhat restored between China and Japan.

The question that needs to be addressed is why Konoe made such a blunder, contradicting his own desire for an early settlement of the incident. In his book *Konoe Fumimaro: Emperor, Military, and Nation*, Okada Takeo argues that there was a great chance to achieve peace before the fall of Nanjing.[43] According to him, the Nationalist party was critically divided. The faction led by Wang Ching-wei was eager to compromise with Japan for the sake of ending the war. Also, in view of the fact that the continuous resistance against Japan was actually enhancing public support for the Communist Party of China and therefore threatening the leading position of the Nationalist Party, Chiang Kai-shek himself was inclined to have a more conciliatory policy toward Japan. Internationally, the Anglo-Saxon nations were still conciliatory toward Japan, at least during the beginning phase of the Sino-Japanese War, if not in rhetoric. Furthermore, at the Brussels Conference held by the signatory nations of the Nine Power Treaty on November 3–24, 1937, to assess the situation of the Sino-Japanese War, only the Soviet Union showed any willingness to take any major sanction against Japan. Okada argues that all these considerations made Chiang move unexpectedly toward accepting the peace terms offered by Japan.

It is true, as Okada points out, that there was a division in the Nationalist government of China and also that the international community, at least during the period of late 1937 through 1938, was rather conciliatory to Japan. Nonetheless, Okada's assertion that Chiang was accordingly inclined to have an early peace settlement with Japan is difficult to sustain. On the contrary, the opposite was quite true.

In December 1936, Chiang Kai-shek, who had unleashed the Sixth Extermination Campaign in Sian against the Communists, was kidnapped by his own bandit suppression chief, Chang Hsueh-liang.[44] After two weeks of confinement, upon the consideration that murdering Chiang Kai-shek would result in full-scale civil war, only benefiting Japan by letting it take advantage of the chaotic situation, Chiang Hsueh-liang released Chiang. This so-called Sian Incident, tossing away the long-lasting hostilities between the Nationalists and the Communists to create a coalition front line against Japanese aggression, drastically altered the nature of the Sino-Japanese conflict. As it turned out, it was to be a fatal blow to Japan. Since the Sian Incident, therefore, despite the split within the Nationalist government, China as a nation was unified, at least at this juncture. Through the ongoing Japanese aggression that peaked when the notorious Nanjing massacre took place in early January of 1938, nationalism in China was raging. Any attempt to compromise with Japan would be fatal to the Nationalist government or any other party. On the other hand, the strong stand against Japan became a driving force for China to achieve national unification. Chiang clearly understood this and politically calculated that it was time for national unification, not for the battle of an ideological unification.

Unable to see the magnitude of this rapidly rising nationalism in China, Konoe made a wrong assumption, thinking that Chiang would be forthcoming and cooperative with Japan's fundamental aim, the establishment of an East Asia totally free from Western imperialism. To Konoe, Japan, as part of East Asia, shared the same fate as China, fighting against their common enemies: Western imperialism and Communist intrusion.

The problem for Konoe was that China had a different way of looking at Japan's standing in East Asia. To China, Japan became a Western nation in East Asia. With Japan's rapid and drastic modernization and industrialization, Japan began to portray itself like a Western imperialist, particularly in the eyes of Japan's neighbors. It was becoming increasingly difficult for China to see Japan as its brotherly nation. It was this failure to see these changing characteristics of the Sino-Japanese relationship that led Konoe to make a regretful statement. Realizing his mistake, as stated earlier, Konoe took various steps to carry "damage control."

Meanwhile, as the military expansion in China continued, Japan's wartime policies also took concrete shape, especially after Konoe's statement of "No deal with the Nationalist government." At the Seventy-third Diet in December 1938, three bills were passed: the national mobilization bill, the national control of electric power bill, and the farm land adjustment bill. With the legislation of these three bills, Japan was becoming an increasingly regimented society under the military-controlled government. Particularly under the national mobilization law, the national economy and the daily lives of the people were put under strict control by the military and the government's bureaucracy.

Along with the other two bills, the national mobilization bill, which would put Tosei-ha in control of the army, was expected to pass. There was, however, a far more realistic incentive for such mobilization. Facing a potentially catastrophic financial crisis regarding international revenue and expenditures because of Japan's isolation in the world community, the Japanese economy was in a crisis. Furthermore, because of the expanded war effort, the military budget was skyrocketing. Japan could no longer afford to indulge in business as usual. If it did, Japan would appear to be choking itself with its own hands, leading to a "national bankruptcy."[45] This is exactly why Konoe, despite his awareness that the policy of national mobilization was driven by the military, made all the efforts to implement the bill.

With the nation heading rather rapidly toward totalitarianism, the constitutionality of the national mobilization policy inevitably became an issue under the leadership of the political parties. Both Minseito and Seiyukai argued that, depending on how it was implemented, the law of national mobilization would infringe upon the constitutionally guaranteed right and duty of the people and also would render parliament literally powerless toward it.[46] They urged Konoe not to submit the bill. Konoe was unwilling to accept the wish of the political parties, and the military, led by Army Minister Sugiyama, was determined to make sure that the bill would be submitted.

Thus, the Konoe cabinet, despite opposition from both Seiyukai and Minseito, submitted the bill during the Lower House general session on February 28, 1938. Konoe was absent because of his sickness. Foreign Minister Hirota took the role of providing the reason for the bill's submission. Facing a sharp attack and criticism by both parties, the Konoe cabinet was obliged to provide a rather embarrassing explanation: this law would not be adopted to deal with China Incident directly, but rather it was designed in anticipation of the time when Japan faced a larger-scale war in the future.

Under intricately divided political circumstances of the conflict between the military and the political parties, including the internal split within the parties (pro-military and anti-military) over the national mobilization bill, the consideration of the national mobilization bill at the committee level was hardly going forward. On March 2, Konoe, who was still sick, forced himself to attend the House to smooth out the situation. Konoe's effort, however, was not successful. The very next day, at the committee meeting, when Sato Kenichi representing the Ministry of the Army was explaining the army's standing on the national mobilization bill, Miyazaki Chokichi from Seiyukai interrupted Sato by saying to the chairman, "How long are you going to allow Sato to go on?" The chairman ignored Miyazaki and allowed Sato to continue. Then Miyazaki said to Sato, "Don't continue such trivial explanation." Outraged, Sato shouted at Miyazaki, "Shut up!" In this clamorous atmosphere, the meeting was adjourned.[47] Then the headquarters of Minseito and Seiyukai were occupied by the right-wing organization with the slogan of "Defend the nation from Communism," followed by the assault on Abe Isoo, chairman of the Shakai Taishuto, by the right-wing nationalists.

Despite these incidents, the political parties continued to fight in order to stop the national mobilization bill from becoming a law. In the end, however, they had to give in to the pressure from the military-controlled Konoe cabinet. The bill became a law when the Lower House passed it at the general conference on March 16, 1938. At the same conference, Nishio Suehiro from the Social People's Party said in his supporting speech, "A war in the future is a war of national power. It is essential to integrate manpower, economic power, and spiritual power." Specifically to Konoe, he said, "Like Mussolini, like Hitler, and like Stalin, in a bold and straightforward fashion, [you must] choose a direction in which Japan should be heading." Minseito and Seiyukai both protested against Nishio's remark, saying, "How dare you ask Japan's Prime Minister to be a dictator!"[48] Because of his remark, Nishio ended up losing his seat in the Lower House.

As this episode indicates, with the inclination of the socialist parties to back the army on the national mobilization bill and the rapid increase in the number of members of Minseito and Seiyukai who were becoming supportive of the pro-military position on the bill, the general mood of the nation on this issue was becoming increasingly pro-military. The leaders of Minseito and Seiyukai felt that unless something was done, they would be helpless in defending parliamentary politics and turning Japan away from disaster.

Through this apprehension, the movement toward establishing a new party began. Sensing the growing political crisis caused by the right-wing nationalists, Home Minister Suetsugu Nobumasa advised Konoe that the root of the political instability was a lack of unity, as seen in the split of the political parties over legislating the national mobilization bill.[49] Suetsugu urged Konoe to dissolve the Lower House, seek the advice of the various political parties, and establish a new political foundation.

While Konoe was hesitant, members of the Konoe cabinet such as Arima Yoriyasu, Nagai Ryutaro, Nakajima Chikuhei, and Kido Koichi agreed to dissolve the Lower House. They insisted, however, that there was no point in re-establishing the political foundation under the leadership of Minseito or Seiyukai: it had to be done under a new political party. That belief was shared by the nation as a whole. They agreed that, as stated in one of the newspapers, it was totally up to Konoe if such a new party would be established or not. If Konoe agreed to be the head of the party, it could be done, but without his approval, it could not succeed. Konoe himself had some interest in creating not necessarily a new party, but a sort of a national organization. He thought that if such an organization were set up to galvanize the whole nation, it would be possible to have some control over the military, the bureaucracy, and the political parties, and then it might also be possible to unify the government, bringing the war to an end.[50]

Hence, there was an expectation that Konoe would take a leadership role if a new party was to be set up along the lines that he envisioned. As will be discussed below, Konoe would later decide to create such an organization. At this juncture, however, having had no precise idea of how and in what shape it should be created, he was unwilling to go forward. Annoyed by the persistence of the political parties, Konoe said to Harada, "With regard to unifying the Minseito and the Seiyukai by creating a new party, they constantly entreat me to lead a new party. I have no intention of doing so. I cannot say so, however. If I do, it might cause some disorder. I really do not know what to do."[51] All his close associates, such as Kido, Saionji, and Harada, agreed that Konoe should not accept a plea from the political parties at this juncture. In the end, an attempt to create a new party was abandoned.

Meanwhile, in early April 1938, shortly after the Seventy-third Diet ended, Konoe was forced to stay home for about 20 days to recover from fatigue and sickness. Once again it was rumored that Konoe would resign. In fact, Konoe himself had been debating the choice of either resigning or reforming the cabinet. He understood that in order to overcome the grave situation the nation was then facing, there had to be cabinet reform. Such reform, however, would be meaningless unless the Army Minister was also replaced. Knowing how difficult that would be to carry out, Konoe contemplated the other option, his resignation in order to rejuvenate Japan's stagnant politics.

First Konoe went to see the Emperor and told him how difficult it was for him to continue to serve as Prime Minister. He said to the Emperor that a person like him who enjoyed wide popularity did not actually possess real power but had a tendency to be treated like a "mannequin" without being informed of anything. Then Konoe saw Kido and told him about his intention to resign. Kido responded by saying, "It is not time to quit. By reforming the cabinet, you should remain the Prime Minister, at least until September or October."[52] Finance Minister Kaga Okinori, Kazami Akira, Harada Kumao, and all of Konoe's other associates agreed with Kido. When Harada told Saionji about Konoe's desire to resign, Saionji, although sympathetic to Konoe because of the enormous difficulty Konoe was facing, again strongly opposed it. He said to Harada, "There should not be even any talk that Konoe would be resigning. Konoe's resignation is out of the question. If his health is the problem, he should go someplace to concentrate on restoring his health. If necessary, he should appoint a temporary replacement so that he can have sufficient time for recuperation. It is impossible to reissue the Imperial Order after Konoe's resignation. Konoe has to stay on."[53] Saionji asked Harada to tell the Home Minister that he should have the Emperor tell Konoe not to quit.

Facing all this opposition, Konoe once again refrained from resigning. Now cabinet reorganization was essential and had to be carried out rather promptly. As mentioned earlier, cabinet reorganization was meaningless if there was no replacement of the Army Minister. Konoe told Harada on April 1, 1938, about the Army Minister's trip to North China. He did not know anything about the purpose of the trip. Except for Konoe, the Navy Minister, and the Foreign Minister, no cabinet members knew about the trip. This was, Konoe lamented to Harada, the way the Army always acted: when any wrongdoing took place, the Army always blamed the government. So, in order to end such distressful conduct of the army, Konoe thought it was essential to select as his successor someone who know the weak point of the army to control it. Konoe thought General Ugaki Kazushige would be an ideal choice.[54]

With the special status of the military operating under protection of the Imperial Code and also the revived rule of selecting an Army Minister from active army generals, Konoe knew the task of replacing the Army Minister was next to impossible. After the blunder of his earlier statement "No deal with the Nationalist government of China," however, if there was any chance for Konoe to make up for his mistake and bring the Sino-Japanese War to a successful end, cabinet reorganization and replacing the Army Minister were indispensable. Konoe was determined to carry out these tasks.

Although it was quite desirable for Konoe to choose someone from the Kodo-ha as the Army Minister, when he realized that all his associates and the Emperor opposed it, he knew it was almost out of the question. Then Konoe chose Itagaki Seishiro, who was conducting military operations in the front line of Xuzhou. Itagaki was strongly in favor of containment regarding the China Incident and was relatively less tainted by factionalism. Furui Inosuke from Domei Tsushin was dispatched to convey Konoe's message to Itagaki. Furui said to Itagaki, "Despite the government policy of non-expansion, the China Incident is continuously expanding. There has to be a change of policy from non-expansion to a peace settlement. It is therefore essential to appoint someone as the Army Minister who is able to carry it out. Konoe hopes that you are the one."[55] Itagaki believed that in order to achieve peace, Japan had to withdraw completely from China, and so he had no reason to reject the offer.

Having an informal consent from Itagaki, Konoe began his maneuvering to replace Sugiyama. Sympathetic to Konoe's position, the Emperor and the Chief of General Staff Prince Kan'in were willing to pressure Sugiyama. In fact, Sugiyama was advised to resign by Prince Kan'in and Prince Nashimoto. Under this growing pressure, Sugiyama complained to Harada, "Everything is moving toward my resignation. Nothing can be done to stop it. Political interference by the military has been often noted, but this is an interference into a military matter by politics!"[56] Sugiyama resigned and was replaced by Itagaki Seishiro. Konoe wrote in his memoir that he was very pleased about accomplishing this replacement of the Army Minister since it was done under an initiative of the cabinet itself.[57]

Konoe also wanted to replace Foreign Minister Hirota. Expectations for Hirota's performance as Foreign Minister had been high, the results were disappointing to Konoe. According to Konoe, the Foreign Ministry under the leadership of Hirota originally presented the statement of "No deal with the Nationalist government."[58] The replacement of Hirota was not something, however, that Konoe could easily accomplish, because it was Konoe who had appointed former Prime Minister Hirota as the Foreign Minister, despite Hirota's reluctance to accept. Fortunately, however, Hirota was willing to step down. He told Konoe that he wanted to resign anyway if the cabinet reorganization was to be carried out.

Konoe had Ugaki in mind to replace Hirota. Initially Ugaki turned down Konoe's offer because of his inexperience in foreign affairs. He was told, however, that unless he accepted, Ikeda Seihin, another important appointee as Finance Minister, also would reject Konoe's offer. Then Konoe most likely would have to resign, and he would be solely responsible for it, so Ugaki decided to take Konoe's offer.[59] Ugaki raised the following conditions for his acceptance:

1. Strong cabinet unity would be established.
2. A policy of achieving prompt peace would be adopted.
3. Peace negotiations with China would begin.
4. Konoe's statement (no deal with the Nationalist government) would be withdrawn on January 16 when it became necessary.

Upon Konoe's acceptance of Ugaki's conditions, Ugaki became a member of Konoe's newly reorganized cabinet, making the rest of the appointments relatively smooth. Ikeda Seihin became Finance Minister, replacing Kaga Okinori.[60] Kido Koichi decided to be the full-time Minister of Health and Welfare. Then Araki Sadeo succeeded Kido as Minister of Education. On May 26, 1938, the newly reorganized cabinet was set up.

The impact of this new cabinet was almost immediate, particularly in terms of the diplomatic effort to settle the Sino-Japanese War. Shortly after Ugaki entered the Konoe cabinet, he received a telegram from Chang Ch'un, the director of the Foreign Division of Chiang Kai-shek's government and an old friend of Ugaki's. In the telegram, Chang Ch'un said, "It is very nice to hear that you have become the Foreign Minister. It is great news for East Asia. I have met you many times to exchange our opinions on East Asian issues. I am sure all those opinions you have mentioned would be realized now." Ugaki responded by saying, "It is quite regretful to see both China and Japan in an unfortunate situation. I will do my best to make the thoughts and opinions we exchanged come true."[61]

Then Chang Ch'un suggested starting peace talks between the two nations immediately and indicated his willingness to be directly involved in the talks.[62] Afraid that peace talks with such a pro-Japanese official like Chang Ch'un would actually have a negative effect on the peace effort, Ugaki told Chang Ch'un that he preferred to have an unofficial talk with someone who was relatively unknown and had little to do with Japan. When Chang Ch'un requested that Ugaki select someone, Ugaki chose K'ung Hsiang-hsi, Administrative Director of the Nationalist government. He did so because he remembered that K'ung, who was in London when the Sino-Japanese Incident took place and needed to go back to China hastily, made the remark to the press on a stopover in Singapore, "It is quite foolish that Japan and China began to fight against each other. It is a great misfortune for the Orient. There has to be an effort to achieve an early peace settlement."[63]

The preliminary talks started in Hong Kong in early June. Then K'ung suggested of having a third party as mediator — either the British or the United States — in the peace talk. Considering that third-party involvement often complicates a settlement, Ugaki opposed it. In the end K'ung agreed with Ugaki. The unofficial but direct talks between the two nations began.

Upon inquiry from K'ung about the conditions under which Japan wanted to start the talks, Ugaki told K'ung that even when the replacement of the government took place, Japanese foreign policy always stayed consistent under the cabinet or Foreign Ministry, so there was no change in the terms of the conditions from those his predecessor, Foreign Minister Hirota had raised.[64] Then Ugaki specified the following conditions:

1. The independence of Manchuria would be recognized.
2. North China and Mongolia would be considered special areas.
3. China would pay indemnity to Japan.
4. Natural resources would be jointly cultivated under an economic cooperation.
5. Japanese troops would be allowed to be stationed in certain areas.
6. Advisors and other leaders would be set up in China.

K'ung responded by saying, "There should not be any talk about the independence of Manchuria. With regard to having special areas, it is all right to consider Mongolia as a special area but not North China. About indemnity, China is not capable of paying because of the cost of the long-lasting war. It should be removed from the list of the conditions. Lastly, China has no objection to having advisors and the joint cultivation of natural resources."[65] K'ung, however, added his apprehension about the possibility of demanding the resignation of Chiang Kai-shek, saying that "Although Chiang Kai-shek himself is ready to resign if it is necessary to have a peace treaty, I am afraid that there is no other leader who is able to carry out the treaty in a proper fashion."[66]

Then K'ung suggested direct talks between him and Ugaki. Finding K'ung's response basically unacceptable, Ugaki also saw that it was necessary to have such direct talks and invited K'ung to Nagasaki to see him. Meanwhile, Ugaki met British Ambassador Robert Craigie and American Ambassador Grew to inform them in advance about his talks with K'ung. Ugaki did so in order to avoid any complication of the Sino-Japanese negotiation process because of the third-party interference.[67]

While all these preliminary preparation talks were going on, Ugaki faced strong opposition from the military and a segment of the Foreign Ministry itself toward the peace talks. They argued, "If we start peace talks now, we'll lose face with the troops. We are trying to suppress China with 'Sword,' not 'Talk.'"[68]

They could not, however, oppose the peace talks publicly, so they pushed the idea of establishing an Asian Development Board. Separate and independent from the Foreign Ministry, this Asian Development Board was designed to primarily deal with China issues, aiming to have more effective policies to promote an early settlement of the China Incident. To Ugaki, however, this was clearly designed to stop the peace talks that he was contemplating by transferring the diplomatic authority toward China from the Foreign Ministry to the new board. Army Minister Itagaki, while in public expressing his support for Ugaki's peace talks, urged Konoe to speed up the establishment of the Asian Development Board.

Seeing that Konoe was rather inclined to agree with Itagaki, Ugaki made up his mind to resign. He said to Konoe, "It is foolish to treat China like a colony by establishing this type of special board. It will make other powers suspicious toward us, aggravate China, and also make our diplomacy further polarized. So, I absolutely oppose it. I decided to enter your cabinet with a chief mission to solve the China issue. Therefore, removing the China issue from my authority [by setting up a new board] is the same as asking me to step down."[69]

Contrary to Ugaki's above assertion, there were heated debates over deciding what actual role the board should take. The ad hoc Five Minister Conference (Prime Minister Konoe Fumimaro, Army Minister Itagaki Seishiro, Navy Minister Yonai Mitsumasa, Foreign Minister Ugaki Kazushige, and Finance Minister Ikeda Seihin) was held in September 1938.[70] Facing determination from both the army and the Foreign Ministry not to give in to each other, the resolution at the conference was far from being reached. Then, on September 24, the Konoe cabinet came up with the idea of a compromise that the Asian Development Board was only a provisional organ set up for the purpose of assisting in achieving a settlement of the China issue. Hence, the fundamental authority for conducting foreign affairs still belonged to the Foreign Ministry.

Although there was still some disagreement over this compromise plan between the Foreign Ministry and the army, both agreed to entrust the Five Minister Conference with the settlement of the issue. Shortly before the conference, Ugaki showed up at the Prime Minister's residence to see Konoe. As soon as he was taken to the office of the Prime Minister, he took out his resignation letter and began to read it. Believing that the issue of the Asian Development Board had been basically worked out, and the only thing remaining to be done was an adoption of the bill setting up the board at the Five Minister Conference, Konoe was, therefore, dumbfounded by Ugaki's action. Without saying a word, he received the resignation letter from Ugaki. After Ugaki left, Konoe said to his secretary, "I do not see why Ugaki has to resign."[71]

On December 16, 1938. Konoe Fumimaro and the members of the Asian Development Board at their first conference (© Mainichi Photo Bank).

Konoe was not alone. Many others felt the same way. The idea of setting up a central organ to deal with the China issue had already been raised in early 1938, before Ugaki became Foreign Minister.[72] The China Incident was rapidly expanding. Along with it, there was a rapid increase in the number of occupied areas. There was, however, no unified policy to deal with these developments. In order to remedy this situation, many felt it was essential to set up a central organ. This issue, however, had been controversial, dividing the central government into two camps. The army, which controlled the cabinet, insisted on a comprehensive, united diplomatic front; the other camp insisted upon a single diplomatic channel, led by the Foreign Ministry.

In fact, Navy Minister Yonai, although he denied it, allegedly attacked Ugaki. To Yonai, Ugaki's opposition as Foreign Minister to a central organ made no sense because Ugaki, understanding the necessity of such an organ, was strongly endorsing it when he was a member of the cabinet counselor system.[73] Yonai found Ugaki's resignation disturbing. Although he could only speculate, Yonai saw a couple of the reasons why Ugaki actually resigned. One was Ugaki's realization of the danger to his life because of the controversy; he wanted to resign before anything happened to him. The other was that after the controversy, Ugaki knew that now he had to deal with not only the army but also the navy as well. Therefore, to Yonai, there was not any rationale for Prime Minister Konoe taking responsibility for Ugaki's resignation. After all, Ugaki did not himself make clear why he was quitting.[74]

Although Konoe did not necessarily think he was in any way directly responsible for Ugaki's resignation, it once again inflamed Konoe's desire to resign. It was easy to move Konoe in that direction. Seeing Ugaki's resignation as an indication that he had little chance to succeed in his "quest," he had already made up his mind that if Ugaki quit, he would do the same. On the same day that Ugaki turned in his resignation, Konoe asked Kido to see him at the Prime Minister's residence. Konoe told Kido that he desired to resign, taking responsibility for the disunity of his cabinet. Disagreeing with Konoe, Kido said, "With regard to the disunity of the cabinet, the issue of the Asian Development Board has been worked out at least officially, and therefore, the argument concerning cabinet disunity does not make sense. Upon considering Ugaki's motivation for resigning and the current situation of internal and external circumstances, any hasty resignation has to be restrained. It should not be your choice to dissolve the cabinet but to fully concentrate on saving the situation."[75]

Under strong urging from Kido and his other close associates to remain in office, Konoe once again refrained from resigning. As Yabe Teiji points out, however, Konoe's resignation was still only a matter of time.[76] Refraining from resignation this time did not mean he had decided not to resign. In fact, Konoe by this time had already asked his chief secretary of the cabinet, Kazami Akira, to prepare a statement of his resignation. It was the same resignation statement Konoe used when he finally resigned on January 4, 1939. In short, Konoe was still looking for the right time to resign.

Regarding the selection of Ugaki's successor, Konoe had in mind the Japanese ambassador to the United States, Saito Hiroshi. Because of his sickness, however, Saito could not serve. The young secretaries of the Foreign Ministry strongly demanded the appointment of Shiratori Tohsio. Army Minister Itagaki recommended Matsuoka Yosuke. Knowing that both men were pro-military, Konoe had no intention of accepting either recommendation. Although not fully satisfied in the end he chose Arita Hachiro as Foreign Minister, when Finance Minister Ikeda Seihin and also Shiratori Toshio recommended him.

Thus, Ugaki did not meet Konoe's expectations as Foreign Minister. Yet Konoe praised Ugaki's diplomacy, knowing that Ugaki's poor performance was due to the uncontrollable problem of the army's interference, which Konoe himself knew firsthand, not Ugaki's inability or negligence as Foreign Minister.[77]

Konoe's positive attitude toward Ugaki was partially due to the positive role Ugaki played in the Changkufeng Incident. The incident began when the Japanese military deciphered two encoded Soviet telegrams in July 1938, shortly after Konoe finished the structural reform of his cabinet. One of them said, "We [the Soviet border guards] need a supply of ammunition which has been lowered to only half of what we usually have." The other said, "Changkufeng located on the national border line should be conquered before Japan does."[78] Proving what those telegrams said, the Soviet troops began to appear on the top of Changkufeng.

While considering the conquering of Changkufeng of little strategic merit, Koiso Kuniaki, commander of the Korean troops, decided that it did not matter even if the Soviets put Changkufeng under their control; the General Staff Office still insisted on attacking the Soviet troops. They argued that attacking the Soviets at Changkufeng would give them a great opportunity to see what the Soviets were up to and what military capacity they had. In the end, this argument prevailed. The military clash between Japanese and Soviet troops lasted for more than two weeks, ending with the devastating and humiliating defeat of the Japanese army with 21 percent casualties out of about 7,000 troops.[79]

From the beginning of the incident, fearing the possibility of a large-scale war against the Soviets, Konoe, Kido, Saionji, Ugaki, Navy Minister Yonai, and the Emperor all opposed army involvement in a military conflict against Soviet troops. When Itagaki met with the Emperor in order to have more troops dispatched to Changkufeng, the Emperor bluntly said to Itagaki, "In essence, the way the army has been behaving is disturbing to me. Like the Mukden or Marco Polo Bridge, they arbitrarily create an incident. It is not the way the military should act. From now on, without my orders, sending even one soldier should not be allowed."[80] Taking the Emperor's harsh words against the military as the Emperor's disapproval, Army Minister Itagaki almost decided to step down. Only Konoe's persuasion stopped him from doing so.

Meanwhile, both Saionji and Kido strongly urged Konoe to step down if the war against the Soviet Union broke out. Saionji said to Harada, "If Japan uses the military against the Soviet Union and the war comes, I think Konoe should resign. It will be better for his future and for the nation's as well." [81]Kido, sharing Saionji's thought, made a similar remark.

Facing this added circumstance, Itagaki urged the troops to withdraw from Changkufeng. On August 10, Ugaki contacted the ambassador to the Soviet Union, Shigemitsu Mamoru, and encouraged him to have a cease-fire settlement under the following conditions: (1) Prompt settlement, (2) Withdrawing troops from both sides of the line of July 29, (3) Locally deciding a new border, and (4) No entry of the Japanese troops beyond a 1 km line from the Changkufeng border. The efforts of Ugaki and Shigemitsu paid off. The Soviet Union basically agreed to the above conditions and the cease-fire treaty was concluded on August 12.

While Konoe, avoiding the worst scenario of war against the Soviets, momentarily felt relieved, the Sino-Japanese conflict had become bogged down. On October 12, 1938, the Japanese army carried out a surprise landing on the Gulf of Bias. Then, on October 21, they conquered Canton and on October 26, Wu-han. Militarily, it was a quick advancement. Still, Chiang Kai-shek showed no sign of submitting to Japan's demands, and such an expanded war was bringing Japan to political and financial chaos. To Konoe and even to the army, it became clear that settling this quagmire by military means alone was impossible.

It was in this setting, on November 3, that Konoe made an official statement called *Establishment of New Order for the Far East*. In it, he stated that Japan hoped that China, recognizing Japan's sincerity in its effort to establish a new order for the Far East, would share the responsibility for it and respond favorably to Japan's hopes. Here, Konoe even made conciliatory remarks that Japan would not necessarily remain persistent on its previous position to reject the Nationalist Government of China if China shared Japan's effort to establish a new order and also agreed to change the government's leadership structure.[82]

As discussed earlier, this statement was intended to remedy his previous announcement of "No deal with the Nationalist government." It is apparent from the content of this statement, however, that Konoe did not mean necessarily dealing with Chiang Kai-shek when he said, "We will not dare to reject the Nationalist government." What he had in mind when he made his statement was an on going backdoor policy of creating a new regime under the leadership of Wang Ching-wei, who was inclined to agree to Japan's scheme of establishing a new order in the Far East and was therefore conciliatory to Japan's peace conditions. Then they would set up a coalition government between the new regime and already established local puppet governments, including Chiang's Nationalist government, which was to be downgraded to only one of several provincial governments.

The origin of this backdoor policy was traced back to the secret diplomacy that was started in February 1938 between Japan and China. The Japanese side was represented by Colonel Kagesa Sadaaki, a chief of the Division of Military Affairs in the Ministry of the Army; Lieutenant Colonel Imai Takeo, from the General Staff Office; and Inukai Ken, son of former Prime Minister Inukai Tsuyoshi. The Chinese side was made up of Kao Tsung-wu, a head of the Asia division of the Nationalist government in Hong Kong; and Mei Ssu-p'ing, a former university professor and governor of Chiang-ning Prefecture. They produced an agreement called "Basic Conditions for Adjustment of the Sino-Japanese Diplomatic Relationship."

According to the agreement, Japan would withdraw its troops as the restoration of peace progressed, station the troops in Inner Mongolia, return its occupied territories, and abolish extraterritoriality. In return China would recognize Manchuria.[83] Then they made the following arrangement that, as soon as the Japanese government accepted the agreement, Wang Ching-wei would leave the Nationalist Party and escape from Chungking. After Wang's escape, the Japanese government would make an announcement of the Sino-Japanese peace plan immediately, and, simultaneously, Wang would make a similar announcement.[84] Then, on November 30, 1938, at the Imperial Conference, the Japanese government adopted the "New Relation Adjustment Plan" based on the above agreement.

The escape of Wang Ching-wei was set for December 8. Konoe decided to make an announcement of the new plan, as adopted at the Imperial Conference, on December 11 in Osaka. When Konoe was about to leave Tokyo for Osaka, a telegram from Wang Ching-wei came, saying, "Chiang Kai-shek, who was in K'un-ming, suddenly came back to Chungking. I will not, therefore, be able to make the planned statement. I do not know how long Chiang will stay in Chungking. I will, however, do it as soon as Chiang leaves. I would like Prime Minister Konoe to postpone his announcement."[85]

In response to the telegram, Konoe expressed his apprehension to Harada. Although Konoe did not really think that it was a trick, he knew that if it was, his cabinet would have to take responsibility it by dissolving itself.[86] Seeing no point in going to Osaka, Konoe called off the trip, excusing himself due to sickness.

It turned out to be no trick. On December 21, a telegram came, saying that "Overall, the escape of Wang Ching-wei was successful. Wang has fled to Hanoi."[87] Then Konoe, on the following day, announced his China policy, the so-called Konoe Declaration.

In his declaration, Konoe stated that, while expecting the Nationalist government of China to cease completely its anti-Japanese movement, Japan, along with the people of China who shared Japan's quest, would make fullest effort to establish the New Order for the Far East. Also, people in various places in China began to demand creation of a new China. Accordingly, if a new China had actually been created, Japanese government would have found it necessary to adjust its relationship with China and expect it to be crystal clear regarding its policies toward Japan. Konoe put an emphasis on the benefits of the unity between the three nations: Japan, Manchukuo, and China. According to Konoe, the New Order would bring to these nations an enormous advantage in three major areas: good neighbor relationships; common defense against Communism; and economic cooperation. Konoe pointed out, however, that all this depended on how cooperative China would be. China had to be forthcoming in its diplomatic relationship with Japan by being unbiased and open minded; it was essential for China to recognize the foolishness of its anti-Japanese movement and to accept sovereign status of Manchukuo.

With regard to how to stop any influence of Comintern forces in the Far East, Konoe stated that Japan and China had to come up with an anti-Communism cooperation treaty, similar to the Japanese-German anti-Communism cooperation treaty, in order to realize and accomplish the purpose of this anti-Communism cooperation treaty, China had to allow Japan to station Japanese anti-Communism troops in Inner Mongolia and concede it as a special anti-Communism cooperation area during the effective period of the treaty. As to the Sino-Japanese economic relationships, Konoe pointed out, there would be no Japanese monopolization and no nation would be discriminated against in seeking economic profits as long as the New Order for the Far East was recognized; also, based on the principle of equality in the Sino Japanese relationship, China had to allow Japans citizens to have complete freedom to stay and have businesses in China. From the standpoint of the Sino-Japanese historical and economic relationship, Japan had to demand that China cooperate with Japan to promote economic benefit for both nations, particularly for the development and utilization of the natural resources in North China and Inner Mongolia.

Konoe concluded by saying rather conciliatorily that was all Japan demand from China; Japan had no desire to seek any territory or reparation from China, but only assurance that Japan to be equal partner in establishing the New Order for the Far East; and Japan would fully respect Chinese sovereignty by abolishing extraterritoriality and returning the occupied territories to China.[88]

Promptly responding to Konoe's statement, Wang Ching-wei made his own. Thus, this backdoor policy seemingly was on the way to achieving its purpose, resisting Communism and establishing peace. As Konoe himself stated, however, facing the army's unwillingness to fulfill the principles raised in the Konoe Declaration but willingness to use it to achieve the fall of the Nationalist government, it was doomed to fail.[89] Rather than being seen as a peace movement, it was seen as Wang's traitorous action.

No matter how the backdoor policy was unfolding, however, Konoe saw it as a good opportunity to resign. By the end of 1938 his cabinet was in an almost helpless situation. Although there was still a slight hope for the backdoor policy, "despair" was the best word to describe the state of the Sino-Japanese Incident. Internally, also, under the policy of restructuring Japanese society to carry on the war effort, the nation's endurance was reaching its limit.

To make matters worse, there was a further widening of the ideological rift between the Konoe cabinet and the army over shifting the Germany and Italy Anti-Communism Pact to the military pact. Such a shift had begun already in early 1938 in talks between the military officer at the Japanese Embassy in Berlin, Oshima Hiroshi, Ambassador Shiratori Toshio, and the Nazi Foreign Counselor Ribbentrop.

The issue was greatly advanced when the Changkufeng Incident in July 1938, as discussed earlier, ended with Japan's military defeat, revealing that Soviet military strength was far greater than Japan had anticipated. It boosted the demanding voice of the pro-military pact.

Apprehensive due to this new development, Finance Minister Ikeda Seihin, Vice Minister of the Navy Yamamoto Isoroku, and those who firmly believed that such a military alliance with Germany and Italy would result in antagonizing the British and the United States and bring dire political and economic consequences for Japan vehemently opposed Japan's military pact with Germany and Italy. This became a critical factor in weakening Konoe's leadership and pushed him to be more firm and forceful in governing.

Ikeda, when he met Harada on December 16, 1938, said, "It is impossible for the Japanese economy to survive if Japan has to confront the British and the United States as our adversaries. I am very apprehensive [about the direction Japan is heading], seeing Konoe so worried. He has to remain firm. Although I was physically weak, health was not my concern at all [but serving the nation] when I became Finance Minister. If Konoe pulls himself up and is determined to take a strong leadership position, I will serve him to the end."[90] Yamamoto also, from the military point of view, warned, "The military pact generates the possibility of war against the British and the United States. If a war really comes, the naval capacity of Japan is hardly enough to win."[91]

Despite these voices asking Konoe to stand firm and to remain in office, Konoe's decision to resign was unshakable this time. Then, gradually, those who firmly opposed Konoe's resignation previously began to realize that it was pointless to hold onto a leader seemingly so wavering and uncommitted to overcoming the difficult time Japan was facing. Although critical of Konoe's governing, even Saionji was sympathetic. Saionji told his secretary, Harada, that he had absolutely no idea about what Konoe actually had accomplished as Prime Minister, but he was sympathetic toward Konoe, who was leading a nation in a difficult time. Although Saionji had no desire to see Konoe resign hastily, he realized that it would be better for the nation as well as for Konoe if he stepped down at an appropriate time. Kido also made similar remarks.

Konoe wanted to resign immediately if possible. Army Minister Itagaki strongly opposed it. He argued that since the backdoor policy of creating a new regime under Wang Ching-wei was seemingly going well, if Konoe resigned, it would be perceived that Konoe and the army were in discord, which would have a negative impact on the backdoor policy. Harada, sharing similar thoughts with Itagaki, told Kido on December 15, 1938, that a change of government at the end of the year would be unwise, showing the political and economic instability of the nation, particularly when the backdoor policy was under way.

Kido, as well as Konoe himself, agreed with Harada. On December 30, Konoe told Harada that there would be a general resignation on January 4, 1939. Konoe had Hiranuma Kiichiro, the Chairman of the Privy Council, in mind as his successor. Although some apprehension about Hiranuma's inexperience in foreign affairs was raised, basically the choice of Hiranuma was accepted. Hiranuma himself was not so enthusiastic about the offer. He indicated, however, that his intention was to accept if Konoe would succeed him as Chairman of the Privy Council. There was a last-minute attempt to block Konoe's resignation when Itagaki directly appealed to the Emperor to persuade Konoe to remain in office. Konoe resigned, however, on January 4, 1939, followed by Hiranuma's acceptance of the Imperial Order.

In his resignation statement, Konoe said, "Entering into a new phase of the Sino-Japanese Incident, it is time for us to fully concentrate on the establishment of the new order to secure an eternal peace in the Far East. I am convinced, in order to deal with this new situation, it is necessary to renew our thinking by having the new policies and ideas under a new cabinet." [92] Yet as Ikeda Seihin said later, "I really have no

On November 3, 1938, Prime Minister Konoe Fumimaro giving a radio broadcast to make an official statement of "Establishment of a New Order for the Far East" (© Mainichi Photo Bank).

idea why Konoe quit." [93]Indeed, no one was really sure why Konoe had to resign. It should not be difficult, however, to speculate why. Having thought that he had done everything he could, yet with no success, Konoe might have been simply tired mentally and physically, without the will to carry on.

4

From New Order and Tripartite Pact to Konoe's Second Cabinet

Considering the contrasting characters of Hiranuma and Konoe, the selection of Hiranuma as his successor is interesting. Konoe was known as a reformer and a man of new ideas who never hesitated to express them. As his critics often noted, however, he appeared to lack executive ability. On the other hand, Hiranuma was laconic and made suggestions of reforms only if he had absolute confidence they would be carried out. Despite their contrasting characters, both were fundamentally right-wing nationalists. Disagreeing with the general characterization of Hiranuma as an extreme right-wing-fascist, Konoe considered Hiranuma a moderate. Facing a delicate situation on both internal and external fronts, Konoe believed Japan should have someone moderate and steady in governing at this juncture. To him, Hiranuma was ideally fit to lead the nation.

Saionji agreed with Konoe. Although he had been known to be critical of Hiranuma's position of anti-party politics and ultranationalism, by this time Saionji began to see Hiranuma becoming less extreme. When asked by Harada about Hiranuma as a candidate for premiership, Saionji said only one word, "Elastic," meaning that Hiranuma was so flexible in thought that, once he assumed a responsible position, he would not do anything drastic.[1]

It was not Saionji, however, who recommended Hiranuma as a candidate for Prime Minister. It had been customary for Genro to recommend a candidate for Prime Minister to the Emperor. As the sole remaining Genro, Saionji had taken that responsibility for some time. Because of his advanced age and difficulty in keeping in touch with political affairs, however, Saionji wished to be removed from this duty. Granting his wish, a decision was made to hold the Lord Keeper of the Privy Seal responsible for the duty of making this recommendation after consulting with Genro.

It was Yuasa Kurahei, therefore, who recommended Hiranuma to the Emperor.

Hiranuma accepted the Imperial Order, but with one condition: that Konoe would succeed Hiranuma as the president of the Privy Council. Upon Konoe's acceptance, Hiranuma began to form his cabinet with the slogan "National Unity." Konoe turned out to be right in his assessment of Hiranuma. Seven out of the thirteen members of Hiranuma's cabinet were former members of the Konoe cabinet. On January 21, 1939, in his speech of administrative policy at the seventy-fourth regular Diet session, Hiranuma emphasized the need to eliminate domestic discord, to reinforce the national mobilization structure, and to increase production in order to end the Sino-Japanese War. All this clearly indicated that Hiranuma had no intention of altering the fundamental policies of his predecessor, Konoe Fumimaro. This also explains why the Hiranuma cabinet was relatively well accepted by the military, the bureaucrats, and the political parties.

The only controversy the formation of this cabinet brought was Konoe becoming a cabinet member without a portfolio while serving as the president of the Privy Council. The demand that Konoe remain in the cabinet as minister was mainly attributed to the ongoing Wang Ching-wei situation initiated under the Konoe cabinet. Consulted over the issue by Hiranuma and Yuasa, Saionji repeatedly indicated his opposition, emphasizing the inappropriateness of any political involvement by the president of the Privy Council.[2] Despite such opposition, the issue of Konoe's membership in the cabinet was pushed forward and, in the end, became a reality. It turned out to be a minor issue, however. Konoe remained as the minister until the end of the Hiranuma cabinet. He did not find himself in the center of any controversy because of his service as a member of the cabinet.

Although widely accepted, the Hiranuma cabinet did not last long. With his moderate style of governing, Hiranuma did not make any major errors internally, but external affairs eventually brought down his cabinet. Hiranuma inherited two major external issues from Konoe. One was the Wang Ching-wei situation and the other was the issue of the Tripartite Pact. As mentioned in the previous chapter, Wang Ching-wei had fled to Hanoi on December 21, 1938. Both Konoe and Wang made declarations simultaneously in their effort to bring the Sino-Japanese War to a peaceful end. However, because of the Japanese army's unwillingness to go along with Konoe in the maneuvers, this issue became stagnant. Then, in March 1939, the Nationalist government tried to assassinate Wang Ching-wei.[3]

Although it was a failed attempt, Hiranuma was alarmed by this incident and held a Five Minister Conference, where they decided to move Wang Ching-wei to the Japanese occupied territory. Wang requested, however, to go to Shanghai rather than the Japanese occupied territory. Wang insisted, "If I move to any place under the occupation of the Japanese military, it would give the impression to the Chinese people that my peace movement is being carried out under the protection of the Japanese military. Compared to the Japanese occupied territory, Shanghai, although considered dangerous because of many raging terrorist acts, is under various foreign influences. It is foreign nationals who control the city government and the judiciary system. It will be easier for the Chinese to get involved in politics there. My comrade, Mei Ssu-p'ing, is already in Shanghai to make preliminary arrangements."[4]

Wang's wish was granted, and he went to Shanghai in early May 1939. A few weeks later, he visited Tokyo and began talks with Japanese officials including Prime Minister Hiranuma and Army Minister Itagaki concerning the establishment of his regime. During his visit, Wang also met with Konoe. Deeply moved by Konoe's warm reception, Wang said about Konoe, "Prince Konoe is an excellent politician. With him, Japan will have a bright future."[5]

Wang believed that if there was to be any success in the peace effort, it was essential for Japan to carry out what was stated in the Konoe Declaration. He outlined conditions for establishing his new regime: (1) No change in the use of the national flag, (2) Adoption of Sun Yat-sen's Three Principles of Democracy, (3) Clarification of the timing for withdrawal of the Japanese troops from China, and (4) Return of any Japanese possessions in the occupied territories.

Despite some disagreements over Wang's outline, both sides made compromises and agreed to the following conditions: (1) Use of the existing national flag with a distinguishable symbol attached, (2) Adoption of the Three Principles of Democracy, (3) Declaration of an anti-Comintern policy by the Wang regime, (4) Recognition of the sovereign status of Manchuria by the Wang regime, and (5) Withdrawal of Japanese troops only after the restoration of peace. The Wang regime was finally established in March 1940, not under the Hiranuma cabinet but the Yonai cabinet. The Wang regime was destined to fail, however. As seen in Konoe's prompt announcement of his regret over his declaration, "No longer deal with Chiang Kai-shek," Konoe had never hold high expectations for Wang Ching-wei's maneuvering from the outset. He used it rather as a political tool to deal with Chiang Kai-shek. As will be discussed later, after Konoe failed to create a new political structure and also saw the disappointing development of the Tripartite Pact movement, Konoe fully focused on the

U.S.-Japan diplomatic negotiations, believing that was the only means left for Japan to solve the Sino-Japanese Incident. By this time, Wang Ching-wei's maneuvering was a dead issue. The war between Japan and the United States eventually broke out, and Wang Ching-wei died in Japan, to the disappointment of Japanese leaders.[6]

While the staging of Wang Ching-wei's ascension was under way, the Hiranuma cabinet was facing another challenging issue, the rapidly growing concern over establishing the Tripartite Pact. Facing strong pressure from the army to strengthen the anti-Comintern treaty with Germany and Italy and ultimately create the Tripartite Pact, Hiranuma was inclined to agree with the army. In fact, Hiranuma, once considered one of the most radical right-wing nationalists, did not have any reason to disagree to having the pact. Contention rose, however, over the nature of the pact, that is, whether the pact was designed to deal with the Soviet Union only, or with Britain and France as well. At the Five Minister Conference on January 19, 1939, except for Army Minister Itagaki, all the attendees— Prime Minister Hiranuma, Foreign Minister Arita, Navy Minister Yonai, and Finance Minister Ishiwatari — agreed to reject the German proposal that specified that Britain and France would be covered by the Tripartite Pact.

Realizing, however, that, in a frenzy of opinions from both the army and the public demanding acceptance of the German proposal, a flat rejection was impossible and would hinder the effort of the Hiranuma cabinet to achieve national unity, Foreign Minister Arita came up with a compromise. Although the Soviet Union was the main adversary of the pact, the three nations of Britain, France, and the United States could be considered to be adversaries, depending on the political circumstances. In dealing with the Soviet Union, military assistance surely would be given. In the case of the British, the French, and the Americans, however, it would depend on circumstances. The treaty should be concluded as soon as possible. An effective period of the pact should be five years. Lastly, an explanation of the pact to the three Allied nations would state that dealing with the Comintern was the sole object of the pact.[7] This created room for avoiding any military assistance to Germany and Italy in the case of the Allied nations' involvement. Because the last article disguised the inclusion of Great Britain, France, and the United States as adversaries and allowed for avoidance of military assistance against them, the compromise plan was adopted.

As special correspondents, Minister Ito Nobumi and two other officers from the army and the navy were dispatched to Berlin and Rome to convey the decision of the central government to the ambassador to Germany,

Oshima Hiroshi, and the mbassador to Italy, Shiratori Toshio. Both Oshima and Shiratori, however, saw such a compromise plan as virtually unacceptable to Germany and Italy. When they were asked by the Foreign Minister of Italy, Gaieazzo Ciano, whether or not Japan would join the war if Germany and Italy had to go to war against the Allied nations or were under attack by them, they took the liberty to say, "Yes."[8]

Oshima and Shiratori's answer to Ciano created a heated debate among top government officials and also infuriated the Emperor. Foreign Minister Arita attempted to have both ambassadors take back their words. "If they do not," said Home Minister Kido Koichi, "they should be summoned back."[9]

Army Minister Itagaki disagreed. He argued that under the Tripartite Pact, Japan could not take the position of neutrality, but had an obligation to assist Germany and Italy. Therefore, the remarks of Oshima and Shiratori were not inappropriate and should not be renounced. With regard to neutrality, Hiranuma shared Itagaki's opinion. To Hiranuma, as a signatory nation Japan could not stand neutral, and also in the compromise plan, Japan specified that military assistance to Germany and Italy, when they were at war against the Allied nations, would take place depending on the circumstances. Hiranuma argued that the neutrality issue did not really matter anyway because, circumstantially, Japan, neither today nor in the future, could be in the position to assist the signatory nations militarily.

Despite Itagaki and Hiranuma's arguments, both Foreign Minister Arita and Navy Minister Yonai, apprehensive about the calamity Japan might face by taking the position of non-neutrality, desired to have the word "neutrality" specified in the Tripartite Pact. Agreeing with Arita and Yonai's argument, the Emperor said to Army Minister Itagaki, "In essence, it is a violation of the sovereign power of the Emperor that two ambassadors consented to join a war without having any consultation with me. Over this issue, it is very disturbing to me to see [the army's] indifference to the violation."[10] Awestruck Itagaki was infuriated and wondered who gave such details to the Emperor.

Saionji also expressed his concern. To him, since Germany and Italy were already treating Japan as a minor power, it did not make much sense for Japan to join Germany and Italy. Saionji believed that if Germany and Italy became victorious in the fight against England and France, they would get even more aggressive and overpowering, leaving Japan almost nothing to gain. Indeed, Saionji was greatly troubled by the inability of Japanese government to see his view.[11]

Hiranuma was struggling to bring the nation, increasingly divided over the issue of the Tripartite Pact, into some sort of consensus. Meanwhile, Germany was running out of patience and wanted to have the pact concluded as early as possible. Friedrich Gaus, the treaty director of the German Foreign Ministry, came up with his own proposal regarding the Tripartite Pact. It was almost identical to the original draft of the pact suggested by Germany. The Japanese Embassy in Berlin suspected that it was actually drafted by the Japanese army and sent through an attaché to the German Foreign Ministry. Meanwhile, German Foreign Minister Ribbentrop contacted Ambassador Oshima, asking when a treaty nation entered into a war situation against a third nation, whether or not Japan should be considered to be in a war, even though it was not providing any military assistance. Oshima without hesitation stated, "Yes."

Infuriated by Oshima's repeated dogmatism, and apprehensive of growing pressure from Germany and Hiranuma's inclination to go along with the army, Arita told Hiranuma that he was no longer able to take responsibility as Foreign Minister and, therefore, wished to resign. Although Arita, persuaded by Hiranuma and Yamamoto Isoroku, Vice Minister of the Navy, agreed to remain in office, his decision showed nothing but Hiranuma's inability to put his own house in order over the issue of the Tripartite Pact.

To make the situation worse for Hiranuma, the Japanese army suffered a devastating defeat by Soviet and Outer Mongolian troops in the military confrontation known as the Nomonhan Incident. It broke out on May 12, 1939, when Outer Mongolian troops invaded the Manchurian territory called Nomonhan, located in the remote area of the Khalka River, the border between Manchukuo and the Soviet Union client state, Outer Mongolia. It rapidly escalated into a major fight between the Soviet troops and the Kwantung Army. The Japanese troops proved no match for the far superior Soviet artillery and tanks. When the cease-fire treaty was concluded on September 15, 1939, Japan had suffered a devastating defeat with nearly 18,000 casualties, 73 percent of the total Japanese troops.[12]

Already deeply disturbed by these developments, Hiranuma was further dismayed by the news of the conclusion of the Non-Aggression Pact between the Soviet Union and Germany on August 23, 1939. It dumbfounded not only the Hiranuma cabinet but the nation as a whole, who believed that Germany was urging Japan to join the Tripartite Pact primarily in order to stop an intrusion of the Soviet Comintern.

Continuing negotiations for the Tripartite Pact became pointless to Hiranuma. He summoned the Five Minister Conference on August 25 and declared an end to negotiations. While sending a letter of protest to Germany for violating the anti-Comintern treaty, Hiranuma dissolved his cabinet on August 28 in order to take responsibility for not being able to detect in advance this sudden change in German foreign policy.

Konoe, Kido, and Yuasa all agreed that former Prime Minister Hirota should be the successor. Hirota, however, wanted Konoe to succeed Hiranuma and, as he had done in Konoe's first cabinet, he would serve as Foreign Minister under Konoe. In the end, because of the strong opposition from the army, Hirota's cabinet was not formed. Then the army recommended General Abe Nobuyuki to be Prime Minister. Although there was apprehension about Abe's lack of experience in governing and the fact that he had been recommended by the army, Abe was chosen because of his "freshness" as a politician.

The Abe cabinet, however, was even more short-lived than the Hiranuma cabinet, lasting only four and a half months, from August 30, 1939, to January 14, 1940. Formed almost simultaneously with the outbreak of the European war, his cabinet was too weak to deal with the growing external and internal turmoil. Facing skyrocketing military expenses, Abe was particularly interested in financial reform. He attempted to set up a Trade Ministry in order to have a more integrated trade practice, but it caused strong opposition from the Foreign Ministry. In the end, the financial sector and even the army abandoned Abe.[13] Urged by the political parties to resign, Abe stepped down.

Voices demanding Konoe for Prime Minister flared up again. Kido, Arita, and General Sugiyama all agreed that Konoe ought to be chosen. Despite such strong demands, Konoe had no intention of forming a cabinet. He argued that it was time to select someone who had a deep understanding of financial policies, and he hardly had such knowledge. Despite such reasoning, his refusal began to raise criticism, suggesting that Konoe was selfish and unpatriotic.

Konoe recommended that either Ikeda or General Ugaki be selected. General Sugiyama opposed Konoe's recommendation of General Ugaki. When he himself was encouraged to be Abe's successor, Sugiyama stated that, in the past, when an active general such as General Ugaki, General Hayashi, or General Abe served as a leader of Japan, none had succeeded in his task as a premier, which underminded the image of the Army. He had absolutely no intention to take a role of premiership.[14]

Realizing that Ugaki could not be the choice because of the army's opposition, Konoe strongly urged the selection of Ikeda, a financial expert and the Minister of Finance under the Konoe cabinet. When Home Minister Yuasa began to recommend General Yonai Mitsimasa, Konoe argued that, considering the need for someone with strong command of the financial field, he could not endorse Yonai.

Nonetheless, with the help of maneuvering by General Okada Keisuke to promote Yonai, and also with the agreement of Saionji, Yuasa managed to recommend Yonai to the Emperor. On January 14, 1940, the Imperial Order was issued for the formation of the Yonai cabinet.[15] This cabinet, however, was also destined to share the fate of the two previous ones. Its foreign policy of non-involvement, particularly regarding the Tripartite Pact, made the Yonai cabinet unpopular. Under strong pressure from the army, it ended its six short months of governing on July 16, 1940. Thus, in only one and a half years, since Konoe's rather sudden resignation on January 4, 1939, three cabinets had been formed. There was a general impression that all three cabinets were merely transitional, waiting for Konoe to return to power.

While this political discord was continuing, the military situation in Europe was rapidly unfolding. Since the spring of 1939, Germany had been unstoppable, succeeding in the conquest of Norway, Holland, and Belgium. In June, Italy joined Germany in the war of conquest. On August 23, 1939, Germany concluded the Non-Aggression pact with the Soviet Union. A week later, on September 1, Germany invaded Poland. The outbreak of the European war created a power vacuum in China and Southeast Asia. Apprehensive that such a power vacuum would entice further aggression of the Japanese military in these regions and threaten U.S. interests, the United States began to put pressure on Japan. The U.S. government unilaterally abrogated the 1911 Treaty of Commerce and Navigation with Japan, and this was followed by an export ban on certain commodities to Japan.[16]

This intensification of the international situation, and the inability of the Japanese government to deal with it, enhanced the voices demanding that Japan seize this momentum and enact the Tripartite Pact with Germany and Italy. The slogan "Do Not Miss the Bus" began to be heard across Japan. At the same time, various Japanese leaders and the public in general realized that structural changes in Japanese politics were urgently needed in order to consolidate the national defenses and develop an effective foreign policy to deal with the rapidly changing world situation. The status quo was no longer tolerable. All agreed that Konoe should be in charge if such structural changes were to be successful.

This was not the first time Konoe had been asked to help create a new political structure. As stated in the third chapter, in early 1938, having seen parliamentary politics threatened by the Army's strong demand for passage of the national mobilization bill, the leaders of Minseito and Seiyukai urged Konoe to form a new party to overcome the crisis. Although Konoe was not totally uninterested in the creation of a new party or some

On October 20, 1939, from left, Prime Minister Abe Nobuyuki, Chairman of the Privy Council Konoe Fumimaro, and Minister of the Railroad Nagai Ryutaro waiting for the Emperor's arrival at Yasukuni Shrine (© Mainichi Photo Bank).

sort of a national organization, he was not enthusiastic enough to give serious consideration to it. This time, however, the demand for creating a new political structure was far greater because of the incomparably grave situations in the international arena. Konoe could not afford to be indifferent.

As Konoe's postwar memoir recalls, when the Saito cabinet was formed in 1932, Konoe strongly opposed Saionji's idea of having a compromise cabinet. Unfortunately for him, the political trend was in favor of Saionji. Since the Saito cabinet, all, including Konoe's own, had been compromise cabinets. Because of this, the military command and the civilian government had grown farther apart. The military became almost autonomous, making it extremely difficult for the civilian-controlled government to function effectively. Konoe took the ending of the Sino-Japanese War, which began a month after he assumed the role of premiership, not only as his official but also his personal responsibility. By the end of his first cabinet, however, Konoe convinced himself that the end of the war would never come unless the replacement of a compromise cabinet took place, and the arbitrary and monopolistic power of the military was contained. To Konoe, relying on the existing political parties to achieve those goals became hopeless. There had to be a galvanization of public

support. Konoe began to contemplate the creation of a national organization. Konoe believed that since the May Fifteenth Incident and the February Twenty-six Incident, the political parties had been ineffective; hence
it was useless to rely on the political parties alone to put the military under
the government control. Konoe was convinced, therefore, that the only
way to control the military and settle the China Incident was to establish
a government fully backed by a new national organization, which was to
be quite a contrast to the existing political parties. According to Konoe,
his main concern was to study how to set up such a national organization
when his first cabinet was about to end, and it was his top priority to actually set it up when he was forming his second cabinet. Coincidentally,
when Konoe was contemplating all this in the spring of 1940, the nationwide movement to create a new political structure began. Konoe believed
that the time was right.[17] Konoe had an idea of what the new structure
ought to be like. He had, however, neither confidence nor any clear plan
to achieve it.

At the outset, Konoe was strongly concerned with the notion that
right-wing nationalists, particularly the army, would make use of this new
movement as a political tool to bring down the Yonai cabinet. He said,
"This movement to create a new political structure is said to be advocating the end of party politics in order to overthrow the cabinet. Particularly with the army contemplating a war based on the Nazi idea of 'One
Nation/ One Party' and right-wing nationalists such as Hashimoto, Nakano,
and Suetsugu planning to support the army, public opinion, although var-
ied, is inclined toward [overthrowing the Yonai cabinet]."[18] There was
even an assertion that Konoe was actually one of the conspirators planning to bring down the Yonai cabinet. According to a remark Harada indicates, however, that assertion had no substance. Harada argued that Konoe
did not necessarily disagree to the need for creating a nationally supported
political structure. Because of the gap between the on-going movements
of creating a new political structure as a party and his own vision of new
structure, Konoe, however, did not have any desire to be part of such
movement. According to Harada, Konoe actually hoped that Yonai would
continue his governing.[19]

Despite Konoe's apprehension, the creation of a new political structure was moving forward swiftly. Konoe himself had to realize that,
whether he liked it or not, circumstances no longer allowed him to remain
inactive. Konoe resigned on June 24, 1940, from his position as president
of the Privy Council to show his readiness to devote himself to creating a
new political framework. In his resignation speech, he said, "In order to
deal with the unprecedented internal and external changes we are facing,

no one disagrees, there is a need to establish a nationally supported political structure. Today, by resigning as president of the Privy Council, I
would like to devote myself to creating the new political structure. It would
be quite desirable if the recent movement for establishing a new party is
designed to achieve this new political model. If, however, this movement
is a mere plot for the creation of a coalition party consisting of the existing political parties or the acquisition of political power, I do not have any
intention of going along with it. After hearing various opinions about
developing a national structure and giving careful thought to them, I will
devote my efforts to achieving this new framework."[20]

Encouraged by Konoe's resignation and subsequent statement, the
political parties rushed into developing a new party with Konoe Fumimaro
as president. The Social Populist Party dissolved itself on July 16, followed
by Seiyukai on July 30. Although Minseito was somewhat cautious, when
Nagai Ryutaro's faction left the party, it had no other choice but to dissolve, finally breaking up on August 14. Thus, Japan entered a no-party
era for the very first time in its history of constitutional politics.

As strong advocates of anti-parliamentary politics, the right-wing
nationalists opposed the idea of creating a new party. Like Konoe, they
wanted to have a national organization that was not just a coalition of the
political parties but was characterized by the galvanization of every element of the nation.

Although they shared the idea that Konoe had to be head of a new
national organization if there was to be any success, these right-wing
nationalists were divided into two conflicting factions: the so-called revolutionary right wing and the ideological right wing. The revolutionary
right wing, linked with Tosei-ha (Control faction) of the army, was strongly
inclined to follow the Nazi style of governing. Their aim was the creation
of a "One Nation/One Party" system. Naturally they were in favor of the
Tripartite Pact and believed that Japan ought to advance south, even though
it would likely create a confrontation with the British and the United States.
On the other hand, the ideological right wing, linked with Kodo-ha (Imperial way faction), strongly advocated the creation of a national organization that would reflect and defend the "national polity." Accordingly, they
vehemently opposed the Nazi-style "One Nation/One Party" system, saying that the creation of such a system would make the new national organization equivalent to Bakufu.[21] To them, the most imminent threat to
Japan was the Comintern. Accordingly, they believed that Japan ought to
move north.

While the revolutionary right wing, reflecting the unstoppable German expansion in Europe, was gaining more political ground, Konoe was

inclined to agree with the ideological right-wing nationalists. Sharing their beliefs and also considering his own family background as a prestigious aristocrat, Konoe was most afraid of creating Bakufu with a Nazi-style single-party system. Konoe argued that such a party, being autocratic, would occupy every political organ and be able to have ideological control and oppressive power over the assembly. It would be a constitutional violation of the rights of freedom of speech and assembly. If that took place, there would be no election and no parliament. Worst of all, it would render the sovereign power of the Emperor meaningless.[22]

Konoe spent the early summer of 1940 at a resort, Karuizawa, located in Nagano Prefecture. Although officially his stay was for recuperation, in actuality it was to develop a new political structure with help from Yabe Teiji, a professor of political science at Tokyo Imperial University, who accompanied Konoe.

Asked by Konoe to write a new structure plan, Yabe could not help but feel at a loss. As discussed above, the creation of a new party out of the existing parties could not be realized. Neither was the Nazi-style single-party system acceptable. A problem for Yabe was that if Konoe was to create a new political blueprint, it was certain that all the political parties would be a part of it. Having no opposition party, there would indeed be a great possibility that a new structure would be like the "One Nation/One Party" system.[23]

A question that Konoe and Yabe had to address, then, was how to establish a new political framework without the risk of creating a "One Nation/One Party" system. Here even the name of the new political system itself became an issue. Konoe wanted to avoid the use of the word "party." With suggestions from Kazami Akira, Konoe named the new political structure simply the New Structure, which later became Taisei Yokusankai (National Service Association).

Although it was a difficult task, Yabe managed to come up with the basic guideline for the New Structure. According to Yabe, first of all, based on the national vocational and professional organizations such as economic groups or cultural groups, the activities of each organization ought to be related to politics; by doing so, it would become possible for the people to participate in policy making directly. At the same time, by creating organizations that were capable of letting an established national policy penetrate people's lives, it would be possible to remedy the problem of detachment of bureaucratic regulations from the reality of people's lives, on the one hand, and to make up the disconnection between politics and people on the other. Finally, by creating a core body consisting of talented people from such national vocational and professional organizations and

the existing political parties, it would be possible to have a national movement.

As Yabe himself points out, there was one crucial obstacle to creating such a national movement allowing each citizen to participate. That
is, under Article I of the Peace Police Law, certain vocational and professional groups such as bureaucrats, teachers, students or religious activists
were prohibited from taking part in political activities. So, without removing this obstacle, if a new structure were to be created, it would have to
be like a national mobilization system with emphasis on the spiritual aspect
only, with no political aspect involved.[24] Despite such an obstacle, based
on Yabe's guideline, the creation of the New Structure moved forward.
The New Structure Preparation Committee was set up on August 23, 1940.

Meanwhile, in the midst of this New Structure movement, Konoe's
second cabinet was formed. As discussed earlier, realizing that Prime Minister Yonai was strongly against the Tripartite Pact, the army wanted to
see the Yonai cabinet fall and be replaced by Konoe. A familiar tactic was
used — a resignation of Army Minster and the army's refusal to provide a
successor. Sensing such a movement was on the way, on July 15, 1940, Yonai
summoned Army Minister Hata Shunroku and said to him, "You have
been conducting the movement to bring down my cabinet for some time.
To keep arguing for this matter is pointless. After all, I am a solider and
so are you. I want you to make up your mind and say whether you want
to resign or not."[25] Then, taking no time, Hata turned in his resignation.
The next day, Yonai asked Hata to recommend his successor. Informed
that it would be difficult, Yonai went to the Imperial Palace and told the
Emperor that he had no confidence that he could carry on and wanted to
resign. The Emperor accepted Yonai's resignation.

That very same day, Kido Koichi, now Lord Keeper of the Privy Seal,
after replacing Yuasa Kurahei, who had resigned because of his poor health,
discussed with the president of the Privy Council, Hara Yoshimichi, and
the former Prime Ministers, Wakatsugi Reijiro and Hirota Koki, who ought
to succeed Yonai. It was a unanimous decision that no one but Konoe
should be recommended.

Konoe, however, had little desire to return to the premiership. He told
Harada that even if he made up his mind to form a cabinet, no new political structure would be set up. He also said it was rather odd for him to
become a premier again because one reason he resigned as the president
of the Privy Seal was to dedicate himself to creating a new structure, not
taking premiership. Konoe thought that since it was the army that brought
down the Yonai cabinet, the army should be leading the nation.[26] Sharing
Konoe's thoughts, Saionji also had little enthusiasm for seeing Konoe

assume the premiership. Asked by Harada for his thoughts, Saionji said, "It is an outdated idea, today, to govern a nation based on popularity."[27]

Konoe's and Saionji's wishes hardly had any effect on reversing the decision to recommend Konoe as the Premier. When the chief secretary of the Lord Keeper of the Privy Seal, Kido Koichi, was sent to Saionji to get his consent for the recommendation, Saionji responded, "I am old and sick. I do not comprehend well what is going on internally and externally. To agree or to answer questions from the Emperor by pretending that I do understand would be disloyal. Therefore, I would like to refrain from giving my response."[28]

Kido met the Emperor on July 17 and said to him, "Since Saionji responded in such a manner, it would be unwise to force him to be more definitive. Saionji knows Konoe very well. If he thinks [the selection of Konoe] is not good for the nation, he would say so. His response, 'I do not know,' therefore, only means he does not necessarily oppose it. It should be okay to proceed as it is."[29]

The Emperor agreed with Kido. On the night of July 17, the Emperor summoned Konoe to the Imperial Palace and ordered him to be Yonai's successor. Upon acceptance, Konoe promptly started forming his cabinet. Konoe decided to appoint the Army, Navy, and Foreign Ministers and have a Four Minister Conference with them in order to discuss basic policies. If there were no disagreements, the rest of the cabinet members would be appointed.

The army recommended Lieutenant Tojo Hideki to be Hata's successor. Yoshida Zengo remained as the Navy Minister. Konoe selected Matsuoka Yosuke to be the Foreign Minister. The selection of Matsuoka was to have grave consequences later. Seeing Matsuoka as too pro-Axis and anti–Anglo-Saxon, a great number of people questioned his selection. Konoe said to Harada, "At first, the Navy Minister was startled by Matsuoka's remark of going to war against the United States. Soon, however, he realized that what Matsuoka was saying was actually rather moderate. It seems to be Matsuoka's weak point to surprise other people by saying what he does not actually mean."[30] As this remark indicates, although he could not help having some apprehension about Matsuoka, at least, at this point, Konoe did not see Matsuoka as too radical. Konoe appointed Matsuoka because he believed that Matsuoka, known as a man with strong nerve, spirit, eloquence, and artifice — qualities that Konoe did not have — would be helpful in controlling the Army.[31]

On July 19, after the appointment of the above three ministers, the Four Minister Conference was held at Konoe's house in Ogikubo, Tokyo. This is what later became known as the Ogikubo Conference. With no disagreements on major issues, the following points were adopted as the basic policies for a new cabinet:

I. In order to deal with the settlement of the Sino-Japanese Incident and the rapidly changing world situation, the domestic and international policy making of our nation should be based on strengthening our wartime economic policies. Hence, it is essential to have a unilateral economic policy executed by the government, except those elements that are essential for the military.

II. Global Policies

1. By strengthening the power of the Axis (Japan, Germany, and Italy) to cope with the rapidly changing world situation and to build a New Order for East Asia, the East and West have to mutually cooperate to carry out important policies. How and when to do this should be determined according to the world situation.

2. By concluding the Japan–Soviet Union Non-Invasion Treaty over the borders of Japan, Manchuria, and Mongolia (effective period of five or ten years), Japan will solve promptly any existing disputes with the Soviet Union and at the same time establish an almost invincible military power to deal with Soviet Union during the effective period of the Non-Invasion Treaty.

3. In order to put any British, French, and Dutch colonies in East Asia and the neighboring islands into the orbit of the New Order of East Asia, Japan will make an effort to remove European powers from those areas.

4. Although Japan must try to avoid any unnecessary confrontation with the United States, with regard to establishing the New Order of East Asia, Japan must firmly commit itself to stop any interference by the United States.

Soon after this conference, Konoe appointed the rest of the cabinet members. It was done without even setting up a headquarters for the cabinet formation. On July 22, 1940, Konoe's second cabinet was established. Some of the major appointees were Foreign Minister Matsuoka Yosuke, Home Minsiter Yasui Eiji, Finance Minister Kawada, Army Minister Tojo Hideki, Navy Minister Yoshida Zengo, Minister of Justice Kazami Akira, and Chief Secretary Tomita Kenji.

What Konoe was expected to achieve was clear. The whole nation put their expectations on Konoe that, upon his agreeing to lead the nation, the things that mattered most would move forward again. Indeed, at the beginning of Konoe's second cabinet, important decisions were made one after another. On July 26, only four days after the establishment of Konoe's cabinet, through almost daily conferences, and based on the decisions made

at the Four Minister Conference, they came up with the
"Basic Guideline for the
National Policies." On the
following day, July 27, the
"Basic Policies to Deal with
the Current Changes in
World Circumstances" pro-
posed by the Imperial Headquarters were adopted.

With these two deci-
sions, the direction in which
Japan was to head, although
somewhat vague was deter-
mined. This was to have
grave consequences for the
fate of Japan. Konoe was
painfully aware, however,
that although things were
moving forward at the beginning, a bumpy road lay ahead
for the nation.

On July 22, 1940, Prime Minister Konoe Fumimaro and Army Minister Tojo Hideki after the
first meeting of Konoe's second cabinet (©
Mainichi Photo Bank).

Domestically the most
crucial issue Konoe had to deal with was the ongoing development of a
new political framework. On August 28, 1940, the New Structure Preparation Meeting was held. It was "Goetsudosen," meaning it was the meeting attended by the representative of every segment or interest group of
the nation such as democrats, socialists, the revolutionary right wing, the
ideological right wing, politicians, economists, and the military. Based on
Yabe Teiji's guidelines, a declaration of the new structure was issued. A
few months later, on October 12, Taisei Yokusankai (the National Service
Association) was set up.

As Yabe himself, more than two decades later, correctly pointed out,
the most crucial obstacle Konoe had to face was that this National Service
Association was a mere congregation of mutually competing groups fighting over the hegemony of leading the nation by utilizing Konoe's fame and
popularity. It was not anything created based on commonly held ideology
or beliefs.[32]

The political parties were eager to establish a new party. Strongly
opposing party politics, the revolutionary right wing wanted to establish
a Nazi-like single-party system. The ideological right wing was vehemently

against such a system, arguing that it was equivalent to establishing another Bakufu, when what was needed instead was a spiritual movement to defend the national polity. In addition, there were bureaucrats who desired to see the National Service Association used as a supplementary organ for governing. Lastly, there was the financial world, which, afraid of the negative impact of the association on their economic interests, began to claim that the National Service Association was Communist oriented.

When it became increasingly likely that the revolutionary right wing would achieve their goal — a "One Nation/One Party system" — all others opposed it and began to seriously question the merit and nature of the National Service Association itself. There was even the argument that the creation of the National Service Association was a constitutional violation. Facing such fervent opposition, in the end, the National Service Association became a mere symbol of a spiritual movement.

In his celebration speech for the establishment of the National Service Association on October 12, Konoe simply said, "The general principles of this movement are nothing but national service and its sincere execution. There is no other principle and I have nothing else to declare," and he quickly stepped down from the stage.[33] It puzzled the audience, who had expected to hear an uplifting speech of the solid guidelines of the association.

It is clear from this speech that Konoe, even before the National Service Association was set up, already knew his attempt to achieve unity between the civilian government and the military had failed. He then lost his passion and had no desire to carry on. Yabe Teiji argues, "If Konoe's intention to achieve a settlement of the China Incident by creating a nationally backed political organization to put the military under control was correct, his failure to do so has to be the biggest crime Konoe committed."[34] Yabe was not alone. It has been repeatedly argued that Konoe was ultimately responsible for the failure of the National Service Association. Critics typically assert that it was Konoe's character flaw of easily giving up what he started when things did not go smoothly that failed him.

Although it may be true that Konoe had such a character flaw, in the case of the National Service Association, Yabe's above assertion seems unfair. In his memoir, Konoe wrote that he was ready to resign from his position as the president of the Privy Council in order to seriously contemplate how to lead the national movement to create a new political organization; however, the Yonai cabinet came to end sooner than he expected, and he had to form a cabinet quickly. As a result, Konoe was hardly able to contemplate the creation of the National Service Association. Moreover, Konoe continued to argue, because of the formation of the cabinet before the establishment of the Association, the Association did not reflect the national opinion. The National Service Association was expected to be a political structure to achieve its far most important goal: the unification of the government and the army. As Konoe lamented, the movement to create the National Service Association evolved into something totally different from what Konoe wanted to take place. It was becoming more like a "political circus" as the different groups (such as the existing political parties) aimed to create a new party by dissolving themselves: the army officers led by the chief for military affairs, Muto Akira, wanting to create a military oriented One Nation/One Party system; the ideological right wing led by Hiranuma Kiichiro seeking to create a more spiritually oriented service association; and the radical group led by Suetsugu, Hashimoto, and Nakano hoping to create a Nazi-like "One Nation/One Party" were trying to utilize the movement to achieve their own goals. In the end, what Konoe wanted to see least became reality. The group wanting to create a Nazi-like One Nation/One Party became dominant. With no desire to carry on, Konoe then decided to turn the movement into the spiritual and service oriented organization advocated by the right wing nationalists such as Hiranuma. Thus, as Konoe correctly pointed out, because of the military interference and the unexpected and too hasty self-dissolution of the Yonai cabinet followed by the political parties, the attempt to create a national organization designed to control the military failed.[35]

Most scholars, including Yabe, do not dispute most of the points Konoe raised in the above statement. An argument many have raised, however, was that if Konoe had been a little more tenacious and decisive, the National Service Association would have ended up being the new structure he had envisioned.

Again, raising such a criticism seems unfair. As previously discussed, it was not Konoe who initiated the movement for creating a new structure. It was a result of the demand from the nation. There was no segment of society that initially questioned the merit of creating a new political structure. It was almost a nationwide frenzy. Eventually, a national movement succeeded in leading the reluctant Konoe to his decision to be part of it. Further, it was not Konoe but the surrounding segments of society, as Konoe's above statement indicates, that did not meet Konoe's expectations when he made a decision and began to embark on the creation of a blueprint for a new structure, in such unfortunate events as the too hasty self-dissolution of the political parties, the unexpectedly early fall of the Yonai cabinet, and above all, the lack of consensus in creating a new structure in the face of the self-interest of each segment. The only consensus was their realization that Konoe's fame had to be utilized, no matter which segment took a lead in the movement for creating a new structure. A point that should be made is that the National Service Association was already destined to fail before any argument about Konoe's decision even became an issue. It failed even before it was initiated. In short, it was pointless to question Konoe's commitment and whether the National Service Association could have been something different.

Yabe argues, however, that Konoe accomplished a very important unintentional achievement through the movement for creating the National Service Association.[36] According to Yabe, it was the failed attempt to create the National Service Association that prevented a dictatorship of "One Nation/One Party" politics plotted by the army and the revolutionary right-wing nationalists. If there had not been the movement to develop the National Service Association and the helpless and untrustworthy political parties had been left alone, there would not have been sufficient resistance against the demand from the Army and the revolutionary right-wing nationalists to create the "One Nation/One Party" system.

Understandably, it was a painful and disappointing experience for Konoe to see how this movement ended. Konoe had no time, however, to comfort himself from such a painful experience. He was facing one other vital issue on the external front: the ongoing issue of the Tripartite Pact. As stated earlier, the Tripartite Pact was considered an extension of the anti-Comintern treaty among Japan, Germany and Italy. It was designed to deal with the Soviet Union. Under the Hiranuma cabinet, this issue was vehemently debated. Facing strong opposition from the navy, however, it became stagnant. In the end, after having met more than 70 times to discuss it, the issue became almost moot when Germany abruptly concluded the non-aggression treaty with the Soviet Union.

By the time Konoe formed his second cabinet, however, the issue re-emerged. The aggression of Germany in Europe peaked in the summer of 1940. On June 14, without facing any resistance, German troops entered Paris, followed by the German victory in Dunkirk and the extensive German air bombing over England. An invasion of the British mainland by Germany appeared to be imminent. Meanwhile, as German expansion continued in Europe, U.S. apprehension of the threat of Japanese expansion toward its interest in Southeast Asia also reached new heights, resulting in further economic pressure against Japan by the United States and, conversely, an anti–United States movement in Japan. Under these circumstances, a strong voice demanding the Tripartite Pact was regaining its momentum. It is important to note, however, in terms of the object of the pact, it was no longer the Soviet Union but the United States and the British.[37]

At the outset, the Konoe cabinet did not necessarily focus on having the Tripartite Pact but rather a reinforcement of the anti-Comintern treaty. At the Ogikubo Conference on July 19, Foreign Minister Matsuoka, although he stated the importance of the Tripartite Pact, emphasized that a settlement of the China Incident should be considered a top priority. Therefore, the new cabinet policies needed to be directed toward achieving a coherent unity between the central government and the overseas military action.[38]

The Tripartite Pact suddenly began to move forward, however, when Heinrich Stahmer came to Japan on September 7, as a special envoy for Foreign Minister Joachim von Ribbentrop with a secret mission with regard to drafting the pact. On September 9, Matsuoka invited Stahmer to his home for a private talk that was strictly between him and Stahmer. As a result of this meeting, a decision was made to formally conclude the Tripartite Pact.[39] According to the record of their conversation, both agreed to the following basic guidelines, primarily based on Stahmer's suggestions for the pact:

1. Germany does not desire the war in Europe to expand into a world war, hopes for a quick settlement, and strongly desires to prevent the United States from entering the war.
2. Germany does not seek Japanese military assistance in its military operation against the British mainland.
3. What Germany wants Japan to do is to restrain the United States from joining the war in Europe by utilizing every possible means. Although Germany so far assumes that the United States would not enter the war, it cannot be said that there is absolutely no possibility.
4. Germany believes that it would be to Japan and Germany's advantage, based on a mutual understanding or agreement, to sufficiently prepare for any crisis at any time. Thus, a prevention of U.S. entry into the present war and also the prevention of the outbreak of any conflict between the United States and Japan are essential.
5. It is essential to understand that the only way to control the United States is to make it so clear to them and the world how determined Japan, Germany, and Italy are so that there would not be any room for misjudgment. On the other hand, showing weakness or lack of resolve would bring only contempt and crisis.
6. Germany hopes that Japan, with a clear grasp of the current situation and a recognition of the reality and importance of a possible crisis in the Western Hemisphere, will act promptly and decisively by conclud-

ing a treaty with Germany and Italy so that the United States and other powers will not make any misjudgment or speculation.

7. In terms of rapprochement with the Soviet Union immediately follow-ing a conclusion of the treaty, Germany will be ready to be an honest mediator for establishment of a friendship treaty between Japan and the Soviet Union. Germany does not think that there is any obstacle exist-ing between the two nations. Accordingly, it should be done without difficulty. Contrary to British propaganda, Germany is on good terms with the Soviet Union and the Soviet Union has been sincere in its rela-tionship with Germany.

Then, Matsuoka presented his own guidelines for the Tripartite Pact:[40]

1. In terms of establishing a New Order in Europe, Japan recognizes and respects the leadership of Germany and Italy.
2. Germany and Italy recognize and respect Japan's leadership in estab-lishing a New Order in greater East Asia.
3. In order to achieve the above-mentioned goal, Japan, Germany, and Italy vow to cooperate in finding an effective and appropriate means to overcome any obstacles.
4. Believing it is possible to build the foundation for a fair and perma-nent peace only by establishing a New World Order capable of coping with the currently changing world situation, each nation — Japan, Ger-many, and Italy — pledges to make its own effort clear for achieving this goal.

Although he basically agreed to Matsuoka's guidelines, Stahmer sug-gested the need to modify the third article. According to it, "Japan, Ger-many, and Italy, based on already stated conditions, will mutually cooperate and maintain dialogue. Also, if one of these three nations comes under attack by a nation not involved in the current war in Europe or the Sino-Japanese conflict, Japan, Germany, and Italy will mutually assist politi-cally, economically, and militarily."[41]

Upon Matsuoka's acceptance of Stahmer's modification, the final guidelines for the Tripartite Pact were completed. Prevention of the U.S. entry into the European war, rapprochement between Japan and the Soviet Union with assistance from Germany as an honest mediator, recognition of leadership zones — Germany and Italy in Europe and Japan in East Asia — and political, economic and military cooperation emerged as the central points of the pact.

Although it was to be adopted, the ratification of the pact did not go through unopposed. Navy officers, particularly Admiral Yamamoto

Isoroku, foreign ambassadors such as Kurusu Saburo to Germany and Shigemitsu Mamoru to England, Saionji Kinmochi, and Harada Kumao all opposed the pact, expressing their apprehension over the likely further deterioration of the U.S.-Japan relationship if ratification were to take place and their doubt about the trustworthiness of the German pledge.[42]

Sharing these apprehensions, the Emperor showed strong concern over this trend of moving toward ratification of the pact. According to Harada, when Konoe met the Emperor on September 16 to report on the ongoing cabinet discussion of the pact, the Emperor said to Konoe, "After giving this matter deep consideration, I think the ratification of the Tripartite Pact today is unavoidable if there is nothing else to be done to come to peace terms with the United States. I wonder, however, how well the navy would do if Japan faced confrontation with the United States. I often hear that, according to maneuvers outlined on the map at the Naval Academy, Japan is always defeated by the United States."[43] Then, the Emperor continued to say, "I am very much apprehensive about the current situation. What would happen if Japan loses the war? Would the Prime Minister share any hardship with me if that really takes place?" Konoe was normally able to remain calm and keep his cool, regardless of the situation he faced, when he heard these words from the Emperor, he could not help himself from becoming emotional and began to sob. Then, in order to alleviate the Emperor's apprehension, although Konoe was not sure about its authenticity, Konoe told the Emperor the story the Count Kaneko Kentaro had told him. According to the story, the Meiji Emperor decided to declare war against Russia at the Imperial Conference. He invited Prime Minister Ito Hirobumi to discuss the upcoming war. Expressing his apprehension about the war, the Emperor asked Ito what he would do if Japan were defeated. Ito told the Emperor in response that he would give up everything and be ready to fight as a mere solder to defend the nation and above all to honor the Imperial Family. Emperor Meiji was deeply encouraged by Ito's words. After telling this story to Showa Emperor, Konoe said that he was apprehensive too about the war and had no intention to spare his devotion to serve the nation and the Emperor to the very end.[44]

Later Konoe mentioned at the cabinet meeting what the Emperor said to him. Overwhelmed, Matsuoka suddenly began to cry, making everyone else at the meeting emotionally besieged. When Konoe saw it, he was not able to maintain his usual composure and he too could not help but be emotional. Then, Konoe repeated the same thing at the New Structure Preparation Committee. Matsuoka once again cried. So did everyone at the meeting. Believing politicians to be old stagers and seeing them from time to time act unlawfully, Konoe found the politicians' behavior rather surprising. Contrastingly, Koneo found it amusing that the bureaucrats who were believed to be always solemn were actually unemotional.[45]

The Tripartite Pact was ratified at the Imperial Conference on September 19, 1940. Matsuoka wished to have the signing of the pact at Tokyo. Facing strong insistence by Germany to have it in their country, Matsuoka gave in. The signing took place in Berlin on September 27.

It was welcomed with enormous exultation both in Tokyo and Berlin. In the midst of such frenzy, Matsuoka and Konoe could not help but be somewhat apprehensive. Both knew that the success of the Tripartite Pact was largely based on speculation. When Harada expressed his doubt about keeping the Soviet Union on the side of the Tripartite Pact, Konoe responded by saying, "I agree with you. There is too much speculation that Japan has to rely on. After conquering Paris, Germany has been sending huge numbers of troops to East Prussia [toward the Soviet Union]. I have some concern about how the relationship between Germany and the Soviet Union will unfold. What would be the worst scenario for Japan is that, if the British defeat Germany, both the United States and the British would be formidable foes in the Pacific."[46] Matsuoka had similar concerns. Knowing that the success of the Tripartite Pact depended so much on having the Soviet Union as part of the pact, to him, the chances of the pact successful were only 50 percent.[47]

Questions to consider are why both Konoe and Matsuoka desired to have the Tripartite Pact in spite of their anxiety, and how they managed to make it possible to have the pact. Answering the latter question first, although, as mentioned earlier, Germany's seemingly imminent victory in the European conflict boosted enthusiasm for the pact's supporters, the change in the navy's assessment of the Tripartite Pact was another important factor. From the beginning, the navy's opposition was a formidable barrier for those who wished to have the pact ratified. That, however, dramatically changed when Navy Minister Yoshida Zengo resigned because of his deteriorating health and Oikawa Koshiro replaced him. Representing the navy, Oikawa gave his consent to the Tripartite Pact. Konoe, finding this sudden reverse of the navy's position difficult to understand, asked the Vice Minister of the Navy, Toyoda Teijiro, to provide an explanation. Toyoda responded by saying, "Although the navy actually opposes the Tripartite Pact, upon consideration of the current political situation, it is no longer possible for the navy to continue to oppose it. The navy has to accept, therefore, ratification of the pact even if it is against our will. Our navy acceptance of the pact, however, is only based on political considerations. From the military point of view, the navy has no desire to fight against the United States."[48] Then Konoe said, "That is very strange to hear. Don't you think that politics are something only politicians should be concerned with? There is no need for the navy to worry. It would be far more faithful to the nation if the navy, taking the issue into consideration strictly from the military point of view, says that it has no confidence in victory and, therefore, has to oppose the pact."[49] Toyoda defensively argued, "In today's situation, please try to understand the position the navy has to take. Now there is only one thing we can and should focus on. That is, with diplomatic means, to prevent the creation of any circumstances that might obligate Japan to carry out military assistance under the Tripartite Pact."[50]

When Konoe told Admiral Yamamoto about his conversation with Toyoda, Yamamoto expressed his disappointment with the navy, saying, "Today, the navy is much inclined to take things too politically."[51] Then Konoe asked Yamamoto what he would think about the fate of Japan if war broke out between Japan and the United States. Yamamoto responded, "I would be able to fight favorably for Japan for the first six months or a year. I have no confidence, however, if the war continues for two or three years. Since the Tripartite Pact has been ratified and there is no point in expressing regret, I would like you to do your best to avoid a war against the United States."[52]

Now, understanding where the navy stood with regard to the Tripartite Pact, Konoe was further convinced that Japan was taking a chance for catastrophe by signing the Tripartite Pact. It was essential, therefore, in the actual utilization of the pact, that Japan act with extra caution and eschew military confrontation with the United States.

Konoe made it clear that one of the main points of the pact was that, if one of the treaty nations was under an attack by a nation that had no involvement in the European war nor in the Sino-Japanese War, the other treaty nations had an obligation to provide political, economic, and military assistance to the nation under attack.[53] What it more specifically meant was that, if the United States came into the war against Germany, Japan would assist Germany militarily, and vice versa. Konoe continued to say that there was, however, circumstantially almost no possibility that the United States would wage a war against Japan. On the other hand, it was more likely that the United States would get into a war against Germany if U.S. assistance to the British increased. It was, therefore, Germany's desire that Japan play a role in reducing this likelihood. Accordingly, Konoe emphasized that one of the main objectives for ratifying the Tripartite Pact was the prevention of U.S. entry into the war in Europe so that an expansion into a worldwide conflict could be avoided.

To Konoe, it was clear that entry of the United States into the Euro-

In July 1937, Konoe Fumimaro in disguise as Hitler. Beside him at right center, in female dress, is younger brother Hidemaro. As Prime Minister of imperial Japan, Konoe was believed to have been deeply interested in the Nazis (© Mainich Photo Bank).

pean conflict meant British victory over Germany, rendering it more difficult for Japan to come to terms with China. Indeed, it would be the end of the goal that both Konoe and Matsuoka were trying to achieve, the establishment of a New Order. On the other hand, a German victory would give Japan much-needed leverage in handling the seemingly insoluble Sino-Japanese Incident and would also make the United States submit to Japan's goals in East Asia. To Konoe, as long as Germany and Japan were able to keep the United States out of the European conflict, a major risk involved in the ratification of the Tripartite Pact could be minimized. It was, however, greatly dependent upon whether or not Germany and Japan could bring the Soviet Union onto their side as part of the pact. Konoe stated in his memoir that, fortunately, according to Stahmer, Germany was on good terms with the Soviet Union and was committed to an effort to expand its relationship with the Soviet Union into a triangular relationship among Japan, Germany, and the Soviet Union.[54] Konoe argued that, with Germany's pledge as one of the premises for ratification, the Tripartite Pact was signed. To further limit any risks, Konoe continued to argue that interpreting the Tripartite Pact as narrowly as possible was also essential so that Japan could have autonomy over a decision about entry into the war.[55] Accordingly, Konoe disagreed with Matsuoka, who considered even the U.S. convoy for the British non-military ships as military action against Germany. The definition of a military attack by the United States had to be narrowly interpreted, and Japan should not be obliged to take military action automatically when a war actually broke out between Germany and the United States. Instead Japan should be given autonomy in deciding when and how it would enter the war. Although Konoe, as stated earlier, still could not help but have some doubt about German trustworthiness, he believed that the risks would be worth taking and greatly minimized as long as Germany and Japan strictly interpreted the Tripartite Pact based on the premises above and acted accordingly. Only then, according to Konoe, would the benefits of the pact outweigh the risks. It was still a gamble, but one worth taking.

Although Matsuoka basically shared Konoe's views, as already mentioned above, Konoe faced a counterargument that, by stimulating U.S. emotion toward Japan in a negative fashion, the Tripartite Pact actually would produce further deterioration of the U.S.-Japanese relationship and eventually cause war to erupt between Japan and the United States.[56] Responding to such arguments, Konoe stated in his postwar memoir that it would not be permanently found out whether the Tripartite Pact really prevented the United States from war in Europe because Japan declared war on the United States before the United States entered the war against Germany.[57] Konoe added, however, that no one could deny that the war between Japan and United States did not break out until more than a year after the ratification of the Tripartite Pact. Furthermore, when the U.S.-Japanese negotiations began in April 1941, the United States considered the nullification of the pact as one of its main objectives, indicating that the Pact had been a diplomatic obstacle for the United States. Konoe emphasized, therefore, that at least it could be said that the Tripartite Pact was effective as deterrence against U.S. entry into the war in Europe.

In his concluding argument over the Tripartite Pact, Konoe further stated that it was logically and factually false to say that the war between Japan and the United States broke out because of the Tripartite Pact. Konoe argued that according the Tripartite Pact, Japan was obligated to declare war against the United States only when war broke out between the United States and Germany: what really took place, however, was Japan's war declaration against the United States before the outbreak of any military exchange between Germany and the United States; furthermore, Japan's declaration of war against the United States did not mention anything about Japan's obligations under the Pact, so, it was a logical conclusion to

Konoe that the war did not take place because of the Pact. He recognized that the British and the United States became more critical of Japanese policies toward China after the ratification of the Tripartite Pact, and Konoe also argued that the British and the United States had been critical toward Japan since the 1931 Manchurian Incident; furthermore, the United States' abrogation of the 1911 Treaty of Commerce and Navigation with Japan came during the Hiranuma Cabinet, far before the conclusion of the Tripartite Pact, and it was ten months after the ratification of the Pact that the United States froze Japanese assets as a sanction against the Japanese invasion of French Indo China. Thus, to Konoe, there was literally nothing to support an assertion that the U.S. polices against Japan were further intensified as a direct result from the ratification of the pact. As the most compelling evidence, Konoe pointed out the U.S.-Japan negotiations, which was, according to Konoe, initiated by the U.S. request "six months" after the ratification of the Pact.[58]

Yabe Teiji refutes Konoe's argument, pointing out that, contrary to what Konoe stated, the British and U.S. reaction against the Tripartite Pact was great. Yabe stated that the United States along with the British began to think about the possibility of a Pacific war following ratification of the pact. Also the encroachment policy by ABCD (American, British, Chinese, and Dutch) against Japan and the economic sanctions of freezing Japanese access to raw materials were further intensified.[59]

Yabe was by no means alone in his assertion. A close observation of U.S. reaction to the pact, however, does not support Yabe's view, but that of Konoe. Joseph C. Grew, U.S. ambassador to Japan, who had been critical of U.S. economic sanctions against Japan and had urged the U.S. government to make conciliatory gestures toward Japan, sent a telegram to the Department of State on September 12, 1940.[60] In it, reversing his previous position, Grew stated that now he had to support economic sanctions against Japan. In his testimony before the congressional investigation of the Pearl Harbor attack, Grew made the following remark: "The Japanese Army was steadily encroaching further into the Far East and into East Asia. They were potentially threatening our vital interests. And from that point of view the situation had very much changed indeed. That, I think, was the main reason why I sent that telegram, but one must remember that my so-called green-light telegram was not something, which had developed in a matter of a few hours or a few days. It meant a progressive line of thinking over a period to the crux of the situation."[61] What one should note here is that the telegram was sent on September 12, 1940, nearly two weeks before ratification of the Tripartite Pact, meaning Grew's reversal of his position had nothing to do with ratification of the pact. As indicated in his testimony, it was a result of his apprehension over the growing threat to U.S. interests in Southeast Asia by the intruding Japanese troops. In fact, in his memoir, *Turbulent Era: A Diplomatic Record of Forty Years, 1904–1945,* Grew hardly mentions the Tripartite Pact.

The Secretary of State, Cordell Hull, also made a similar remark in his public statement after meeting with President Franklin D. Roosevelt over the issue of the Tripartite Pact.[62] According to Hull, the Tripartite Pact did not, in the view of the U.S. government, in any drastic fashion alter the situation that already had existed for several years. Instead, it merely made clear what the U.S. government had known for quite sometime regarding the relationship among the three treaty nations. Furthermore, like Grew, in his memoir, Hull indicates almost nothing to suggest any major concern over the terms of U.S. policies toward Japan because of ratification of the Tripartite Pact.

The Tripartite Pact might have played a role as Konoe desired, bringing the Sino-Japanese War to a diplomatic settlement. Unfortunately for Konoe, his concern about the possibility of the rupture of the Russo-German relationship became a reality when Germany invaded the Soviet Union on July 22, 1941.

Contrary to Japan's hope to have Germany as a mediator to improve the Russo-Japanese relationship, Germany's relations with the Soviet Union were deteriorating. In November, through the talks between German Foreign Minister Ribbentrop and Foreign Commissar Vyacheslav M. Molotov, the former proposed a draft agreement regarding mutual respect and protection of the spheres of interests among the Tripartite Pact nations and the Soviet Union and a conclusion of the Four Power Treaty.[63] Moscow responded to the draft agreement, saying they would not accept it unless Germany acknowledged the Soviet military buildup in Finland and the Dardanelles Strait and the Soviet-Bulgaria Alliance.[64] Finding it too much to accept, Germany began to think that military confrontation against the Soviet Union might be necessary.

It was the spring of 1941 when Japan became convinced about possible military confrontation between Germany and the Soviet Union. On March 12, Matsuoka left Japan for Berlin to discuss the Four Power Treaty. At Berlin, Matsuoka was told of the growing tension between Germany and the Soviet Union. In fact, German Foreign Minister Ribbentrop said to Matsuoka, "In order to eradicate our European problems, we may need to confront the Soviet Union militarily."[65] Matsuoka responded, "If such a situation emerges between Germany and the Soviet Union, Japan would suffer immensely from it. It is difficult for me, therefore, to give any consent to a military confrontation against the Soviet Union." Rather ironically, Mastuoka continued to say to Ribbentrop, "On the way back to Japan, I will stop by Moscow in order to advance the talks for adjusting the Russo-Japanese diplomatic relationship."[66] Then Ribbentrop responded, "Since the Soviet Union is untrustworthy, such talks will not work out."

Contrary to Ribbentrop's prediction, Matsuoka succeeded in concluding the Japan-Soviet Neutrality Treaty. Responding to this news, Ribbentrop said to Ambassador Oshima Hiroshi, "I told Matsuoka so clearly that a war against the Soviet Union was inevitable. Yet he concluded the Neutrality Treaty with the Soviet Union. It is difficult for me to comprehend Matsuoka's action."[67]

Apprehensive over the increasingly deteriorating German-Soviet relationship, on May 28, Konoe sent a message under the name of Foreign Minister Matsuoka to Ribbentrop. It said, "Taking into consideration the current international and national situations, as the Foreign Minister, I would like the government of Germany to make as much effort as possible to avoid a military confrontation with the Soviet Union."[68] In response, Ribbentrop said, "Today it is impossible to avoid a war against the Soviet Union. If the war really comes, however, I am convinced that it will be over within a few months. Please trust me on this. In this war Germany does not need any help from Japan. Moreover, the outcome of the war will favor Japan."[69]

With this response, Konoe knew the war between Germany and the Soviet Union was imminent. On June 22, less than a month later, war broke out between Germany and the Soviet Union. With the United States and Britain immediately pledging their assistance to the Soviet Union, Konoe's wish to have the Soviet Union as an ally to the Tripartite Pact nations became completely hopeless, making the pact pointless for Japan. Understandably feeling deceived, Konoe stated that during the Hiranuma cabinet, Germany betrayed Japan by suddenly concluding the non-invasion treaty with the Soviet Union while Germany and Japan were still conducting bilateral talks regarding the Tripartite Pact to deal with the Soviet threat. To Konoe, if that was Germany's first betrayal of Japan, the German decision to go to war against the Soviet Union while promising Japan they would bring the Soviet Union as an ally to the Tripartite Pact and to conclude the Pact with Japan based that promise was clearly the second betrayal.[70]

The Tripartite Pact, designed to prevent the United States from coming into the war first in Europe and then in the Pacific, was now becoming a possible cause for the war between Japan and the United States. Konoe wanted to reconsider the Tripartite Pact. He consulted Army Minister Tojo Hideki about Japan's withdrawal from the pact. According to Konoe, Tojo, expecting a quick victory by Germany against the Soviet Union, had no intention of listening to him. Konoe then realized that, circumstantially, reconsideration of the pact would be impossible and unwise. Even though Japan was betrayed by Germany, abolishing the pact that had been concluded less than a year earlier would damage Japan's reputation in terms of international trust. So then, what became vital for Japan was rapprochement toward the United State's. According to Konoe, before the conclusion of the Tripartite Pact, there was almost no chance for rapprochement. After ratification of the pact, however, it became possible. The United States did not want to get into a military confrontation with Japan so that they could focus on rescuing the British in the European war. As will be discussed later, Konoe had no idea at this point how wrong he was in his view of rapprochement. Contrary to Konoe's optimism, rapprochement was to be next to impossible.

5

Konoe's Last Endeavor: U.S.–Japanese Negotiations

As discussed in the previous chapter, the most important goals of the Tripartite Pact were the prevention of U.S. entry into the war in Europe and the settlement of the China Incident through mediation by the United States. Konoe understood, however, depending on the impact of the ratification of the Tripartite Pact, that there was a good chance the pact would produce the opposite outcome, meaning that the pact would not prevent but rather cause the U.S. entry to the war. Konoe spared no time, therefore, in his diplomatic efforts to make the necessary adjustments in the U.S.-Japan relationship.

Admiral Nomura Kichizaburo was dispatched to the United States as an ambassador. Because of his lack of experience in foreign affairs, Nomura was first reluctant to take the assignment, but he gave in to the pressure from Konoe and the military. Nomura left Japan for the United States in February 1941.

Under Nomura's leadership, the U.S.-Japanese negotiations began. They were conducted in a secret manner in order to avoid any interference until the basic agreement was reached. Then in April the negotiation began to move forward rapidly when both governments agreed to produce a mutual understanding over the various issues regarding the U.S.-Japan relationship. In order to produce the so-called Japanese-American Draft Understanding, the intensive negotiations began between Ambassador Nomura and U.S. Secretary of State Cordell Hull.

The background of these negotiations goes back to November 1940 when Bishop James E. Walsh and Father James M. Drought, representing the Catholic Foreign Mission Society of America at Maryknoll, New York, met with Ikawa Tadao, an executive officer of the Central Bank of the Industrial Association in Tokyo, and asked him about the possibility of starting negotiations between the United States and Japan in order to improve their deteriorating relationship.[1] Having a positive reply not only from Ikawa but also other prominent Japanese leaders, Walsh and Drought returned to the United States to report on their visit to President Roosevelt and Secretary of State Hull. Roosevelt and Hull also gave them encouraging words, showing their interest in such negotiations. Informed by Walsh and Drought of a positive reply from the U.S. government, Ikawa Tadao and Colonel Iwakuro Hideo, chief of the military section of the Army Ministry, went to the United States in February and March, respectively. They joined Nomura, Walsh, and Drought for talks to adjust the U.S.-Japanese relationship.

After going through repeated negotiations, they produced the first draft of the Japanese-American Draft Understanding on April 5. Then, after examining this draft, they generated the second draft on April 16. Cordell Hull invited Nomura twice on April 14 and 16 for their first meeting and indicated his desire to shift negotiations from the civilians to an unofficial negotiation between him and Nomura and start it based on the second draft.[2] At the same time, Hull handed Nomura the four principles that the United States specified Japan had to accept if there was any chance for negotiations to succeed. Those four principles were: (1) Respect for the territorial integrity and the sovereignty of each and all nations; (2) Support of the principle of non-interference in the internal affairs of other countries; (3) Support of the principle of equality, including equality of commercial opportunity; and (4) Non-disturbance of the status quo in the Pacific except by peaceful means.[3]

Upon Nomura's agreement, the following Japanese-American Draft Understanding was adopted:

1. The concepts of both Japan and the United States regarding the international relations and the national character: As the neighboring powers in the Pacific, both nations mutually recognize their equality, sovereignty, and independence. Both governments agree to the establishment of a new era for the two nations based on respect, trust, and cooperation. Both nations declare that it is their traditional belief to support and protect their equality as nations and races; their right to pursue spiritual and material welfare in a peaceful fashion.
2. Approach of both nations toward European war: The Japanese government makes it clear that the purpose of the Tripartite Pact is for defense and to prevent the escalation of the war by nations that are not involved in the European war. The Japanese government has no intention of neglecting its duty as a member nation of the Tripartite Pact. Japan makes it clear, however, that it will carry out its duties only when Germany is under attack by a nation that is not currently in the European war. The

U.S. government makes it clear that the U.S. approach toward the European war is not based on any offensive alliance like supporting one nation while attacking the other. The United States strongly condemns an act of war. Accordingly, the U.S. approach toward the European war is strictly in the interest of defending its own security and welfare.

3. The relation between the two nations over the China Incident: The President of the United States recognizes the conditions mentioned below and will advise the Chiang regime to have peace with Japan only when Japan assures that it will follow up on those conditions.
   a. Sovereignty of China.
   b. Withdrawal of Japanese troops from Chinese territory based on an agreement between China and Japan.
   c. No acquisition of Chinese territory.
   d. No indemnity.
   e. Re-adoption of an Open Door Policy — how to apply and interpret this point, however, both nations will discuss at an appropriate time in future.
   f. Establishing a joint government between the Chiang regime and the Wang regime.
   g. Japan's restricting mass immigration to China.
   h. Recognition of Manchukuo.

   When the Chiang regime accepts the advice of the President of the United States, Japan will immediately begin peace negotiations as a partner in establishing a new and unified Chinese government. This is placed within the framework of the previously mentioned conditions and based on the principles of the mutual friendship prevention act against Communist intrusion and economic cooperation.

4. The issue of naval and air power, and marine transportation in the Pacific:
   a. Both Japan and the United States hope to maintain peace in the Pacific. Accordingly, neither nation will adopt a policy of deploying Naval and Air power in order to avoid creating a threat against the other. Details about this matter will be determined through U.S.-Japanese negotiations.
   b. Should an agreement be reached between the two nations, each nation will dispatch its naval fleet to the other as a symbolic gesture to recognize the establishment of peace in the Pacific.
   c. When the China Incident is settled, responding to the U.S. request, the Japanese government will move those ships that can be set off duty to the Pacific. The number of tons of those ships will be determined through negotiations.

5. Agreements in commerce and finance: When both nations ratify the draft understanding, each nation promises to supply goods that the other nation needs. Both nations will take necessary measures to restore the proper channels of commerce with each other. When they desire to have a new commerce treaty, both nations will discuss it at the U.S.-Japanese negotiations and conclude it according to regular customs. In order to promote economic agreements between the two nations and also to improve the economic situation in the Far East, the United States will provide monetary credit to Japan.

6. Economic activities of both nations in the Southwest Pacific: Since Japan pledges that Japanese advancement in the Southwest Pacific will not rely on military means but on peaceful measures, the United States will give its cooperation and support to Japan so that Japan can produce or obtain any desired goods and materials.

7. Policies of both nations with regard to political stability in the Pacific: Both Japan and the United States will not tolerate any future territorial annexation in East Asia and the Southwest Pacific by the European nations. Both Japan and the United States will guarantee the sovereignty of the Philippines and take into consideration how to defend it when they are under attack by a third nation. Japanese immigration to the United States and the Southwest Pacific would be treated in an equally friendly fashion, as are the other nationalities.

8. Japan–United States Conference:
   a. Prime Minister Konoe representing Japan and President Roosevelt representing the United States will hold a conference at Honolulu. The number of delegates from each nation has to be five or less.
   b. There will be no observer from a third nation for the conference.
   c. After reaching an agreement on the draft, both nations will hold the conference immediately.
   d. Re-discussion of each article will not take place at the conference. Both nations will talk over the already decided agenda and how to put it in statutory form. The two nations will discuss elaboration of the agendas.

Appendix: *Both nations agree to treat this draft understanding in a secret fashion. Both nations will discuss when and how much they are going to publicly announce about this draft understanding.*

On April 17, 1941, the telegram from Ambassador Nomura conveying this Japanese-American Draft Understanding came to Tokyo. On the following day, at the cabinet conference, Vice Foreign Minister Ohashi (Matsuoka was on the way back to Japan from his trip to Europe) informed

Konoe about the draft. Ohashi, however, could not say anything to Konoe about the four principles Hull raised, because Nomura refrained from saying anything about them in the telegram. Nomura was afraid that the Japanese-American Draft Understanding with such "strings" attached would be difficult for Japan to accept, thus delaying Japan's response to the U.S. proposal on the draft understanding.

Responding to Nomura's telegram, Konoe promptly held a liaison conference between cabinet members and military officials. The major attendees were Prime Minister Konoe, Home Minister Hiranuma, Army Minister Tojo, and Navy Minister Oikawa from the government, and Head of the General Staff Office, Sugiyama; Head of the Military Commanding Office, Nagano; Chief of Army Military Office, Muto; Chief of Navy Military Office, Oka; and Chief Secretary of the Cabinet, Tomita, from the Supreme Command.[4] Konoe, Tojo, and Oikawa basically agreed to accept the draft understanding. They argued that it would be the most helpful for Japan in solving the China Incident.[5] Without having any positive result from the Wang Ching-wei maneuver, it had been difficult for Japan to have any dialogue with Chungking. Rapprochement between Japan and the United States was now the only way to settle the China Incident.[6] The only disagreement they had was over whether or not they should inform Germany in advance before Japan and the United States reached any settlement. Some said that since it was an important matter, Japan had to be faithful to Germany by informing them, that others opposed, arguing that if Germany knew in advance, it would surely protest. In the end, Japan would miss the chance to solve its problem, so, there was no other choice but ensue without informing Germany.[7] In addition to this disagreement, they also had some apprehensions about the violation of the Tripartite Pact by negotiating with the United States. Taking all these things into consideration, they chose to wait for the return of Matsuoka and hear what he would say before they made any definitive decision.

When Matsuoka arrived at Dairen on April 20, Konoe made a phone call to Matsuoka to inform him about the ongoing U.S.-Japanese negotiations and urged him to return to Japan as early as possible. Matsuoka was very pleased with what he heard and said to his associates, "This proposal from the United States is perhaps due to what I told U.S. Ambassador to the Soviet Union, Laurence A. Steinhardt."[8] During his trip to Europe, Matsuoka had a chance to talk to Ambassador Steinhardt and told him about his interest in having a summit meeting with President Roosevelt in order to discuss a possible role Roosevelt could play in bringing the China Incident to a peaceful end. In fact, on April 8, Matsuoka sent a telegram to Konoe about his meeting with Steinhardt.

On April 22, Matsuoka arrived at the Tachikawa Airport in Tokyo. Considering Matsuoka's complex character, Konoe decided to meet Matsuoka to tell him personally abut the Japanese-American Draft Understanding. It did not go as Konoe planned, however. When Matsuoka, just before he got into the car, started saying that he desired to go to the Imperial Palace to worship at the Niju Bashi (Double Bridge), Konoe changed his mind and chose not to ride with Matsuoka to tell him about the draft understanding. Unlike Matsuoka, Konoe disliked the political spotlight. He could not stand Matsuoka's seeking publicity about his achievements in Europe by acting like a movie star in front of big crowds of press correspondents and broadcasting staff.[9]

The delicate role of telling Matsuoka about the draft understanding went to Vice Foreign Minister Ohashi Tadaichi. When Ohashi told Matsuoka, as expected, Matsuoka became very displeased, realizing that this draft understanding had nothing to do with his talk with Steinhardt.[10] To him, it was a shattering blow, ending his grand plan to settle the Sino-Japanese dispute through the mediation of President Roosevelt and then go to the United States to adjust the U.S.-Japanese relationship, remove all the disputes between the two nations, and finally, together with Roosevelt, bring the European war to an end.[11] After speaking with Hitler and Mussolini and then concluding the Japan-Soviet Neutrality Treaty, to have a summit talk with Roosevelt was the final stage and the highlight of his career as a diplomat. The diplomatic maneuvering Konoe and his cabinet did without any consultation with Matsuoka while he was gone to Europe took the glory away from Matsuoka. As will be discussed later, this began Konoe's troubling political relationship with Matsuoka.

On the night of Matsuoka's return, Konoe held a liaison conference. True to his character, Matsuoka purposely came to the conference late to show his displeasure. He dominated the conference and utilized it as an occasion to boast of his achievements in Europe. Then, when it came to the discussion on the Japanese-American Draft Understanding, Matsuoka made a passionate argument. He said that regardless of how the army and the navy saw the policy of accepting the U.S. proposed draft understanding, he could not agree to it. To him, it was a weak policy and also went against Japan's obligation to and trust of Germany. Then, having some doubt about trustworthiness of the United States, Matsuoka told the conferees that during World War I, the United States signed a treaty, so-called "the Ishi-Lansing Treaty," with Japan in order to remove a threat from Japan in the Pacific and quickly revoked it as soon as the war was over; that was the way the United States conducted its foreign affairs always. So what emerged from the U.S. draft understanding was full of deception and little sincerity.[12] After stating all these facts, Matsuoka said that that he was not fully recovered from the trip to Europe and he needed more time to contemplate the issue of the U.S. draft understanding and to make up his mind about it.[13] Afterward, he simply left the conference.

The conference continued without Matsuoka. Despite Matsuoka's remark, Konoe and the rest of the cabinet members made a decision to push the draft plan forward as it was. The next day, April 23, Konoe invited Matsuoka alone to his home for a further talk about the U.S.-Japanese negotiations. All Matsuoka said was, "I would like you to let me think it over. I have just come back from Europe. I need time to rest."[14]

Understandably, Matsuoka's behavior created ill feelings toward him among the other cabinet members. The anti-Matsuoka mood became high, particularly among the top army and navy officers. Some even demanded his resignation. Seeing Matsuoka as a person with a complex character, Konoe thought it would be better to wait and leave the situation as Matsuoka desired until he formed his opinion.

Then, almost simultaneously, both Konoe and Matsuoka became ill. Both had to stay at their own homes for about a week to recuperate. At the same time, understanding the significance of giving a prompt response to the U.S. proposal, the army and the navy continued to put pressure on Matsuoka. While showing no sign of giving in to such pressure, despite his sickness, Matsuoka made an effort to have the draft understanding modified.[15]

On May 3, the Konoe cabinet held the third Liaison Conference, and Matsuoka presented his modified draft understanding. All at the conference basically agreed to accept it. The modification specified the following: (1) To remove the fourth article of the draft, *The Relation Over Naval and Air Power, and Marine Transportation in the Pacific*; (2) Regarding the approach of the two governments toward the European war, to have a new article of mediating the military conflict between the British and Germany by Japan and the United States; (3) To refrain from publicly announcing peace conditions for the settlement of the China Incident; (4) To eliminate the Japanese pledge not to advance southward; (5) To eliminate the arrangements regarding the Japan–United States Conference.[16]

While the voices demanding to immediately send this modified "draft understanding" were dominant at the conference, Matsuoka insisted that Japan should first propose that the United States conclude a neutrality treaty between the two nations. His insistence prevailed.

Then Matsuoka sent two telegrams to Nomura. One was an oral statement directly addressed to the Secretary of State, Cordell Hull. In it, In the statement, Matsuoka said that Germany and Italy were confident that they would win the European war and that the U.S. entry would cause nothing but prolongation of the war and ultimate ruin of the entire civilization. Therefore, it was out of the question for Japan to end its alliance with Germany and Italy.[17] The other was the proposal to establish the neutrality treaty between Japan and the United States.

Upon receipt of these telegrams, Nomura met Hull on May 7. Hull did not show any interest in the neutrality treaty. Regarding the oral statement, Nomura, considering that the content of the statement might be offensive to Hull, did not give the telegram to Hull and did not even finish reading it.

Meanwhile, the Emperor could not help but be strongly concerned with these diplomatic developments. Such concern was further intensified when Matsuoka said to the Emperor, "If the United States joins the war, Japan has to be on the side of Germany and Italy and must attack Singapore. The U.S. entry will prolong the war, and there will be a great possibility of a military clash between Germany and the Soviet Union. If that happens, Japan has to abolish its neutrality treaty with the Soviet Union and, joining Germany, advance to Irkutsk."[18]

Informed of Matsuoka's remark to the Emperor, Konoe secretly met Army Minister Tojo and Navy Minister Oikawa on May 9 to discuss how to deal with the behavior of Matsuoka. On the following day, Konoe met the Emperor and told him that Matsuoka's remark was one of the options Japan might take only if Japan faced the worst outcome of the current diplomatic effort. Also, it was only Matsuoka's idea. A decision had to be made through the cabinet conference in the presence of the executive officers of the military. Therefore, Konoe told the Emperor that there was no need to worry.

Meanwhile, Matsuoka wanted to delay the delivery of Japan's amended draft understanding until a response from Germany arrived. There was no sign of such response from Germany, however. Unable to wait any longer, on May 12, Matsuoka sent the telegram to Nomura, instructing him to begin negotiations based on the Japanese amended draft understanding. Nomura met with Cordell Hull on May 11 and 12 to explain the amended draft. At the same time, Matsuoka sent a message directly to Hull. In it, Matsuoka stated that Japan had two basic reasons for its decision to have negotiations with the United States: one was to prevent U.S. entry into the European war, and the other was to have the United States urge Chiang Kai-shek to begin peace talks with Japan immediately. Matsuoka emphasized that the U.S.—Japanese negotiations had to be conducted based on the above two points.[19]

Predictably, Hull's reaction to the amended draft and Matsuoka's message was negative. In his memoir, Hull wrote the following: "Very few rays of hope shone from the document. What Japan was proposing was mostly to her own advantage. In effect, it called for a species of joint overlordship of the Pacific area by Japan and the United States, with Japan the baron of the part that embraced nine-tenths of the population and the wealth, and with little consideration for the rights and interests of other nations."[20] Despite the negativity in Hull's reaction, upon consideration that the outright rejection of the Japanese proposal would not only shut off a rare chance to settle the fundamental problems existing between the two nations but also increase the possibility of military confrontation against Japan when U.S. entry into the war against Germany was becoming more imminent day by day, Hull indicated his desire to continue the negotiations.[21]

Shortly after Japan sent its response to the United States, the reply from Germany finally came. In it, Germany stated that the true intention of the U.S. effort to continue the U.S.-Japanese negotiations was to make the U.S. entry into the war against Germany possible, and, therefore, Germany expected Japan to recognize the following: (1) The U.S. patrol and convoy of British vessels should be considered as an act of war, and therefore, if they take place, Japan will be obliged to enter the war; (2) Only when the United States refrains from the above actions will Japan consider the U.S. proposal; (3) Japan informs Germany about its final response to the U.S. proposal before it is sent.[22]

On May 19, German Ambassador Ott expressed Germany's formal protest against the U.S.-Japanese negotiations. It stated that any treaty between one of the signatory nations to the Tripartite Pact and a non-signatory nation would weaken the war effort of the other signatory nations. Accordingly, Japan had to specify its obligation and the obligation of the U.S. government not to interfere in the war between the British and the Axis nations based on the Tripartite Pact.

Influenced by such strong protests from Germany, Matsuoka became more dogmatic, uncompromising, and, consequently, increasingly isolated in the Konoe cabinet. At the meeting with Konoe on May 23, Matsuola bitterly criticized the army and the navy. He told Konoe that the top officers of both were seemingly trying to achieve Japanese-American understanding even if that meant betraying Germany and Italy; nothing worried him more than such a timid approach.[23]

By the end of May 1941, Matsuoka also became increasingly resentful toward Ambassador Nomura.[24] At the May 23 meeting, Matsuoka expressed to Konoe his indignation toward Nomura, saying that the proposal from the United States actually was not from the United States but from Nomura himself, and he was clearly overstepping his authority.

Despite Konoe's efforts to convince Matsuoka that it had to be a misunderstanding, Matsuoka was further aggravated by finding out that Nomura allegedly told Hull that, while the Emperor and all members of the cabinet, including the Army and Navy Ministers, supported the U.S. proposal on the Japanese-American Draft Understanding, Matsuoka alone had opposed it. Matsuoka quickly sent a telegram to Nomura, asking him to take back his remark to Hull. Nomura responded by saying, "I have absolutely no clue about how you got such an idea. Asked by Hull, I told him, however, that Japanese diplomatic policy could not be determined by the Foreign Minister alone."[25] With Matsuoka's acceptance of Nomura's elaboration of the alleged remark, Matsuoka's political relationship with Nomura did not deteriorate further. It was, however, becoming increasingly clear to Konoe that Matsuoka's stand-alone diplomacy was becoming a serious obstacle in the ongoing U.S.-Japanese negotiations. Hull indicated that seeing such disunity in Japanese diplomacy made him somewhat doubtful of Japan's sincerity in carrying on the negotiations.

Despite such difficulty, the Nomura-Hull negotiations continued. With neither nation showing any desire to compromise over the treaty on the Pacific areas, the Tripartite Pact, and the China issue, the negotiation was hardly moving forward.

Facing such uncertainty and difficulty on the diplomatic front, particularly with regard to dealing with Matsuoka, and also being informed repeatedly by Ambassador Oshima Hiroshi about the possible outbreak of war between Germany and the Soviet Union, Konoe began to consider resigning. When Konoe met the Lord Keeper of the Privy Seal, Kido Koichi, and Home Minister Hiranuma Kiichiro on June 21, he told them that if war broke out between Germany and the Soviet Union, it would have a great impact on the Tripartite Pact just like during the Hiranuma cabinet; then his cabinet had to take the responsibility.[26] Kido, disagreeing with Konoe, told him that the Hiranuma cabinet had to dissolve itself in order to take the responsibility for failing to detect German rapprochement with the Soviet Union, but this time there had been information suggesting possible war between Germany and the Soviet Union; so even if the war did break out, Konoe did not necessarily need to feel the same way as Hiranuma did.[27] Agreeing with Kido, Konoe refrained from resigning.

Then, as anticipated, on June 22, 1941, the war between Germany and the Soviet Union broke out, changing drastically the nature of diplomacy. Just a day before the outbreak of the war, Cordell Hull finally responded to the May 12 Japanese-American Amended Draft Understanding by proposing the anti-amended draft understanding. It was filled with a harsh and bitter tone. In it, Hull specified three basic principles: (1) Japan's pledge not to move southward militarily; (2) Japan's pledge not to provide military support for Germany when the United States gets involved in the European war; (3) Withdrawal of Japanese troops from China. According to this new proposal, only when Japan agreed to accept these three principles would Japan be given a chance to join the party of peaceful nations as the lowest-ranked nation and live peacefully by being allowed to earn a living through hard work in order to feed the overpopulated nation, but nothing more.[28]

Now both nations rejected the Japanese-American Draft Understanding, indicating the difficult nature of the U.S.-Japanese negotiations. What is significant to note here is that, as shown in the strong tone of the response, Hull seemingly knew about the outbreak of the German-Soviet war in advance and had waited until the last minute to announce the U.S. response.

Matsuoka quickly responded to these ominous developments. Right after the outbreak of war between Germany and the Soviet Union, he went to see the Emperor and told him that, due to the beginning of the war between Germany and the Soviet Union, Japan had to participate in the war to support Germany. To do so required Japan to suspend its southward expansion for time being; it was inevitable, however, soon or later, for Japan to resume its expansion and eventually confront a simultaneous fight against the United States, the Soviet Union, and the Great Britain.[29]

Konoe disagreed with Matsuoka. Now the Soviet Union as an enemy of Germany was on the side of the United States and the British. Joining Germany to fight against the Soviet Union was almost the same as declaring war against the United States. Besides, it was impossible to fight against the United States and the Soviet Union simultaneously. Japan's decision to join the Tripartite Pact was to prevent the United States from coming into the war in Europe by keeping the Soviet Union on the side of the pact nations, and subsequently Japan would be able to settle the China Incident through the mediation of the United States. Germany's betrayal, however, shattered all these calculations. Therefore, to Konoe, it did not make any sense to join Germany in a fight against the Soviet Union.

Konoe convened the Liaison Conference almost daily from June 25 to July 1. Then, at the Imperial Conference on July 2, despite Matsuoka's vehement argument to join Germany against the Soviet Union, the decision not to take any hostile action was made. This did not mean, however, keeping the status quo. The military demanded action. Facing ABCD economic sanctions against Japan and a crisis concerning the dwindling stock of natural resources, they were particularly eager to move southward, more precisely toward French Indo-China. The decision to move southward was made. As Konoe explained, it was made to some extent to satisfy the demand of the military and avoid creating direct confrontation with it. Konoe naively believed that it was possible to move southward and still keep the peace with the United States through maintaining dialogue.[30]

Now it was more essential than ever for Japan to have a speedy settlement with the United States over the Japanese-American Draft Understanding. The biggest obstacle for Konoe to achieve this was Matsuoka. In his effort to make Matsuoka cooperate, on July 4, Konoe sent the following notes to him:

1. Japan should not have any military expansion southward and should adjust its relations with the United States until the northern issues reach some settlement. According to the navy, it is impossible for Japan to fight against the United States and the Soviet Union simultaneously. From this point of view, if necessary, expansion into French Indo-China needs to be halted.
2. Japan cannot meet all the demands from Germany if there is to be some adjustment in the U.S.-Japan relationship. Although the adjustment might cause ill feeling among the signatory nations of the Tripartite Pact toward Japan, we cannot help it.
3. The adjustment in the U.S.-Japan relationship is necessary to strengthen national power by obtaining natural resources from overseas, to prevent rapprochement between the United States and the Soviet Union, and to have rapid settlement with the Chunking government.
4. From the above points of view, it is necessary to continue the ongoing negotiations with the United States.

Lastly, Konoe added that as Prime Minister with a heavy responsibility, he had to do his best to reach a compromise with the United States even when Matsuoka saw it impossible; furthermore, the Emperor was deeply apprehensive so a compromise had to be reached, even if it required Japan's concession to the United States.[31]

Matsuoka responded by saying that he did not necessarily disagree with Konoe, and, no matter what other people said about him, he was truly concerned with the U.S. issue and was not afraid of Germany. Matsuoka added, however, that Japan still should not do anything to undermine the Tripartite Pact. To Konoe's surprise, Matsuoka continued to say that from now on he would give more effort to the U.S. issue. He also said that he would leave Konoe cabinet if he became impediment to dealing with the U.S. issue.[32]

Meanwhile, the United States was greatly concerned with how Japan would react to the outbreak of war between Germany and the Soviet Union.

Roosevelt sent a message to Konoe on July 6, saying, "We have information that Japan is going to take military action against the Soviet Union. We would like to have an assurance from Japan that such information is not based on fact."[33] In response to the message, Konoe sent a copy of Matsuoka's letter to Soviet Ambassador C. Smetanin, which clearly denied any intention of Japan taking hostile action against the Soviet Union. At the same time, utilizing this opportunity, Konoe retaliated by inquiring whether or not the United States would join the war in Europe.[34] The response from the United States on July 16 was bitter, saying, "It is a matter of self-defense. So it is natural for the United States to join the war. Any nation which demands us to stay away from the war in Europe should be considered as an aggressor."[35]

The message from Roosevelt was strictly addressed to Konoe, indicating the U.S. desire not to deal with Matsuoka any longer. Finding out about this secret message, Matsuoka felt insulted. Contrary to what he had told Konoe days before, Matsuoka began to indicate his even stronger opposition to the U.S.-Japanese negotiations and became more uncompromising. On July 10, when Konoe held the Liaison Conference to discuss the June 21 U.S. proposed draft understanding, Matsuoka brought in Dr. Saito Yoshie as his counselor and, with his help, made a vehement argument to express his total opposition to the U.S.-Japanese negotiations. He argued that the U.S. proposal clearly indicated its ill intention to make Japan concede completely; accordingly, there was no other choice for Japan but to deny Hull's oral statement attached to the U.S. proposal and end immediately the U.S.-Japanese negotiations.[36]

Apprehensive of Matsuoka's vehemence, Konoe met with Army Minister Tojo, Navy Minister Oikawa, and Home Minister Hiranuma to discuss the situation. Then, on July 12, at the Liaison Conference, the army and the navy jointly submitted their opinion regarding the U.S. proposal. With Matsuoka basically agreeing to it, the draft response to the U.S. proposal was made. On July 14, after accepting Matsuoka's suggestion to amend it, the final draft was adopted.[37]

The major points that diverge from the June 21 U.S. proposal are the following:

1. To restore the article, "Japan and the United States jointly make an effort to achieve early termination of the European war."
2. Regarding the article about the Tripartite Pact, to amend it to say, "Unfortunately, if the war in Europe gets expanded, the government of Japan, carrying out its duty as a signatory nation to the pact, will determine its action only under the consideration of defending its security and welfare."

3. In terms of the China issues, (a) to follow basically Konoe's principles, (b) to avoid the use of the name "Nanjing Government," and (c) to specify that the United States will urge the Chiang regime to establish peace with Japan.
4. To remove the article about the conditions for the establishment of peace between Japan and China.
5. To change "whole Pacific" into "Southwest Pacific" under the consideration that what is particularly essential for Japan-U.S. economic cooperation is the Southwest Pacific.

While Konoe and everyone else agreed to send this final draft immediately to the United States, Matsuoka insisted on first sending a telegram to reject Hull's oral statement and then, after a few days, to send the draft. In the telegram, Matsuoka stated, "Unless the United States takes back the oral statement, Japan cannot continue the negotiations on the draft understanding." Konoe agreed to send the telegram, but sending it without the draft would provoke the United States and might result in termination of the negotiations. Konoe, as well as the army and the navy, urged Matsuoka to send the telegram and the draft simultaneously. Matsuoka ignored Konoe. On July 14, he ordered his counselor, Dr. Saito, to send only the telegram to the United States.[38] Moreover, on the following day, Matsuoka, through Sakamoto, Chief of the Asian Division in Europe, secretly informed Germany about Japan's final draft. Finding out about Matsuoka's actions, Konoe was astonished and, without telling Matsuoka, quickly arranged to send the draft to Nomura.

In his desperate effort to find a way to manage the diplomatic "mess," Konoe held a cabinet meeting on July 15 and followed up on his consultation with Army Minister Tojo, Navy Minister Oikawa, and Home Minister Hiranuma. Tojo told Konoe, "Considering that removal of the Foreign Minister would have a negative impact in various ways, we have made our best effort to cooperate with him. Now we have reached our limit and have come to the point where we either remove him or have the general resignation of the cabinet."[39] All agreed with Tojo. Konoe was reluctant to remove Matsuoka. It was Konoe who had insisted on appointing Matsuoka as Foreign Minister despite the Emperor's apprehension. Moreover, to Konoe, it would give the impression that Japan had given in to Hull's pressure. So when Hiranuma suggested, "It would be better to have the general resignation of the cabinet from the viewpoint of strengthening Japan's political structure in wartime, not because of the Foreign Minister issue nor U.S. issues," Konoe decided to have the resignation of his entire cabinet.[40]

On the same day, Konoe informed the Emperor about the general resignation of the cabinet. When the Emperor asked Konoe whether it would
be possible to make Matsuoka alone resign, Konoe told him, considering
the situation, it was impossible for the cabinet to carry on as it was. Then
Konoe met with Kido. Asked again whether Konoe could make Matsuoka
alone resign, Konoe told Kido that such an action would surely let Matsuoka say that the Prime Minister has reshuffled the cabinet because he
gave in to the pressure from the United States.[41]

On July 16, at the Five Minister Conference, all agreed to have the
general resignation of the cabinet. Informed of this decision, Matsuoka,
who was home because of illness and did not expect it, became very displeased. Realizing, however, that there was no way to reverse the decision,
he agreed to turn in his resignation.

On July 17, summoned to the Imperial Palace, Konoe was given the
Imperial Order to form his cabinet for a third time. Konoe immediately
began doing so. On the following day, Konoe held his first cabinet conference. The man who replaced Matsuoka was Admiral Toyoda Teijiro. Toyoda had served as Minister of Commerce and Industry for Konoe's second
cabinet and was a strong advocate for maintaining peace with the United
States. Konoe hoped that his choice of Toyoda would be taken as an indication of Japan's strong desire to have successful U.S.-Japanese negotiations.

Contrary to Konoe's expectations, Nomura, not given much information about the formation of Konoe's third cabinet, failed to inform the U.S.
government sufficiently about Konoe's intentions. To make matters worse,
in order to wait for the completion of forming the new cabinet and afraid
of U.S. rejection because of its content, Nomura had not given the U.S.
government Japan's July 15 response to the June 21 draft understanding.
Instead, Nomura sent a telegram urging the Japanese government to inform
him of the policies of the new cabinet toward the United States.

Konoe was understandably frustrated by this failure to inform the
United States of his new cabinet's passion for the U.S.-Japanese negotiations. Konoe's anxiety was further increased as Japan's advancement into
French Indo-China grew nearer. The United States was increasingly skep-
tical about Japan's intention of having the U.S.-Japanese negotiations.
According to Nomura's telegram dated July 24, the United States became
more and more inclined to believe that the negotiations were only a plot
by Japan to gain time to prepare sufficiently for Japan's southward expansion. In the face of such skepticism, the general mood in Japan, particularly that of the press, was becoming more and more anti-American.

In this increasingly deteriorating U.S.-Japan relationship, Nomura met President Roosevelt on July 24 after being told by Deputy Secretary of State Benjamin Sumner Welles that although the United States had been negotiating with Japan patiently, now there was no fundamental reason to continue the negotiations. Roosevelt reiterated the grave concern the United States had with Japan's movement into French Indo-China and made some significant suggestions. He told Nomura that if Japan halted its planned expansion into French Indo-China, the United States would guarantee neutralization of French Indo-China by Japan, the United States, the Great Britain, the Netherlands, and China, and would also guarantee Japan's access to raw materials in French Indo-China.[42]

Shattering Nomura and Roosevelt's expectations, on July 26 the Japanese government announced the advance of Japanese troops into French Indo-China. Almost simultaneously, the U.S. government declared a freeze of all Japanese assets in the United States.

Although, to Konoe this was almost a confirmation of the voices indicating that there was no longer any point in carrying on with the U.S.-Japanese negotiations, he made every effort to keep the hope alive. Expecting that by responding to Roosevelt's suggestion, the negotiations could be resumed, Konoe held a series of Liaison Conferences. The following proposal was adopted as a response to Roosevelt's suggestion:

1. Japan had no intention of moving further south than French Indo-China and would withdraw its troops from French Indo-China after the settlement of the China Incident.
2. Neutrality of the Philippines would be guaranteed.
3. U.S. armament in the Southwest Pacific would be abolished.
4. The United States would cooperate with Japan in its effort to gain natural resources in the Dutch East Indies.
5. The United States would mediate the establishment of Japan-China direct commerce and trade and also recognize Japan's special right in French Indo-China even after Japan withdraws its troops from China.[43]

Konoe's wishes hardly came true, however. On August 6, Nomura handed the Japanese proposal to Hull. Showing no interest, Hull told Nomura that the United States had no intention of carrying on with the negotiations with Japan unless Japan stopped its military expansion.

At this point, Konoe felt that there was nothing left for him to do through the regular channels of diplomacy. Out of desperation, Konoe made up his mind to have a personal meeting with President Roosevelt. On August 4, Konoe met Army Minister Tojo and Navy Minister Oikawa to tell them about his intention to meet Roosevelt and why. He raised the following reasons for his meeting with Roosevelt:

1. As administrators, if we get into war without exhausting completely every option to avoid it, we will feel sorry for the Emperor and the nation. Furthermore, to completely exhaust all options will help us to convince the nation that Japan has no choice but to go to war; this will also help Japan reduce the chance of being portrayed as an aggressor.
2. If both sides try to talk from broader points of view, there is a chance to reach some settlement through negotiation.
3. With regard to the meeting, prompt action is essential. By September, the situation of the war in Europe will become decisive. It is therefore urgent and essential to have the settlement now, particularly in case Germany loses the war.[44]

Oikawa generally agreed with Konoe. Although Tojo could not help but feel some hesitation, in the end he agreed conditionally, and he replied to Konoe in writing. In his response, Tojo stated that it was a mistake for Konoe to meet the President of the United States. He believed that such a meeting not only undermined Japan's imperial diplomacy, which was based on the Tripartite Pact, but also wouldn't go over well domestically. Tojo, however, continued to say that he respected Konoe for his devotion to dealing with the difficult situation and that the Army wouldn't oppose the meeting if Konoe was prepared to go to war against the United States if the meeting failed. Tojo quickly add that the meeting would not take place unless Konoe agreed to two conditions: (1) The meeting had to be with Roosevelt, not Hull, and (2) Konoe could not retire if the meeting failed since his leadership was indispensable in the war against the United States.[45]

On August 6, Konoe met the Emperor to convey his determination to meet with Roosevelt. On the following day, the Emperor summoned Konoe and said, "There is information that the United States would totally ban Japan's importing oil from the United States. So your meeting with the President needs to be prompt."[46]

Before this meeting with the Emperor, Konoe also met with Wakatsugi Reijiro, Izawa Takio, and Shidehara Kijuro to get their views. Izawa said to Konoe, "If you push it through, you will be killed." Konoe responded, "I do not care much about my life." Then, when Izawa further said to Konoe, "It is not just your life. You will be considered a traitor," Konoe simply said, "That is fine, too."[47] According to Yabe Teiji, when he met Ikeda Seihin, Ikeda said the following to Yabe: "During his first cabinet, Konoe was unfocused and unreliable. During his third cabinet, however, Konoe was a completely different person. He was serious and persistent. Particularly, he had a strong sense of responsibility toward the Imperial Household."[48]

On August 7, with high expectations, Konoe sent a telegram regarding his meeting with Roosevelt to Ambassador Nomura. Disappointingly, however, and despite Konoe's commitment, the U.S. government showed little interest in this new proposal from Konoe. Roosevelt was out of Washington for the Atlantic Conference with Churchill. So Nomura handed the telegram to Hull on August 8. Hull told Nomura that unless there were some changes in Japan's policies, he had no intention of conveying Konoe's proposal to Roosevelt.

In the joint declaration at the Atlantic Conference, Roosevelt promised Churchill that if Japan's aggression continued, the United States would be ready to assist any nation under attack by Japan even if the United States itself was not in the military conflict with Japan.[49] Upon a request from Churchill to give Japan a warning, Roosevelt agreed to send an ultimatum to Japan. The Japanese press responded to such harsh words from Roosevelt with an even harsher rhetoric to condemn Roosevelt.

On August 16, facing an increasingly negative mood from both sides of the Pacific, Nomura attempted to explain Japan's true intentions regarding the summit meeting. Although Hull indicated that he had no intention of changing his strong opposition toward Japanese militarism, he somewhat softened his opinion on the summit meeting, saying, "If you think there is a great chance for the summit to be successful, I will propose it to the White House."[50]

Meanwhile, Foreign Minister Toyoda approached U.S. Ambassador Grew and directly asked him to support Konoe's desire to have a summit meeting with Roosevelt. Believing that unless something dramatic took place, the U.S.-Japanese negotiations would fail and leave nothing but war, Grew found the idea of the summit meeting worth trying. He told Toyoda that he would do his best to persuade the U.S. State Department.

In his telegram to the State Department, Grew pointed out the following:

1. This summit meeting between Konoe and Roosevelt provides a chance to avoid the possibility of getting into an absolutely useless war.
2. If this proposal is rejected in some way or if the meeting is held and fails there would be a reform of the present cabinet. This reform or transition would result in the inevitability of war between the United States and Japan by placing the fate of Japan in the hands of the military.
3. Japan understands that there would not be any success for the meeting unless Japan was ready to make drastic concessions.[51]

Despite Grew's effort, the response from the U.S. State Department was not optimistic. Particularly, the Far East political advisor, Stanley Hornbeck, expressed an opposite view from that of Grew. He stated the following:

1. Japan is weak and in a dangerous situation.
2. Japanese leaders are divided and in constant conflict with each other.
3. Japan is the only nation passionately seeking this meeting.
4. This proposal by Japan's leaders is a clear indication of its weakness.
5. True danger exists only in Japan. Accordingly, the United States has nothing to lose, but everything to gain, by sticking to our policies and principles.[52]

In the midst of exchanging such rhetoric over the Pacific, Roosevelt returned from the Atlantic Conference. On August 18, he promptly met Nomura and handed him two proposals: one was a warning against Japan's military expansion to the south and the other was about the summit meeting. In those two proposals, Roosevelt indicated that he basically agreed to have the summit as long as Japan halted its expansion policies and began its effort to establish peace in the Pacific. He added that Japan should make a clear statement expressing agreement to his proposals. Throughout the meeting with Nomura, Roosevelt was in good spirits. He even suggested Juneau, Alaska, as a place for the summit and mid-October as the date. Nomura quickly sent a telegram about his meeting with Roosevelt, asking Konoe not to miss this opportunity to respond promptly to Roosevelt's proposals.

On August 28, at the Liaison Conference, the response to Roosevelt's proposals was adopted. It basically says, "From Japan's point of view, the U.S. proposals are difficult to accept. To establish peace, however, it is necessary to adjust and specify Japan's policy toward the Soviet Union and Japan's southward expansion, and also to see that the U.S. proposal for establishing peace in the Pacific can be applied to the whole world."[53]

In addition to this response, Konoe's message directly addressed to Roosevelt was also adopted. In it, Konoe clearly and straightforwardly expressed why the summit meeting was essential. He emphasized the importance of dealing with the rapidly unfolding current situation by discussing Japanese-American issues from a broader perspective.

Nomura handed these two documents to Roosevelt. Impressed by Konoe's message, Roosevelt said to Nomura, "It is excellent. I would like to have a meeting with Konoe for about three days."[54] As Konoe expressed in writing, this was perhaps the moment of the closest ties in the entire negotiations between the United States and Japan.

Compared to Roosevelt's willingness to meet Konoe, Hull was cautious. On the night of August 28, he invited Nomura to a meeting and said to him, "Serious consequences from the viewpoint of both governments would ensue if the meeting fails. The meeting should therefore have as its purpose the ratification of essential points already agreed to in principle."[55] Hull then emphasized that it was essential for Japan to make its intentions clear before the meeting regarding the China issues, particularly over the question of withdrawing troops and self-defense.[56]

Nomura reported to Tokyo these two contrasting responses to Konoe's proposal for the summit meeting. In the face of such a contrast, there was a mixture of optimism and pessimism in the government's view of the summit meeting, but overall the Konoe cabinet tilted more toward optimism.

This all changed on September 3, however, when Roosevelt handed Nomura his message in response to Konoe's August 26 message to Roosevelt. In it, Roosevelt, no longer showing any sign of optimism, indicated his agreement with Hull over the argument that Japan had to accept four fundamental principles before the summit meeting would ever take place. Roosevelt emphasized to Nomura that it was essential for the Japanese government to let the United States know where it stood over the issue of accepting those four principles.

Now, with Roosevelt's change of viewpoint toward the summit meeting, there was a fundamental gap between the United States and Japan over the reason for having it. Hull and Roosevelt insisted that the summit meeting would be held for ratification purposes only after Japan's acceptance of those four principles. On the other hand, to Konoe, the summit meeting was essential, providing the last chance to find a compromise over the disputed issues between the two nations, including the question of the four principles. Konoe also wanted the summit meeting in order to gain political leverage, which might enable him to control the army, and accordingly, it would be possible for him to make some concessions toward U.S. demands. If the summit were for ratification only, in Konoe's mind, holding it would be pointless. Konoe painfully realized that little could be done to narrow the gap. Accordingly, there was little chance for the meeting to be held.

Meanwhile, another proposal was adopted at the Liaison Conference on September 3. It was a simplified version of the previous draft understanding. Nomura handed it to Hull on the following day. This proposal did nothing but cause confusion and misunderstanding on the side of the United States. The United States took this version as a totally new proposal that had nothing to do with the previous draft understanding. Konoe partially blamed Nomura for this confusion. On July 15, Japan responded to the U.S. June 21 draft understanding. As previously stated, Nomura did not hand this response to the United States because of the regime transition (from Konoe's second cabinet to the third). So receiving another proposal before Japan had responded to the June 21 proposal confused the United States. In the midst of this confusion and the dwindling hope for a successful summit meeting, there was a growing argument over whether Japan should continue its negotiations with the United States or stop negotiating and make up its mind to fight.

As mentioned earlier, in order to avoid the rise of opposition, only Konoe's cabinet members and the top officers of the army and the navy were clandestinely engaged in conducting negotiations for the Japanese–American Draft Understanding. Starting with Matsuoka's reporting of the negotiations to Germany and Italy, however, it gradually became public.[57] Accordingly, those lower-ranked officers, particularly from the army, who were opposed to the negotiations began to voice their concerns. Such voices were getting louder as the United States began to strengthen its economic sanctions against Japan in response to Japan's decision to move into French Indo-China. There was a growing argument that if economic sanctions continued, Japan, which heavily relied on foreign imports of oil and other natural resources, mainly from the United States, would lose its capacity to sustain a military operation. So if the decision to fight was to come, it had to come now. Otherwise, Japan would lose the war without a fight. By the end of August, it was clear to Konoe that the voice demanding an immediate decision to go to war against the United States became rather dominant and increasingly difficult to suppress.[58]

On September 6, the Imperial Conference was held in order to have an outline of the imperial national policies to deal with this increasingly volatile situation. The following outline was adopted:

1. For the sake of self-existence and self-defense and according to our resolution to accept the war against the Anglo-Saxon powers if it has to come, Japan will complete its war preparations by the end of October.
2. At the same time, Japan will endeavor diplomatically to have the Anglo-Saxon powers accept our demands.
3. If Japan is unsuccessful in having our demands accepted diplomatically by early October, to go to war against the Anglo-Saxon powers will be our decision.[59]

One day before the conference, Konoe met the Emperor to report on the outline for the conference. After perusing it, the Emperor said to

Konoe, "According to this, war preparation comes first and diplomatic negotiations come second. It seems to imply that war is a higher priority than diplomacy. I would like to ask a question on this point at the conference tomorrow."[60] Konoe responded, "Such an order does not mean that one is more important than the other. The government will put a priority on diplomacy. Japan will begin preparation for war only if diplomacy fails."[61] Then Konoe suggested that the Emperor summon Army Chief of Staff Sugiyama and Navy Chief of Staff Nagano to pose the question to them, rather than at the conference.

Sugiyma and Nagano were summoned. When asked the question regarding priority, Sugiyama and Nagano gave the Emperor basically the same answer as Konoe did. Then the Emperor asked Sugiyama, "If war breaks out between the United States and Japan, how long does the army need to end the war?" Sugiyama responded, "Regarding the fight in the southern Pacific, we perhaps need three months." Then the Emperor continued, saying, "You were the Army Minister when the China Incident took place. I remember you saying to me at that time, 'The Incident will be solved within a month.' It has been four years since then. It has not been solved yet." When Sugiyama tried to defend himself by telling the Emperor about the vastness of the Chinese interior making the military operation more difficult than anticipated, the Emperor responded by saying, "You say that the Chinese interior is vast. The Pacific is even more vast. So how can you say that you can end the war in three months?"[62] Sugiyama had no response. Then, in order to be certain, the Emperor reiterated the same question regarding the priority of diplomacy over the military operation. Both Sugiyama and Nagano assured the Emperor that would be the case. To Konoe, such an assurance from the army and the navy was nothing but an empty promise. Konoe knew that a chance to achieve a diplomatic settlement with the United States was rapidly diminishing. Something had to be done.

Frustrated, on September 6, upon agreement from Tojo, Oikawa, and Toyoda, Konoe decided to meet U.S. Ambassador Grew after the Imperial Conference. With the presence of Chief Secretary Ushiba and Counselor at the American Embassy Eugene H. Dooman as interpreters, Konoe had a meeting with Grew for more than three hours. Konoe emphasized that he had an agreement from both the Army Minister and the Navy Minister with regard to the summit meeting; therefore, this could be the only opportunity for success; a meeting between him and Roosevelt should be held without delay.[63] Then, when Grew asked Konoe about Hull's four principles, Konoe responded, "Although basically I agree to them, when it comes to the real application, various problems might arise. The summit meeting is indeed necessary to find a solution to those problems."[64]

Agreeing with Konoe, Grew promised to convey what Konoe told him as a direct message to Roosevelt and said to Konoe, "This report would be the most important one since I started my diplomatic career."[65] Then Grew sent the following telegram to Hull:

1. If the United States is too persistent in getting a satisfactory response from Japan regarding the four principles, Japan might take it that the United States is only interested in prolonging negotiations. In the end, Japan will be controlled by a military dictatorship.
2. Despite its alliance with Germany, Japan indicated its intention to negotiate with the United States. This should be considered a concession, showing that there would be a greater possibility for a satisfactory summit meeting.[66]

Sharing what Grew said in this telegram, British Ambassador Robert L. Craigie stated: "The problem with this negotiation is that, when Japan needs a prompt settlement, the United States is trying to prolong negotiations by demanding Japan's complete acceptance of its principles. Such a demand is a clear indication that the United States does not take into consideration the nature of the Japanese mentality and also the internal conditions of Japan that do not allow such delay. I agree with Grew that a chance has arrived and it is foolish to miss it."[67]

Despite Grew's message and Craigie's supporting statement, Cordell Hull showed no concern. Grew wrote in his memoir, "Little or no evidence is apparent in the official correspondence of a desire or of efforts on the part of our Government to simplify Prince Konoe's difficult task or to meet him even part way. So far as we in the Embassy could perceive, the policy of the Administration during this critical time was almost completely inflexible."[68]

Now it became clear to Konoe that Japan had only two choices: either to accept all four principles before the summit meeting as Hull demanded or face the almost inevitable consequence, war against the United States. Moreover, because of the decision at the Imperial Conference, time became the crucial element. Spending most of his days at the Prime Minister's official residence, Konoe held conferences with Foreign Minister Toyoda, Army Minister Tojo, Navy Minister Oikawa, and the head of the Planning Board, Suzuki, almost on a daily basis from late September to early October. In terms of accepting the four principles, although they basically agreed to accept Hull's demand, over the issue of withdrawal of the Japanese troops from China, there was no sign of an agreement. Facing the strongest opposition from the army over the withdrawal issue, Konoe met Tojo alone on October 7. Tojo told Konoe he had absolutely no intention of making any concession about the withdrawal issue.

Desperately trying to find a way to continue negotiations with the United States, on October 12, his fiftieth birthday, Konoe held the last conference with Tojo, Oikawa, Toyoda, and Suzuki. Shortly before the conference, Oka, the Bureau Chief of Military Affairs for the Navy, told Tomiat, Chief Secretary for the cabinet, that although the Navy did not wish to continue the negotiations but wished to avoid war, the Navy could not openly say so. For that reason, Oka continued, the Navy Minister would say at the conference that the Navy had to leave a decision for war or peace to the Prime Minister.[69]

So, as expected, at the beginning of the conference, Navy Minister Oikawa stated that time had come to make a decision, war or peace. The Prime Minister had to make that decision, and whichever decision he made, he had to be definitive. If the decision was for peace, Japan had to stick to it even if some concessions had to be made to the United States. If Japan had to go to war, the decision had to come right away; it would be totally unacceptable to make a decision to go to war after negotiating for a few months simply because things did not go well. Konoe responded, "If we have to decide today, I will decide to continue the negotiations." Then, Army Minister Tojo said to Konoe, "Your decision is too hasty. It would be a serious mistake if we miss a chance [the best time to make a decision to go to war] by continuing the negotiations when there is no prospect of a successful settlement." Tojo continued and asked Foreign Minister Toyoda, "Foreign Minister, do you think we have any chance to have a successful negotiation?" Toyoda answered, "That depends on one condition. The most difficult issue we face today is the matter of stationing Japanese troops in China. There will not be any chance of success in the negotiations if the army does not make any concession at all over this issue. On the other hand, if the army can make concessions, no one can say that there is absolutely no chance for success." Tojo hastily responded, "The issue of having the troops in China is a matter of life and death for the army. The army absolutely cannot make any concession on it." Then Konoe said to Tojo, "In this situation, we should not be concerned with our 'pride' but with what is best for the nation. It is possible to give in to U.S. demands now only on the surface, then, later, to create the same situation as having troops in China in a real sense."[70]

The conference lasted four hours. With Tojo showing no sign of giving in, no agreement was made. Two days later, on October 14, shortly before the cabinet conference, Konoe met Tojo again and asked him to reconsider his view on stationing Japanese troops in China. Konoe said to Tojo, "I am responsible for the China Incident. It has been four years since the Incident took place. Yet it is still unresolved. Hence, it is difficult for me to agree to go into another major war today. We should avoid war against the United States at all costs even if we have to give in to U.S. demands and withdraw the troops from China. Also, considering the situation of our national strength, I think it is essential for us to settle the China Incident first. Although I, myself, desire to have the progress and development of the nation, it is sometimes necessary to concede in order to build up the national strength."[71] Tojo did not show any sign of reconsideration, saying, "If we give in now, the United States will become more haughty and demand further concessions. With regard to withdrawing the troops, although you say that we should forget our pride but concern ourselves with what is best for the nation, I cannot agree at all to the withdrawal of our troops, and we should maintain the good spirit of our troops." Tojo continued to say, "Your argument is too pessimistic. I think it is so because you are too familiar with the weakness of our nation. Don't you think that the United States has its own weakness, too?"[72] Then Tojo ended his remarks over the difference between him and Konoe in viewing the issue of stationing troops in China, saying rather emotionally, "It's all due to the difference in character between you and me!"

It became clear to Konoe that to make Tojo reconsider was out of his reach. In his postwar memoirs, Konoe recalls the following remark Tojo made to him during these repeated meetings: "We as persons sometimes need to jump from the platform of Temple Kiyomizu with our eyes closed (taking a chance even when there is a risk of losing life)."[73] Konoe responded, "We as individuals may face such a situation once or twice in our lifetime. If we consider the two thousand and six hundred years of polity of our nation and the fate of our hundred million Japanese nationals, we as government officials holding responsible positions should not do such a thing."[74]

Konoe also wrote in his memoirs, "I often hear people say 'with spiritual unity' or 'taking a chance as a nation.' Although it may sound exciting, whenever I hear it, I cannot help but feel apprehensive. If I consider the polity of our nation, we cannot thoughtlessly start war when we are so uncertain of the prospect of victory. Even though people might think I am indecisive, it is impossible for me to do such a thing. I firmly believe that we should avoid war unless we are absolutely sure of a favorable outcome."[75]

At the conference, Tojo repeated what he said to Konoe. The other cabinet members were so amazed by his rather abrupt and uncompromising remarks that no one dared to say anything. Without further discussion over the issue, the conference was adjourned.

Later the same day, Muto, Chief of Military Affairs, came to see Tomita, Chief Secretary of the Cabinet. Muto told Tomita that Konoe could not make up his mind whether or not to go to war against the United States because the navy was ambiguous over the issue. Muto continued to say that without insisting that it was up to the Prime Minister, if the navy did not desire the war, it should say so officially to the army so that it would make it less difficult for Konoe to control the army and also easier for the army's top officers to control their subordinates. Muto asked Tomita to make an arrangement so that the navy could make such an official statement to the army. Hence, Tomita met Oka, Chief of Military Affairs of the Navy, and told him about Muto's request. Oka responded by repeating his previous statement: "It is impossible for the navy to say officially, 'The navy does not want the war.' All it can say is that the navy leaves it to the Prime Minister."[76]

On that evening, the head of the Planning Board, Suzuki, visited Konoe at his private residence to deliver a message from Army Minister Tojo. In it, Tojo said, "It seems that the navy does not desire to go to war. Then why doesn't the Navy Minister say so to me? If the Navy Minister specifically tells me so, I have to reconsider it (a decision to go to war). It is deplorable that the navy leaves all responsibility to the Prime Minister. The navy's indecision is the same as invalidating the decision we made at the September 6 Imperial Conference. What it means is that everyone at the conference did not do his duty adequately. So now every one of us should resign, cancel what we have decided, and come up with a new plan. I think, however, no one from the present cabinet is capable of putting the army and the navy under control and coming up with a new plan. Hence, there is no other choice but to ask the Prince to form a new cabinet. Prince Higashikuni would be the most suitable person to take such a role. It is rather difficult to say this to you, but there is no other way. I would like you to recommend Prince Higashikuni to the Emperor as the succeeding Prime Minister."[77]

This was the army's no-confidence statement toward the Konoe cabinet. Konoe said to his close associates, "The army is seeking a war we have no chance to win. The navy says they have no confidence. The Emperor opposes the war. Yet no matter what we say, the army does not understand [the uselessness of going to war]. This is indeed absurd!"[78]

On the next day, October 15, Konoe met the Emperor and, as Tojo had requested, recommended Prince Higashikuni as his successor. The

Emperor was not so excited about it. He told Konoe that it was all right to appoint Prince Higashikuni as Chief of the General Staff, but not as Prime Minister, particularly when the nation was about to engage in war; it was inappropriate and would surely have a negative effect on the Imperial Household.[79] When Konoe met Kido, Lord Keeper of the Privy Seal, on the same day, and told Kido about Prince Higashikuni, Kido was also not so enthusiastic about it.[80]

On October 16, Konoe summoned each cabinet member separately and told them the reason for the general resignation. Upon agreement from the whole cabinet, Konoe's third cabinet came to an end. Konoe

turned in his resignation letter to the Emperor. Konoe's memoirs do not say anything about why he accepted Tojo's recommendation and resigned. It should not be difficult to speculate, however, that Konoe felt by this point that he had done everything he could, and that there was no point in him remaining as Prime Minister. Indeed, Konoe must have thought that his resigning and bringing in someone new would be his only choice.

After the general resignation of Konoe's third cabinet, the Tojo cabinet was formed on October 20, 1941. Former Prime Minister Konoe Fumimaro and new Prime Minister Tojo Hideki at the official residence of the Prime Minister shortly after their succession procedure (© Mainichi Photo Bank).

At the conference for the elder statesmen held on October 17, Kido Koichi insisted that Tojo, not Higashikuni, should be Konoe's successor and concurrently hold his current position as Army Minister. With no disagreement from the other conferees, Tojo was recommended to the Emperor.[81]

Regarding this recommendation of Tojo by Kido, Konoe pointed out, considering that his cabinet came to an end through the discord between his persistence to continue the negotiations and Tojo's attempts to stop Konoe from doing it, it was understandable that this Imperial Order to Tojo to form a new cabinet was taken as a sign of cutting off negotiations and commencing war. According to Konoe, however, Kido did not recommend Tojo because he wished to see war between the United States and Japan begin. He did so because he knew that Tojo, realizing the navy was not fully committed to the war against the United States, was not necessarily wholeheartedly in favor of war by the time of the recommendation. Furthermore, Kido thought that considering Tojo's character of being absolutely faithful to the Imperial Code, he would follow whatever the Emperor wished him to do.

On October 16, Konoe sent a letter to Ambassador Grew to tell him about his resignation. He emphasized in his letter that his resignation did not mean Japan had decided to go to war against the United States, and asked Grew not to be discouraged either by the change of cabinet or by the mere appearance of the new cabinet. Lastly, Konoe expressed his highest gratitude for Grew's friendship.

Grew responded to Konoe's letter, expressing his respect and gratitude for Konoe's long public service and his assurance that he would continue his effort to support the new cabinet to achieve a successful conclusion to the negotiations between the two governments.[82]

In the section of his memoirs dated November 21, 1941, Grew further wrote about Konoe, saying,

> I have often thought about my letter to Prince Konoe, in reply to his letter informing me of the fall of his cabinet, and especially my allusion to the distinguished service which he had rendered his country. Some people might quibble at that statement, on the ground that he had led his country into all sorts of difficulties, including the Axis Alliance. I grant all that, but I put it down more to the nefarious influence of Matsuoka than to Konoe himself, who had his own military people and the extremists to deal with.
>
> The chief reason why I mentioned his outstanding service was the fact that he alone tried to reverse the engine, and tried hard and courageously, even risking his life and having a very close call as it was. Whatever mistakes he made in directing Japan's policy, he had the sense and the courage to recognize those mistakes and to try to start his country in a new direction of friendship with the United States. If only for that, I think he deserves some degree of good will. With the invasion of Indo-China staring us in the face during the Washington conversations, it is difficult for anyone not living in

Japan and understanding the forces and stresses loose in this misguided country to appreciate what Konoe was up against, but I do, and hence that allusion in my letter, I would not change it if I had the letter to write again.[83]

Contrary to Grew's sympathetic and understanding assessment of Konoe's resignation and the formation of the Tojo cabinet, the government of the United States perceived this change of cabinet the same as driving the last nail into the coffin, the end of the already deeply troubled negotiating effort.

In his postwar memoirs, Konoe attributes this failed diplomacy to the familiar argument of the disunity between the civilian government and the military, saying, "In looking back on the history of those difficult U.S.-Japanese negotiations, what we painfully remind ourselves of is the disunity between the government and the military. Each successive cabinet had been annoyed by this disunity. In the U.S.-Japanese negotiations, while the government was seriously engaged in the negotiations, the military was furiously making preparations in case of failed negotiations. Since we were not informed at all about how those preparations were going, we could not keep pace with the military. Naturally, seeing those preparations by our military, the United States did not see any sincerity in our diplomatic efforts. It was indeed troublesome to see no unity between diplomacy and military affairs."[84]

Konoe continued to say that at this juncture, there was only one person who could turn the situation around. That was the Emperor. Recalling the remark Prince Higashikuni made to the Emperor that only the Emperor alone could turn around the situation, and so he had to be firm in his action and statement, Konoe also wished the Emperor to be more decisive. Konoe argued that it was acceptable that the Emperor acted passively when the time was peaceful, but when the nation was facing the decision of either war or peace, the Emperor had to act decisively.

At the same time, Konoe expressed his sympathy for the Emperor. He understood that the passivity of the role of the Emperor had been a tradition. The Emperor had been advised as such by elder statesmen such as Prince Saionji or former Lord Keeper of the Privy Seal, Makino Nobuaki. Also, Konoe was painfully aware of both the Emperor's concern and sincere wish to maintain peace in the Pacific and to have eternal protection of the polity of the nation with 2,600 years of history.

As Kido correctly expected, Tojo, now as Prime Minister, decided to keep hope for diplomatic settlement with the United States alive. At the cabinet meeting on October 30, Tojo came up with three options for dealing with the crucial situation Japan was facing:

1. To continue the negotiations. Even when they failed, Japan must accept the consequences and live with them.
2. To end the negotiations immediately and go to war.
3. To carry on war preparations while continuing negotiations.

Choosing the last option, Tojo sent two new proposals to Ambassador Nomura. For Japan, they were the last proposals, and November 25 was chosen as the deadline for U.S. acceptance. Even though the proposals were conciliatory, the United States, taking those proposals as Japanese ultimatums, flatly rejected them, pointing out that such proposals were only a gimmick from Japan to gain time to prepare for war. With this rejection from the United States, on December 1, at the Imperial Conference, the decision to go to war was adopted. A week later, on the morning of December 7, the assault by the Japanese fleet at Pearl Harbor took place. It was a prelude to Japan's catastrophic fate and equally so to Konoe's personal tragedy.

6

War and Its Aftermath

Japan's attack on Pearl Harbor on December 7, 1941, rendered the inevitable into reality. It was followed by a series of Japanese victories in the early stage of the war. Along with the Pearl Harbor assault, Japan simultaneously attacked Guam, Wake Island, the Philippines, Hong Kong, and Malaya. Within the same month of December, Japan took control of Guam, Wake Island, and Hong Kong. In the Malayan campaign, the Japanese forces shattered the British naval power by sinking the battleship *Prince Wales* (once considered unsinkable) and the cruiser *Repulse* on December 10, rendering the fall of Malaya inevitable. It came on February 15, 1942, when Japan achieved the main objective of the campaign by capturing Singapore. In the Philippine campaign, although faced with persistent guerrilla resistance, Japanese forces finally established a firm control of the islands in early April. General MacArthur had to abandon the island fortress of Corregidore to escape to Australia. While the entire nation was in wild jubilation with these astonishing military successes, Konoe could not help but be apprehensive. He knew what fate was to come for Japan.

When Konoe met one of his associates on January 2, 1942, he told him about the mood at the Imperial Palace on New Year's Day: "The old folks on the Privy Council were over-joyful [about Japan's early success in the war]. They came up to me and expressed their sympathies for me, saying, 'It is pitiful indeed, Mr. Konoe. You ought to be the one receiving the honor!' It is almost unbelievable that these old folks are truly convinced that Japan will keep on winning and actually be victorious in this war. I wonder what they will say to me on the next New Year's Day."[1]

As this remark from Konoe indicates, from the outset of the war, Konoe was bitterly critical toward those expressing optimism about Japan's war effort and never hesitated to be explicit about it. Shortly after the fall of Singapore, Konoe said to one of his close associates, Kiya Ikusaburo, "Both the army and the navy are ecstatic about Japan's victory after victory. We should note, however, we are victorious only because we are fighting against the Malay and the Southern Pacific islanders. It would be awful if we were losing. What is crucial is how we will do in the upcoming fights [against the Western troops]."[2]

Inevitably, Konoe's open critique of Japan's war effort and also his strong belief in the ultimate defeat of Japan earned Konoe censure and ridicule. The Tojo government as well as the general public labeled Konoe as an unpatriotic coward and anti-war activist. Konoe was put under close surveillance by the military police, making it difficult for Konoe to engage in political affairs as well as carry out his private life. Tired of the situation, Konoe began to think of giving up his peer status to retire from politics and move away from the calamitous atmosphere of Tokyo. With Kiya's suggestion, Konoe began to think of moving to Kyoto and setting up his own school. Konoe even went to Kyoto to find out what land was available.

This retirement plan, however, never became a reality. While Konoe was contemplating the idea of moving to Kyoto, the rumor that Konoe had been involved in the Ozaki Hidemi Incident began to circulate. This was an incident linked to the Sorge International Espionage Affair in 1941. A counselor for the German embassy in Japan, Richard Sorge, a critic, Ozaki Hidemi, and many others were arrested and indicted for violation of the Law of National Defense and Security and the Peace Preservation Law. Sorge and Ozaki were sentenced to death in 1943 for their espionage over Japanese imperialism and executed in 1944. Saionji Kinmochi and some of Konoe's close associates were also rounded up. According to the postwar statement by the U.S. army regarding this incident, Sorge had engaged in espionage regarding Japanese politics, military affairs, and the economy for the Soviet Union since 1933. Although Konoe had nothing to do with this incident, he was unable to carry out his plan of moving to Kyoto for retirement. He did not want to be portrayed as a "fugitive"–running away in order to avoid persecution. In the end, however, thanks to the effort of Tomita Kenji, a former chief secretary for Konoe's third cabinet, Konoe's non-involvement in the incident was proven.

Although momentarily pleased with this favorable end regarding his alleged involvement in the Ozaki Incident, Konoe was never able to free himself from his anxiety about the direction the nation was heading and the inevitable outcome of the "journey." Konoe's mind was constantly occupied by one thing — how to get the nation out of this deadlock.

Meanwhile, apprehensive about Konoe's safety due to the growing public condemnation of him, Kiya visited Konoe in the summer of 1942. He told Konoe that, due to Konoe's membership as the president of the advisory committee of Koyasan Temple, even Kondo Hongen, the secretary-general of the Temple, became a suspect as an anti-war activist. Thinking that Konoe's visit to Koyasan might ameliorate the anti-Konoe and anti-Kondo sentiment, Kiya recommended that Konoe go to Koyasan to pray for war victory and also to attend a memorial ceremony for those who died in the war.[3] Konoe agreed with Kiya.

When Konoe's plan to visit Koyasan was reported in the newspaper, Konoe began to face the attack from the right-wing nationalists. They condemned him for going to the Buddhist temple rather than the Shinto Shrine of Ise. Just one day before Konoe was to leave for Koyasan, an ultra right-wing nationalist, former Home Minister Yasui Eiji, visited Konoe and denounced him for going to Koyasan without visiting Ise Shrine. Yasui suggested to Konoe that if he had to go to Koyasan, he should go to Ise Shrine first.

Despite these denunciations from the right-wing nationalists and Kiya's concern about a possible terrorist attack against Konoe, Konoe carried out his visit to Koyasan. Fortunately, it turned out to be a safe trip. Kiya, who accompanied Konoe, later stated that he was ready to sacrifice himself in order to save Konoe's life in case of any assault.

Meanwhile, what Konoe and Yamamoto had anticipated prior to the war became a reality, that is, an early end to Japan's offensive and the beginning of the catastrophic decline in the country's wartime fortune. In fact, it came earlier than expected. On April 18, 1942, the U.S. air force led by Colonel James H. Doolittle dropped incendiary bombs on Tokyo. It was the first air raid over the mainland of Japan and had an enormous psychological impact on Japan. This U.S. air raid was followed by the battle of the Coral Sea in May. Both sides declared victory. It was Japan's first defeat, however, since it failed to achieve the objective of the campaign—to occupy Port Moresby. Then the tide of the war completely turned around when the U.S. fleet almost wiped out Japan's naval force led by Isoroku Yamamoto at Midway in early June.

After this devastating defeat at the battle of Midway, the voices asking for peace began to rise. On June 11, Yoshida Shigeru, who was to be the most influential figure in Japan's postwar reconstruction effort, visited Kido Koichi. He urged Kido, in order to utilize this incident as an opportunity to establish peace, to send Konoe to Europe. In response, Kido said to Yoshida, "Although basically I have no objection to the effort to establish world peace as early as possible, with regard to sending Konoe to Europe, I have to think it over."[4]

Ugaki Kazushige agreed with Yoshida that Konoe should be sent to Europe.[5] Ugaki told Yabe Teiji that, along with Ikda Seihin and Yoshida Shigeru, Konoe should go to either Switzerland or Sweden in a form of a private trip and rather openly engage in a diplomatic effort to find a way to establish peace. Ugaki continued to say that he himself was ready to join if it was necessary. In the end, however, Konoe's visit to Europe never took place. Konoe was not able to make up his mind.

The war situation continued to get worse for Japan. In mid-November 1942, the Japanese navy lost the battle of the Solomon Islands. That was followed by Japan's retreat from Guadalcanal in early February 1943 after the loss of 17,000 troops. At this alarming time Konoe met Kido on February 4 to discuss the prospect of the war, domestic politics, and an intrusion of Communism.[6] Konoe, particularly apprehensive about the Communist threat, told Kido that if the current war situation continued and the internal circumstances of Japan deteriorated further, there would be a subsequent intrusion of Communism, and, therefore, it was essential for Japan to bring the war to an end without any delay. Kido had no reason to disagree with Konoe. He pledged to Konoe his unsparing effort to end the war.

Konoe knew that an early termination of the war quite depended on how cooperative Tojo would be in an effort to change the direction of internal politics. In early 1943, Konoe decided to have a direct talk with Tojo in the presence of other elder statesmen. Although reluctant, Tojo acceded. Konoe's attempt did not go well from the beginning. Knowing that Tojo was a key figure in his effort to achieve peace, Konoe wanted to have a talk with Tojo alone in order to have a frank exchange. Tojo was reluctant to meet with Konoe alone and insisted on having some of his ministers accompany him. Konoe had to give in. The first meeting took place and they met periodically afterward as well. Although Tojo later on began to come to meetings alone, nothing substantial came out of those meetings.

Contrary to Konoe's wish to see Tojo cooperative, Tojo was intensifying Kenpei Seiji (reliance on the military police to govern) because of the Ozaki Incident and also because of growing criticism from the public against Tojo due to the change of the tide of the war in the aftermath of Japan's decisive defeat at the battle of Midway. In September 1942 the so-called Yokohama Incident took place. This was a series of attempts to suppress any political speeches against the Tojo cabinet. First, the military police of Kanagawa Prefecture arrested a journalist, Hosokawa Yoshiroku, charging him with violating the Peace Preservation Law with his article "Trend of World History and Japan" in the August/September issue of *Kaizo.* The article was considered to be anti-war and Communist propaganda. Then, in May 1943, some of the editors from the journals *Chuo Koron, Kaizo,* and *Nihon Hyoron* were also arrested for their alleged relationship with Hosokawa. This suppression of speech continued, and altogether more than thirty people were arrested. Some of them died in prison after being tortured. As a result of this incident, *Kaizo* and *Chuo Koron* vanished from the publishing world in July 1944.

Utilizing this Kenpei Seiji, Tojo also intensified the suppression of his opponents in the political arena, as well exemplified in the fate of a politician, Nakano Seigo. After a career as a newspaper journalist, Nakano entered the political field and was elected as a member of the House of Representatives. In 1936 he set up a political party, Tohokai, and appointed himself as president. Sharing Konoe's view of "Asia for Asia," Nakano closely worked with Konoe. In 1940 he became the general secretary of Taisei Yokusankai. Then in 1942 Nakano opposed Tojo's Suisen Senkyo (an election by recommendation). In the following year, in order to criticize Tojo's Kenpei Seiji, he wrote an article titled "Senji Saisoron" (A View on the Prime Minister under the War Situation) in *Asahi Shinbun*. Infuriated, Tojo prohibited the circulation of *Asahi* and had Nakano arrested by the military police in October 1943 on charge of involvement in the movement to bring down the Tojo cabinet. Although Nakano was released later, he took his own life by committing Japanese ritual suicide (hara-kiri). Allegedly Nakano was forced to kill himself in order to ensure the safety of his own son in the army.[7]

Thus, despite the growing anti-Tojo sentiment, Tojo had no intention of altering his style of governing. On the contrary, in order to solidify it, Tojo forced Army Minister Sugiyama Gen and the Chief of Military Command Nagano Osami to resign and appointed himself as Army Minister and Chief of Staff and Shimada Shigetaro as Navy Minister and Chief of Military Command. Although without any intention to be one, now Tojo was increasingly becoming like a dictator. Some began to call the Tojo government "Tojo Bakufu."

Meanwhile, the war situation continued to get worse for Japan. In September 1943, General Pietro Badoglio replaced Mussolini. During World War II, General Pietro Badoglio led the upper class of Italy, including the royal family and other top military officers, in the uprising against Mussolini. After the arrest of Mussolini, Badoglio set up his own government. Under his leadership, Italy abolished the Fascist system and withdrew from the Tripartite Pact. In September 1943, Italy surrendered unconditionally and joined the war against Germany. To the Japanese public at that time, the Badoglio government became a synonym for a "traitor" and a "loser."[8] Also, by early 1944, the ultimate defeat of Germany was already becoming certain. In the Pacific, Japanese forces were losing battle after battle, retreating from the islands they once occupied.

The fall of the Marshall Islands into the hands of the U.S. forces became only a matter of time.

It was becoming clear to Konoe that Tojo had to go in order to achieve an early termination of the war. In the spring of 1944, Konoe began the so-called Senior Statesmen Meeting with Wakatsuki, Hiranuma, and Okada to contemplate how to bring down the Tojo cabinet. Kido also basically agreed with Konoe. In his diary, Kido wrote on January 6, 1944, "If such a situation (a downfall of Germany and its unconditional surrender) develops, it would be extremely difficult for the Tojo cabinet to go on."[9]

Now there was seemingly a national consensus to demand the termination of the current cabinet. Despite such consensus and demand, Hosokawa Morisada told Prince Takamatsu on March 13 that Tojo was showing no reflection at all and, therefore, some even suggested that the only way to end the Tojo cabinet was the use of a radical measure such as a coup d'etat. Hosokawa thought, however, that there might be a chance to smooth out the situation with an imperial statement.

It was a difficult task, however, to have the Emperor play a role. Tojo and Kido made an effort to keep the Emperor unaware about the war situation and the reaction of the general public by not allowing anyone, even members of the imperial family, to be received by the Emperor, only themselves and their close associates. Shortly after the war was over, Kido stated to Goto Ryunosuke that it was such an arrangement that made it possible to achieve the termination of the war in a relatively smooth fashion.

Prince Higashikuni stated, "I could hardly see the Emperor during the war. Since the Pacific war began, not just me but any member of the imperial family could not see the Emperor under the consideration of keeping the Emperor away from any 'noise.' I do not know whether or not this idea (protecting the Emperor) came from Prime Minister Tojo or Lord Keeper Kido, but along with the military police and the secret police, this was a clear indication about how the close associates of the Emperor were feeling."[10] Except taking a peep at him at the ceremonial occasions, Konoe also had hardly seen the Emperor until February 1945, when the Emperor received him for a formal report.

As mentioned earlier, Kido had realized that it would be difficult for Tojo to stay in power if Germany was to fall. He did not wish, however, the Tojo cabinet to come to an end immediately and continued to support Tojo until shortly before the fall of Saipan. It is easy to understand Kido's reluctance to see Tojo go down. It was Kido who recommended Tojo as the successor when Konoe stepped down from the premiership in October 1941. The downfall of Tojo's cabinet would clearly make Kido vulnerable to the foregone conclusion in the aftermath of the war, that is, a search for those responsible for the war defeat.

On June 11, 1944, however, when enormous U.S. task forces bombarded the Japanese strongholds of Saipan, Tinian, and Guam, Kido had to give up on Tojo. The bombardment continued for three days until June 13 when the U.S. marines began landing. What followed was a ferocious battle. Despite the desperate effort of the Japanese forces to defend Saipan, in mid-July the U.S. marines secured the island when all the Japanese troops and about ten thousand civilian residents perished.

With the loss of this island, which Tojo had once believed unconquerable, retaining Tojo was out of the question for Kido. Even Tojo himself realized that he had to find a way to step down. On June 22, while the Japanese forces were still desperately defending Saipan, Prince Higashikuni said the following to Konoe at a meeting held at the residence of Konoe's friend Nagao Kinya: "This time Tojo seems to realize that he is in a difficult situation. According to Tojo's messenger who came to see me, Tojo stated that he had done his best. He did not think, however, he could go on. So I told him that it was absolutely out of the question for Tojo to quit now, and it would be better if Tojo reshuffled his cabinet and continued. I really think that we should have Tojo serve until the very end, and, when we face the worst situation, hold Tojo responsible for everything. If the [Tojo] cabinet were replaced, it would become difficult to see who should be held responsible. Then there will even be the possibility that the imperial family is held responsible. So it would be better to have Tojo continue."[11]

On the following day, June 23, Akamatsu Sadao, a secretary to Tojo, visited Matsudaira Yasumasa, the chief secretary for Lord Keeper Kido, and told him that Tojo wished to step down if there was someone who was appropriate to replace him. Two days later, Tojo visited Kido. Tojo was not explicit about his wish to resign. Kido recalled that Tojo was quite downcast. They talked for more than an hour but nothing substantial came from the talk. As Yabe points out, perhaps this was because Tojo wanted Kido to be the one to make an initial public remark about his resignation.[12]

Then Konoe met with Kido to discuss what should be done when Tojo resigned.[13] Both basically agreed that it would be desirable to let Tojo continue to govern for the time being and wait for the U.S. heavy bombardment or invasion of the Japanese mainland, and then, in order to establish peace, swiftly form a new cabinet under the leadership of a prince, and that if Tojo quit right away, there was no other choice but to set up a compromise cabinet, which would be expected to last for a few months, and then have a prince form a new cabinet in order to establish peace.[14]

As he said to Hosokawa on June 26, Konoe knew that to establish peace by setting up a new cabinet — whether a compromise cabinet or a cabinet under the leadership of a prince — required support from the general public. To Konoe, such support would be possible only when Japan suffered from another heavy U.S. bombardment or U.S. invasion of the Japanese mainland.

On July 2, Konoe handed Matsudaira his own written paper regarding the current situation Japan was facing. In it, Konoe emphasized how essential it was for Japan to obtain an immediate termination of the war. Konoe stated, "The prime reason for obtaining an immediate termination of the war is to maintain the national polity. If our enemy completes the setup of their military base on Saipan by the middle of this month [July], all of our 60 states or so will be within the air bombing range. Also, as a result of the incapacitation of our combined fleet, there might be [U.S.] attempt to invade our mainland at anytime. If that happens, human and material loss would be ten times or even a hundred times more than what we have lost so far since the China Incident. Then, what we have to take into most serious consideration is the issue of the national polity. For example, according to one authority, the number of disrespectful incidents toward the imperial family is already increasing every year. Also, despite the fact that the Third Comintern has been dissolved and we have not seen the formation of a Communist party in Japan yet, the element of the left wing is ubiquitous. They are planning to instigate a revolution when Japan faces an imminent and inevitable war defeat. In addition, most of the right wing who are unwavering in terms of continuing the war to the end and hoping for total destruction of Japan by the Anglo-Saxon powers are actually converters from the left-wing and we do not know what they are really up to. It is beyond our comprehension to know what they will do by taking advantage of the aftermath of the war. Therefore, continuing the war, when our defeat is inevitable, is the most perilous in terms of maintaining the national polity. In this sense, an immediate termination of the war is absolutely essential."[15]

Such a sense of urgency prompted Konoe to meet with Kido once again on July 8 for further elaboration regarding how to achieve a speedy termination of the war.[16] Through their talk, both agreed that although there was an option to set up a new cabinet right away under a prince in order to achieve a termination of the war on the assumption that the war situation was hopeless for Japan, due to the domestic situation it was almost impossible to carry out this option immediately. So to them there was no other choice but to set up a compromise cabinet and to receive another devastating defeat by going into the last naval battle in order to convince the nation that Japan faced doom.

When Konoe asked who should lead a compromise cabinet, Kido responded by saying, "We still have a few million army troops. Considering the enormity of the task to deal with the aftermath of the termination of the war, I think it is better to have someone from the army. How about General Terauchi to replace Tojo?"[17] Although he did not think that was the best choice, Konoe agreed with Kido since the compromise cabinet was supposed to last for only a few months anyway. As to who should head an imperial cabinet, Kido suggested Prince Higashikuri. Lastly, Konoe told Kido that in order to continue the war to its bitter end, the army was planning to bring the Emperor to Manchuria in case of U.S. invasion of the mainland and was also contemplating replacing the Emperor with another imperial member if the Emperor tried to seek peace. Kido said that the Emperor had absolutely no intention of going to Manchuria.

On July 14, Konoe met with Hiranuma and told him that Kido had Terauchi in mind to replace Tojo. Hiranuma responded by saying, "Terauchi is an indecisive fellow. He needs to be surrounded by competent subordinates. Also, this political transition has to be done promptly. If you select Terauchi, we have to bring him back to [Japan] and that will consume too much time. So I think that Suzuki Kantaro, Vice Chairman of the House of Peers, should be our choice. Whoever becomes the successor, it is likely that General Umezu Yoshijiro will become either Army Minister or Chief of Staff. [If that happens], since many of Umezu's associates are 'red,' the left-wing reformists would dominate the army."[18]

Wholeheartedly agreeing with Hiranuma, Konoe told Hiranuma that losing the war was dreadful, but it was not as dreadful as a left-wing revolution. Konoe continued to say that Japan was moving closer and closer to that end, and the only way to stop it was to have someone from Kodo-ha lead the nation. As this remark by Konoe indicates, by this time Konoe was convinced that all the military movements starting from the Manchurian Incident were the result of the plot by Tosei-ha (converters from the left wing) to have a Communist revolution in the aftermath of the war by bringing Japan in to a Pacific war and ultimate defeat. Konoe could not help but be frustrated because his beliefs were not quite shared by Kido or the Emperor. Recalling that both the Emperor and Kido held the leading figures of Kodo-ha, General Mazaki and General Araki, responsible for the February Twenty-six Incident, Konoe felt it regrettable that the Emperor and Kido were failing to grasp how vital it was to let Kodo-ha lead the nation at this juncture.

On July 13, a day before Konoe met with Hiranuma, the Emperor, apprehensive about the current military situation, summoned Tojo and in a rather firm voice ordered him to reform the military leadership.

Ashamed, Tojo met with the Emperor on the following day and said to him, "With regard to your request for reforming the military leadership, I will step down from the position as Chief of Staff and also have Shimada resign. I am determined to continue to serve [as Prime Minister] by refining the military and reshuffling the cabinet."[19]

Both Konoe and Kido were amazed by Tojo's remark to the Emperor. They had thought that Tojo was ready to step down. Furthermore, it was clear to Konoe that what the Emperor really meant by asking Tojo to reform the military was to express lack of confidence in the Prime Minister. As Wakatsuki said at the elder statesmen conference on July 17, "No matter how Tojo reshuffles his cabinet, since the general public has abandoned him already, it is no use." The Tojo cabinet was doomed.[20]

The one they favored to replace Tojo was Koiso Kuniaki. First, considering the enormity of the task to serve as a new Prime Minister and also the uneasiness that the public might feel if the fate of the nation was handed down to Koiso alone, Konoe suggested setting up a joint cabinet by Koiso and former Prime Minister Yonai Mitsumasa. Konoe believed that Yonai had far more support from the public than Koiso, and also Yonai enjoyed overwhelming popularity among the navy officers. Since Yonai however, when he was asked by Tojo to join his cabinet, had told Tojo that he would never involve himself in politics, Yonai was unwilling to take the premiership. He told Konoe that the only position he might accept was Navy Minister.

On July 20, along with Yonai as an expected Navy Minister, Koiso received an Imperial Order to be the new Prime Minister. The Emperor then told Koiso to respect the constitution and not to provoke the Soviet Union. When Konoe heard the Emperor's remark, he could not help but think that the Emperor made such a remark because of his desire to prevent any intrusion of the Kodo-ha into the Koiso cabinet. Konoe said, "Today, there is no one who wishes to provoke the Soviet Union. On the contrary, what makes me worry is that almost every ministry of the Japanese government is too much in favor of the Soviet Union. There is even a competition about who can be more pro–Soviet Union than the others. Accordingly, this remark by the Emperor is absolutely odd. It has to be the Emperor's intention to preempt any influence of the Kodo-ha on the new cabinet."[21]

Both Konoe and Hiranuma agreed that, although it would be difficult after the Emperor's remark, it was essential to have the Kodo-ha as part of the Koiso cabinet from an ideological point of view. Since Hiranuma was far closer to Koiso than Konoe, Konoe asked Hiranuma to convey their opinion to Koiso.

Although faced with some difficulty due to Tojo's attempt to remain in the government as part of the Koiso cabinet, on July 24 Koiso formed his cabinet. Konoe, however, could not help but be somewhat disappointed. According to Konoe, one of the major reasons for the elder statesmen to recommend Koiso was to achieve unity between the government and the military in order to have coordinated policy making. So Konoe wanted Koiso to serve not only as Prime Minister but also as Army Minister. Konoe's wish did not go anywhere when the army strongly opposed it.

To make matters worse, most of the personnel of both the army and the navy under the Tojo government remained to serve Koiso. Konoe told Hosokawa that the rationale of replacing Tojo with Koiso was almost completely lost and that the Koiso cabinet would not last. Perhaps Koiso himself may have known that his cabinet was to fall soon. Koiso told Konoe that before he was given an Imperial Order to become Prime Minister, he thought that Japan was one of the major powers with substantial military strength. Koiso now realized that Japan was far weaker than he had thought.

Convinced that Japan's defeat was a foregone conclusion, Konoe by this time showed a understandable concern not for bringing the war to an end but, more importantly, what postwar Japan would be like. When an academician, Takada Yasubo, met with Konoe on July 28, Konoe expressed his concern to him. As he told Takada, Konoe believed, in general that in war there were only two outcomes: either winning or losing; there wasn't much one could do about it. What was really bothersome at this juncture was what negative impact the outcome of the war might bring to the Imperial Family. Hence, to Konoe, it was most worrisome indeed that, contrary to his concern, some officials believed that Japan's turning into a communist nation in an economic sense would not have much negative impact on Japan as long as Japan was able to maintain its Imperial Family.[22]

Konoe naturally worried most about how the Allied powers would treat Japan in the postwar era, particularly over the question of the national polity. Konoe spent time studying U.S. thought on imperial rule and also U.S. plans of how to deal with postwar Japan. Konoe worried that, if the United States and other Allied powers demanded an abolition of Japanese monarchism, the polity of Japan would be doomed; so, before that took place, the Emperor had to be in a position to take an initiative in dealing with postwar Japan in order to maintain Japan's national polity.

Konoe was eager to have an opportunity to meet with the Emperor at this juncture and to convey his thoughts on the current situation. As mentioned earlier, meeting with the Emperor had been difficult for almost anyone, even for Konoe, because of Kido and Tojo's effort to keep the Emperor away from anyone except his close associates in order to avoid making the Emperor worried about the war situation and the public reaction to it. Nonetheless, as the war situation continued to deteriorate for Japan, the Emperor became keen to hear from those other than his close associates. For example, on January 7, 1945, when the Emperor heard about the advancement of U.S. troops into Lingayen, he told Kido that he needed to hear from the elder statesmen about the war situation. Also, as a result of the fall of Tojo cabinet and the increasingly deteriorating war situation, Kido himself became subjected to growing criticism. Some even demanded the resignation of Kido as the Lord Keeper of the Privy Seal. Kido could not afford to stay idle regarding the Emperor's wish to hear from the elder statesmen.

At last Konoe met with the Emperor on February 14. It had been nearly three years since Konoe saw the Emperor in person the last time. In his talk with the Emperor, Konoe stated that he was concerned with the ramifications of the war defeat on the national polity. Konoe pointed out that since there had not been any public demand by Britain and the United States for Japan to alter its government structure, Japan had nothing to worry about with regard to maintaining its national policy. Konoe knew, however, that would be quite different if Japan had to confront Communist revolution in aftermath of the war defeat.

Unfortunately, to Konoe, Japan was indeed moving toward Communist revolution. Konoe lamented to the Emperor that Japan was failing to see true intention of Soviet Union — that is, Communization of the entire world. Konoe argued that, although the Soviet Union had adopted the 1935 two-stage revolution tactic and dissolved the Comintern, seemingly distancing itself from hard-line politics, in essence, nothing had changed. The opposite was actually taking place. As seen in the examples of what happened to the Tito government of Yugoslavia or the Polish government, and contrary to the Soviet Union's claim of non-interference, the Soviet Union was actively involved in domestic politics of European nations. Konoe was convinced, therefore, that the Soviet Union would likely take a similar policy toward East Asia.

Under this situation, Konoe believed that the Soviet interference with the domestic politics of Japan was more than likely. He pointed out that, regrettably, Japan's domestic conditions— such the hardships of daily life, the enhancement of the voice of labor, the rise of pro-Soviet sentiment as a reaction to an increase of anti–Anglo-Saxon feeling, the reform movement by the conspirators in the military and related movement by new bureaucrats, and the actions behind the scene by left wing element to manipulate that movement — were creating an increasingly ideal situation for the Soviets to achieve their goal of Communist revolution in Japan.

The most troublesome and worrisome of the above to Konoe was the reform movement pushed by the Communist conspirators. They created a false idea that the polity of Japan and Communism could be compatible. According to Konoe, this idea was very effective in making the military officers vulnerable to Communist teaching since most of these military officers were coming from lower class families.

It was this group of the conspirators, Konoe argued, who brought Japan into the Manchurian Incident and the China Incident, and eventually drugged Japan into the Great East Asian War by escalating those incidents. Therefore, the true purpose of these incidents was not anything external but the domestic reforms. Here, Konoe expressed his deep regret to the Emperor that, without understanding the nature of the demands to have the reforms, he accepted them, believing it necessary to eliminate internal strife and achieve national unity.

Konoe found it particularly lamentable that some right-wing nationalists demanded the "honorable death of the entire nation" rather than acquiescing to the enemy. What was equally lamentable was that these right-wing nationalists were increasingly becoming pro–Soviet. According to Konoe, some of them even demanded that Japan should make an alliance with the Soviet Union regardless of how much risk Japan would be taking. Konoe understood that behind these demands from the right-wind nationalists, there was the left-wing element, which were stirring up the right-wing nationalists to put the nation into disorder and ultimately to achieve a revolution. Thus, it was clear to Konoe that the internal and increasingly detrimental for Japan and were becoming more and more favorable for Communist revolution.

With regard to the prospect of war, Konoe told the Emperor that, since Japan had no chance to change the current course of the war and that the only destiny Japan now faced was defeat, continuation of the war hardly made a sense. All it was doing was assisting the conspirators in achieving their goal, the Communization of Japan. Therefore, if Japan really wished to have any chance to maintain national polity, the war had to be terminated as soon as possible.

Konoe ended his talk with the Emperor, as Konoe himself acknowledged, with a rather naïve view. He told the Emperor that if the government of Japan were somehow able to eradicate the left-wing element from the military, it would be possible to change the military drastically. As a result, the United States, Great Britain, and the nationalist government of China in Chunking might soften their policies toward Japan and began to question the merits of continuing the war. After all, their ultimate goal in this war was to end Japanese militarism, not the termination of Japanese military itself. So, clearly understanding how essential it was for Japan to achieve a quick eradication of the left-wing interferences in the military, Konoe strongly urged the Emperor to make a courageous decision.[23]

The Emperor told Konoe that the United Sates would demand the abolition of Japanese monarchism if Japan decided to end the fighting now. That would endanger the polity of the nation and there was no guarantee for its maintenance. Then, recalling what Umezu said to him — if Japan could lead the enemy to Taiwan, Japan might give them considerable damage — the Emperor asked Konoe if Japan would be able to create a chance to end the war in a desirable way by continuing to fight.[24] Konoe replied to the Emperor by saying that although he did not think U.S. ambassador Grew and the leaders of the U.S. government yet had any intention of abolishing Japanese monarchism, that might change if further deterioration of the internal and external situations took place.[25]

It is difficult to assess how much the Emperor was persuaded by Konoe's statement. One should recall, however, that when the February Twenty-six Incident took place, it was the Emperor who, instead of giving support for the cause of Kodo-ha, ordered the suppression of the coup d'etat, which resulted in the debacle of Kodo-ha in the army. As Konoe pointed out, this debacle made it possible for Tosei-ha to move southward, ultimately leading Japan into the confrontation with the United States. So, even if Konoe's assessment that the series of events from the Manchurian Incident to the outbreak of the Pacific war were the result of elaborate planning by the left-wing element in its conspiracy to achieve Communist revolution in Japan had been correct, it would have been tough for the Emperor to accept it. Regardless of how the Emperor saw it, as Yabe points out, it is significant, however, that Konoe in this statement to the Emperor made it clear that he believed that there was planning by the left wing to bring Japan to Communist revolution and truly regretted that he had failed to detect it.

While Konoe, Kido, and the others were searching for a way to terminate the war, the U.S. offensive was showing no sign of slowing down. In early 1945, the U.S. forces liberated Luzon and Manila and occupied the island of Iwo. The air bombing over the major cities of Japan was increasingly intensified. In February, the Yalta Conference was held. At this conference, Stalin made a pledge to Roosevelt that the Soviet Union would be in the Pacific war within a few months after German surrender.

Facing this dire situation, the Koiso cabinet was going nowhere. In March Koiso tried to establish peace with Chiang Kai-shek through talks

with Chiang's close subordinate, Miao Pin. Considering the difficulty
Konoe faced in establishing peace with Chiang Kai-shek in the aftermath
of the China Incident, Koiso's attempt to have peace talks with China at
this juncture was almost a joke. Why should Chiang come to peace terms
with Japan when Japan was already doomed in the Pacific war? Facing
opposition from both the army and the Emperor, Koiso's attempt came to
an end.

Koiso also tried to reshuffle his cabinet and appointed himself as
Army Minister. Serving both as Prime Minister and Army Minister, Koiso
was rather desperately trying to strengthen his government. Koiso should
have known better, however. By this time, Kido and even Konoe were contemplating a successor to Koiso.

Koiso resigned on April 5. On the same day, the elder statesmen conference was held to discuss succession. The attendees were Konoe,
Iranuma, Suzuki, Hirota, Kido, Wakatsuki, Okada, and Tojo. One consensus emerged from the conference: whoever succeeded Koiso, it had to
be someone from the military in order to have unity between the military
command and the government. Konoe had no objection, but added one
other criterion, saying, "It is better to choose someone who has been free
from the past politics."[26] Agreeing with Konoe, Hiranuma suggested choosing Admiral Suzuki. Suzuki was unwilling to take premiership, however,
saying, "As I told Admiral Okada once, I have the belief that involvement
of a military man in politics often creates a source of national destruction. For example, there are the fall of Rome, the end of Caesar, and also
the fall of the Romanov Kingdom. Such a belief of mine makes it difficult
for me to involve myself in politics. Besides I have a hearing problem. So
I would like to decline the recommendation."[27] Tojo also indicated his
opposition to the selection of Suzuki as a successor. He argued, "Considering the importance of defending the mainland of Japan, it is indispensable to have unity between the military command and the government.
In this sense, the army is key, and also [a successor] has to be an active
military man. I think General Hata would be the most appropriate
choice."[28] Tojo continued, "When we face the possibility of turning the
mainland of Japan into battlefields, we have to be really careful in making a policy. Otherwise the army might turn away from us. If that happens, the new cabinet will fall."[29] In a response to Tojo's remark, Kido
said, "Today there is a strong anti-military mood among the general public. It is possible to see the general public turning away from the army."[30]

Despite Suzuki's reluctance and Tojo's opposition, the agreement was
made at the conference to choose Suzuki as a successor to Koiso. Receiving the Imperial Order, Suzuki formed his cabinet on April 7. Contrary to

Konoe and Kido's expectation that this new Suzuki cabinet would move toward a speedy end to the war, Suzuki did not have an easy beginning. General Anami Korechika, as the conditions for his acceptance to join the Suzuki cabinet as Army Minister, asked Suzuki to pursue three things:

1. To continue the war of the Pacific to an end.
2. To improve the defense power for the mainland battle.
3. To strive for achieving unity between the army and the navy.

According to Yabe, this demand from Anami was not necessarily aimed at the Suzuki cabinet, but it was rather a means to achieve an internal unity of the army.[31] No matter what Anami's intent was, it was the kind of beginning that the Suzuki cabinet wanted to avoid. To make matters worse, the international situation was further deteriorating for Japan. On April 5, the Soviet Union abolished the Russo-Japanese Neutrality Treaty. This was followed by the outbreak of the battle of Okinawa on April 6. Perhaps it is not an overstatement to say that Japan was by this time already defeated.

Despite such a doomed situation, the Kenpei Seiji under the left-wing army officers was showing no sign of ending. On the contrary, as the movement for achieving peace intensified, the actions of the Kenpei Seiji deepened.

On April 15, Yoshida Shigeru, Iwabuchi Tatsuo, and Ueda Shunkichi were arrested by the imperial forces for their alleged involvement in Konoe's February 14 statement to the Emperor. What the army wanted was clear: they wanted to suppress Konoe's maneuvering to achieve peace. A few days later, Konoe said to Kido, "The imperial police officers are eagerly trying to find out the content of my statement [to the Emperor]. Since I do not understand why they are doing that, I am going to see Army Minister Anami and ask him. As an elder statesman, I just gave my view to the Emperor. That is all I did. When I did so, there was no questioning about it. So it does not make sense that I have to be interrogated by the imperial police today. If this continues, I do not think that I will be able to carry out my duty as an elder statesman. So I intend to give up all my status."[32]

Kido told Konoe not to do such a thing and promised Konoe that he was going to talk to Anami. Indeed, Kido met with Anami and told him what Konoe intended to do. Anami then pledged that he would no longer pursue the issue. Konoe was somewhat relieved. As he himself mentioned, however, the attack from the left-wing army officers against Konoe and anyone associating with Konoe meant only one thing: putting pressure on the Kodo-ha in order to halt the peace movement.

Meantime, the war in Europe was coming to an end. On May 7 Germany surrendered. Two days later, Hitler took his own life. Now it was becoming clear to almost anybody that the end of the Pacific war was imminent.

It was certain to Konoe and Kido that Japan was already defeated. Even though Kenpei Seiji was showing no sign of ending, now nothing seemed to be able to suppress the internal peace movement. According to Kido, the Emperor himself inclined toward early termination of the war. With such inclination of the Emperor, both Konoe and Kido were convinced that no matter how the army opposed the termination of the war, such opposition no longer meant much. In fact, even among the army officers, there was growing doubt about any positive result from the war for Japan.

On June 8, Kido drafted a plan for how to achieve a termination of the war. In his plan, Kido said, "Although it is proper that, since the main goal of our enemy is to end [Japanese] militarism, Japan negotiates with the U.S. by having the military propose peace and then having the government decide a policy, [circumstantially] it is almost impossible. If we delay further, however, we will lose a chance to achieve a termination of the war and follow the same fate as Germany. Then we would not be able to even achieve the goals of securing safety for the imperial family and maintaining the national polity. Although it is quite unusual and gracious, we have to ask the Emperor to make a decision [to terminate the war], and, through the imperial decree, we need to negotiate with the United States through a mediator. To negotiate with the United States and the British directly is one policy we could take. It would be better, however, to have the Soviet Union as a mediator in order to make the negotiation somewhat more flexible. As a condition, if we can get an assurance [from the United States] that neutrality of the Pacific is truly maintained, our nation will abolish all the status of the occupation leaders, retreat all the troops voluntarily, and be satisfied with minimum defense power."[33] On the following day, June 9, Kido met with the Emperor and submitted his plan. Wholeheartedly agreeing with Kido, the Emperor commanded an immediate execution of the plan.

On July 12, the Emperor summoned Konoe and asked him about the termination of the war. Konoe responded by saying, "Recently I have seen the army officers quite often. Using statistical data, they explain to me that winning the war is still possible. According to the navy, however, such statistics are unreliable. The uneasiness of the general public is growing. Some say that we have to ask you to take some action, and some even think ill of you. I truly believe that we have to terminate the war as quickly as possible." The Emperor told Konoe that he was thinking about sending

Konoe as special envoy to Moscow.[34] Because Konoe doubted the trust-worthiness of the Soviet Union, he opposed the idea of using the Soviet Union as a mediator. In fact, Konoe believed that there was a great chance the Soviet Union would enter the war against Japan. Nonetheless, considering how much pain the Emperor was bearing about the current war situation, Koneo could not be truthful to the Emperor. He told the Emperor that he would devote himself to a successful mission if he was appointed as an envoy.

Konoe was correct in his assessment of the Soviet Union. There was almost no chance that the Soviet Union would comply with Japan's request. At the Tehran Conference in November 1943, Stalin pledged to Roosevelt and Churchill that the Soviet Union would join the Pacific war against Japan a few months after the defeat of Germany. Stalin repeated this at the Yalta Conference. In April 1945, the Soviet Union had already informed Japan about the suspension of the Russo-Japanese Neutrality Treaty.

On July 12, Foreign Minister Togo sent a telegram to Japanese Ambassador Sato, asking him to hand his message to Foreign Commissar Vyacheslav M. Molotov and tell him that Konoe Fumimaro would come to Moscow to plead with the Soviet Union to take on the role of mediator. In his message, Togo said, "His Majesty worries so much about the great suffering and sacrifice of his people that he appeals to each nation in the war to stop fighting. Nonetheless, [if the United States] adheres to its demand of 'unconditional surrender' in the Great East Asian War, Japan has to carry on its war effort to the end in order to defend the honor of our motherland and its existence. What results from that would be great bloodshed for each fighting nation. That is against his wish. The Emperor hopes for a swift restoration of peace for the welfare of humankind."[35] On the following day, July 13, Ambassador Sato contacted the Soviet government. He was told, however, that the Soviet response to Japan's request would be delayed since Stalin and Molotov had to leave Moscow for Berlin to attend the Potsdam Conference.

Meanwhile, Konoe, although having doubt about any positive outcome from Japan's efforts to use the Soviet Union as a mediator, began to prepare for his mission to Moscow. First, he drafted an outline of peace negotiations for the Emperor to see and then selected those who were to accompany him to Moscow.

On July 18, five days after Sato initially contacted the Soviet Union, Sato received the first response. It turned out to be negative for Japan, for the Soviets pointed out that Japan's request did not contain concrete proposals and also did not indicate clearly what the real mission of the special envoy was; accordingly, it was impossible for the Soviet Union to give a definite answer to Japan. Informed by Sato about this, Konoe responded to the Soviet Union, mentioning that he was to go to Moscow to plead with the Soviet Union to take on the role of mediator for the sake of establishing peace and that he would talk about the concrete proposals after his arrival.

Despite Konoe's effort, the Soviets made no sign of the acceptance. On July 26, the Allied powers issued the Potsdam Declaration. While some spoke up, saying that Japan should immediately reject the Declaration, Prime Minister Suzuki decided to give a little more time for the Soviet Union to respond to Japan's request before Japan gave its response to the declaration. Also, as an obvious reason for Japan's hesitation to accept immediately, Japan was greatly concerned with the ramifications of Japan's unconditional surrender with regard to the fate of the Emperor. President Truman took Japan's decision to delay its response as a flat rejection of the declaration.

On August 6, the United States dropped an A-bomb on Hiroshima, thus opening a new era, an atomic age. When he heard about the new bomb, Konoe knew that the termination of the war was only a matter of time.

Two days later, on August 8, Ambassador Sato met with Molotov to get an official response to Japan's request. It was not, however, the response Japan wanted to hear, but rather a declaration of war against Japan.[36] The following morning, the Soviet troops advanced into Manchuria.

With regard to this Soviet declaration of war against Japan, Konoe stated the following: "The Soviet Union says that, because of Japan's defiance of the Potsdam Declaration, the foundation to restore peace has been lost. It should be noted, however, that the Soviet Union at that time was not a participant in the Potsdam Declaration, had not responded to Japan's July 23 request to have the Soviet Union as a mediator, and also mentioned nothing about Japan's acceptance of the Potsdam Declaration as a condition for the Soviet mediation. Anyhow, because of all this, a chance to dispatch a special envoy to the Soviet Union has been lost."[37]

On August 9, the second A-bomb was dropped on Nagasaki. Although ultra right-wing nationalists such as Army Minister Anami still insisted that Japan continue to fight, it was clear to almost everybody that Japan had to terminate the war immediately. All the cabinet members except the Army Minister agreed to accept the declaration as long as the Allied powers guaranteed the polity of the nation and some assurance of existence of the imperial family. Nonetheless, it was unfortunate that Japan still could not reach unanimity over the decision.

Urged by Konoe, on August 11 Kido met with the Emperor and told him that the only way to deal with this dire situation was an imperial sanction. Kido asked the Emperor to directly appeal to the nation through a radio broadcast in order to achieve the termination of the war.[38] The Emperor showed no hesitation to carry it out. On August 14, at the Imperial Conference, Anami repeated his adamant demand for the continuation of the war. In his response to Anami, the Emperor expressed his intent to end the war. He told Anami that he had no desire to change what he said at the Imperial Conference on August 9, and that, although some still worried about the sovereign power of the Emperor under the Potsdam Declaration, the Allied response to Japan's inquiry was acceptable.[39] Here the Emperor clearly realized that by ending the fight right away, Japan still had a chance to maintain national sovereignty. If the war continued, considering the war potential of the Allied powers, Japan would lose even that chance.

The Emperor did not hesitate with his decision to accept the declaration to end the war, but at the same time, he could not help being deeply agonized about the position he was in. As he told Anami, he couldn't bear to take away the weapons from his dedicated solders and turn them in as war criminals. Not only that, he was also deeply concerned with the ensuing hardship the nation had would have to endure in the postwar era.

Regardless of how he felt, the Emperor knew he had no other choice. The Emperor concluded his remarks by saying that enduring the unendurable and bearing the unbearable, he was ready to do anything, including a radio broadcast, to carry out his decision, and asked Anami and other conferees to do anything they could do to prevent or ease any agitation the nation would likely express when they were told about the fate Japan was about to accept.[40] When the Emperor was saying the above, tears were streaming down his face, bringing everyone at the conference tears.

Now with this Emperor's statement, only a group of the fanatical young military officers dared to oppose. When they heard the word "surrender," these young officers attempted to carry out a coup d'etat. They surrounded the imperial palace in order to prevent the radio broadcast and also assaulted the homes of Prime Minister Suzuki, Hiranuma Kiichiro, and Kido Koichi. The destruction they caused did not go further, however. By the early morning of August 15, their attempt was suppressed. Army Minister Anami killed himself, leaving the statement that he believed the sacred land of Japan would never perish and now he had to make an apology to the Emperor with his death for his greatest "crime"—war defeat.[41]

At noon on August 15, the Emperor himself delivered the radio broadcast, telling the whole nation why Japan was terminating the war. Hearing the Emperor's voice for the very first time, the entire nation wept and repented. It was literally "Ichioku so zange" (nationwide repentance). Although Konoe anticipated it, it must have been one of the most difficult days in his entire life. Konoe's grief was even deepened by his stepmother's death on the same day, shortly before the imperial broadcast. A few months later, Konoe said to his sister heartily, "My mother died at the right time. I envy her. Today there is nothing good to live for. She was always worried about the national polity. Indeed, it was fortunate for her to die without hearing the Emperor's words."[42]

Prime Minister Suzuki resigned on August 15, only three hours after the Emperor's radio broadcast. Asked by the Emperor to select a successor, Kido, after consulting with the president of the Privy Council, Hiranuma Kiichiro, recommended Prince Higashikuni Naruhiko.[43] Insisting that he was not a politician and, since he was a member of the imperial family, it was inappropriate for him to serve as Prime Minister, the Prince was reluctant to accept a premiership. When told, however, that considering the gravity of the situation the nation was facing, he was the only choice, Prince Higashikuni agreed to replace Suzuki with a condition that Konoe would be a member of his cabinet in order to supplement his lack of experience in politics.

With this new Prime Minister, the first and last as a direct member of the imperial family, Japan's postwar era began. At the outset, many expected reactionary moves against the government or particular individuals by elements opposing the outcome of the war. Fearing this, Konoe took the precaution of changing his residence almost day by day. Contrary to such fears, no major terrorist act took place. It turned out to be one of the most serene transitions from wartime to peacetime. As Yabe Teiji points out, it was primarily due to the Emperor's direct appeal to the nation and also the strong and reciprocal trust of the nation in the Emperor.

With the arrival of the U.S. military forces on August 28 followed by General MacArthur's arrival at Atsugi Airport on August 30, the Allied occupation of Japan began. Things were unfolding rather rapidly. On September 2, the Japanese representative, Shigemitsu Mamoru, signed a document of surrender on board the battleship *Missouri* in Tokyo Bay, officially ending the Pacific war. On September 11, Tojo Hideki and 38 others were charged as war criminals. On the following day, Sugiyama Gen took his own life; Tojo also attempted to kill himself but failed.[44]

With regard to punishing the war criminals, Prime Minister Higashikuni and Konoe hoped that the Allied powers would allow Japan to be in charge. When Higashikuni met with the Emperor and told him about it, the Emperor was not so eager. The Emperor stated his concern, saying, "All those sentenced to be war criminals [by the Allied powers] are my loyal subordinates. They merely were carrying out their duties and, therefore, it is unbearable for me to see them punished under my name."[45] Despite this reluctance, the Emperor was persuaded in the end. He agreed to make a request to the Allied powers. Here Konoe should have known better. Such a request got nowhere. Even if the Allied powers had wished to grant such a request, it would have been impossible due to the raging demand from the U.S. general public for severe punishment of those held responsible for Japan's war crimes. Understandably, it was intolerable for the U.S. public to see the authority to punish the war criminals given to the hands of the nation those criminals belonged to.

Meanwhile, on September 13, Konoe met General MacArthur for the first time. Due to the inexperienced American interpreter, the meeting was not productive. Konoe was hardly able to express his thoughts on the various issues. During the meeting, MacArthur told Konoe that Japanese militarism had been destroyed in a structural sense but the ideological foundation for militarism also needed to be rooted out. MacArthur wished Konoe to be the one to take up the task. In his conversation with MacArthur, Konoe well sensed MacArthur's strong hatred of Japanese militarism. What really surprised Konoe, however, was not this hatred but rather MacArthur's ignorance of the background of Japanese militarism. He had almost no knowledge about the major incidents of the 1930s.

Understandably, Konoe felt it disturbing to see someone who had nothing but only a shallow understanding of the very fundamental aspects of Japanese militarism in charge of dealing with postwar Japan. Konoe was eager to have a second chance to see MacArthur to convey his thoughts and more importantly to help MacArthur have a better knowledge about Japanese militarism and the nature of the Japanese political setting. With such eagerness, on October 4, Konoe visited MacArthur once again. In his meeting with MacArthur, Konoe stated that it was true that the military and the ultra nationalists were responsible for shattering the world peace and bringing Japan to ruin. With regard to the roles the conservative force of Japan — particularly the Imperial House — and the financial cliques played, the United States, however, hardly had clear understanding. For example, the United States viewed that both groups conspired with the militarists and brought Japan into ruin. To Konoe, nothing was further from truth. He pointed out to MacArthur that the conservative force and the financial clique actually were suppressors against the military clique. Otherwise, it could not be explained that some of the assassination targets of the militarists were some prominent members of the conservative force and the financial clique.

As he told MacArthur, to Konoe, the true conspirators were the left-wing forces. It was they who were manipulating the military clique and ultra nationalists behind the scenes in order to achieve their goal — the radical revolution in Japan. Konoe emphasized that only by understanding that point could one explain why some militarists and bureaucrats opposed the early termination of the war and sought to prolong it.

Konoe continued to say that the Soviet Union was the imaginary enemy nation for the military clique. Unable to understand how to deal with a total war, the military clique was becoming increasingly apprehensive toward the Soviet Union. The soldiers were mostly the sons of the lower class farming families, and they were therefore resentful toward the landlord class and the capitalists. Konoe argued that all these were making the military clique vulnerable to manipulation by the left-wing.

So, to Konoe, it was clear that the left-wing and its manipulation of the military brought ruin to Japan. It was therefore foolish, Konoe argued, to remove the conservative force and the financial clique along with the military clique and the ultra nationalists. That would surely turn Japan into a Communist nation. Although removal of the military clique was indispensable to build Democracy in Japan, Japan would never achieve its own democracy without the existence of the conservative force and the financial clique. Konoe also pointed out that after the World War I, it was social democracy that saved Germany from Communist revolution. What was comparable in Japan to this social democracy of Germany was nothing but the conservative force and the financial clique. It was true that there were emerging political parties such as the Liberal Party or the Proletarian Party. They still remained insignificant. Konoe ended his remarks to MacArthur reemphasizing his belief that if the stable forces — the conservative force and the financial clique — were removed from Japan immediately, Japan's turning into a Communist nation would be a foregone conclusion.[46]

Impressed by Konoe's statement, MacArthur told Konoe that it was useful and instructive.[47] Then, when Konoe asked for MacArthur's thoughts on the governmental organization and structure of parliament, MacArthur emphasized in response the essentiality of constitutional reform and said to Konoe, "Although you are one of the conservatives, you are a cosmopolitan and very familiar with the global situation, and also you are still young. I would like you to take an initiative resolutely. Along with the other liberals, if you publicly announce constitutional reforms, the parliament will follow your direction."[48] As Konoe took it correctly, in this remark MacArthur was requesting that Konoe be in charge of such constitutional reform.

A week later, on October 11, MacArthur told the new Prime Minister, Shidehara Kijuro, that Japan had to revise the constitution in order to fully comply with the terms of the Potsdam Declaration.[49] Responding to MacArthur's remark to the Prime Minister, the Emperor ordered Konoe to form within the office of the Lord Keeper of the Privy Seal a Constitutional Problem Investigation Committee.

Now Konoe found himself in the center of the constitutional reform effort. Upon the Imperial Order, Konoe immediately began to prepare a constitutional reform plan. It took almost no time, however, before Konoe ran into obstacles in his effort. When Shidehara explained at the cabinet council about the constitutional reform, some members of the cabinet opposed the idea of letting the office of the Lord Keeper of the Privy Seal deal with constitutional reform. They argued that since the constitutional reform was a state affair, it should be dealt with by the cabinet. A similar argument rose from the constitutional scholars.

As Nishi Toshio points out in his book *Unconditional Democracy: Education and Politics in Occupied Japan, 1945–1952,* MacArthur could ignore this oppositions from the Japanese domestic front and let Konoe continue the reform.[50] What could not be ignored was the growing criticism of Konoe from the American public. An editorial in the *New York Herald Tribune* dated October 31 says the following:

> Of all the absurd blunders made by America in the Far East, one of the worst is the selection of Prince Fumimaro Konoye[sic] to draft Japan's new constitution. It is the equivalent of choosing a gunman to devise rules for a reform school. If the prince were in prison awaiting trial as a war criminal there would be no reason to object. His designation, with official American sanction, as the man to write a democratic constitution for Japan is the ultimate in absurdity.
>
> Prince Konoye was Japan's Prime Minister in 1937, when the Japanese attacked China and opened the second world war. He served the militarists of Japan repeatedly during their bloody aggression in the Far East. He announced the "New Order in East Asia" and thus lent his tremendous prestige to Japan's vicious imperialistic program. It is true enough that he posed as a liberal and that he let it be known that he disliked some of the more reckless moves of the militarists. But there is nothing to indicate that anything but caution and intelligence led him, at widely spaced intervals, to try to restrain the Tojos and Koisos.
>
> The evil oligarchy which ruled Japan so long is being strengthened by the use of Konoye to draft a constitution — just as the imperial institution is being strengthened by American use of the emperor to give "commands" to his subjects. The many excellent moves of General MacArthur to encourage the development of democracy in Japan are being nullified by the general's acceptance of Konoye as the man to lead Japan to democracy. Konoye is one of those who used the old constitution as a tool to enslave the Japanese people at home and to enslave other peoples abroad. There is nothing in his

record that shows he is fitted for his present job. He is not the man to prepare a new constitution for Japan unless it can be said that Americans enjoyed the recent war and want to have another one just like it as soon as possible. "[51]

As this editorial indicates, there was growing argument for and demand from the American public for Konoe to be held responsible for Japan's ordeals such as the China Incident, the Tripartite Pact, and the Pacific war, and to sentence him as a war criminal. Giving in to such pressure from the American public and also from its own public, the Shidehara cabinet appointed Dr. Matsumoto Joji to set up the Constitution Problem Investigation Committee, thus creating an odd situation of having two committees simultaneously engage in constitutional reform. To make matters worse for Konoe, MacArthur, giving in to the pressure from the public, made a farfetched statement through the General Headquarters of the Allied powers on November 11 regarding their previous endorsement of Konoe's role in constitutional reform. It says, "Regarding constitutional reform, we did ask Konoe as a vice premier under the Higashikuni cabinet to engage in it. Due to the fall of the Higashikuni cabinet, however, Konoe's engagement has been canceled. What Konoe is doing now is only through the Imperial Order. It has nothing to do with us."[52] Konoe truly believed that his engagement in the constitutional reform was due to MacArthur's request and the Imperial Order. Also, regarding the constitutional reform, Konoe received various advice from George Atcheson, a U.S. political advisor to MacArthur, after the fall of the Higashikuni cabinet. This statement from MacArthur was, therefore, something Konoe never anticipated.

Until this moment, Konoe did not think that he would be considered a war criminal. With this growing criticism and demand from both the Japanese and American public for Konoe to be held responsible for Japan's war of aggression and, more significantly, with the United States giving in to such pressure, Konoe sensed an inevitability that he would be designated a war criminal.

Despite this distasteful development, Konoe continued to make an effort in drafting a new constitution. Konoe turned in his draft on November 22 and on the same day carried out his long-contemplated idea of giving up his status as peer. Then, on December 12, as anticipated, Konoe was charged as a war criminal, literally ending his political career, which Konoe had never wished to have, and, as it turned out, ending his life as well.

Once again Konoe's fate played out in a pattern repeatedly seen in the past events of his life, starting from forming his first cabinet in 1937 despite his reluctance, followed by the China Incident a month later, the

Portrait of Konoe Fumimaro (© Mainichi Photo Bank).

debacle of the National Service Association, the fiasco of the Tripartite Pact, Konoe's abortive and last endeavor to have the summit meeting with Franklin Roosevelt as part of the U.S.-Japan negotiations, and now his failure in his effort for constitutional reform and the disgrace of being charged as a war criminal. Surely Konoe was by no means impeccable in the failures of all these incidents. As this last case of constitutional reform well exemplifies, however, Konoe had little control in determining their outcomes. With a great insight, Konoe once said, "I am a child of fate!"

Conclusion

On December 16, ten days after his being charged as a war criminal, Konoe took his own life. The night before his death, Konoe invited over two close friends and high school classmates, Yamamoto Yuzo and Goto Ryunosuke.[1] In their conversation, Yamamoto asked Konoe about his medical checkup to determine his feasibility to go to the Sugamo Prison in Tokyo to carry out imprisonment. Konoe responded, "According to my physician, I am basically healthy. He told me, however, he had some apprehension about my health with regard to imprisonment and asked me whether he should write a medical report indicating it. I said to him that it was unnecessary." Then Yamamoto asked, "Are you going to the Sugamo Prison tomorrow?" Konoe responded, "No, I intend to ignore the trial." Yamamoto then said, "Are you thinking about the worst situation [committing suicide]?" Shaking his head, Konoe said firmly, "No." Then Goto, joining the conversation, said to Konoe, "I think you should go to the trial and, like Marshall Henri Pétain, defend the Emperor by expressing your view with great dignity." Konoe responded, "I think the reason why I have been considered a war criminal is my involvement in the China Incident. When I think of the Incident, although I cannot say that, as a politician, I do not have any responsibility at all for it, I have little to do with the Incident. [What I apprehend, however, is that], if you press this issue of the China Incident, it ultimately goes back to a question of 'Supreme Command.' Then, in the worst case, the Emperor would be obliged to take responsibility. There is no way, therefore, for me to stand at the trial and express my view." With this remark, Goto was convinced that Konoe had made up his mind to die. Noticing Mrs. Konoe, Chiyoko, and Konoe's second son, Michitaka, standing behind Konoe, Goto could not help but be emotionally overwhelmed. Goto, however, strongly suggested Konoe not repeat the shameful act of Tojo.[2]

Konoe wrote his will shortly before he committed suicide. In it, he wrote, "Since the China Incident, I have made many political blunders. Although I feel deeply responsible for them, it is intolerable for me to be judged as a war criminal in the U.S. court. It is my sense of responsibility for the China Incident that drove me into my firm determination and effort to solve the Incident. Believing that the only chance left to achieve settlement of the China Incident was rapprochement with the United States, I thoroughly devoted myself to the U.S.-Japanese negotiations. Hence, it is quite regrettable to be charged as a war criminal by the United States. I believe, however, those who know me well can see the truth. There must be such people even in the United States. Today, what we see are the presumptuousness of the victor, extreme servility and slander of the loser, and rumors based on hate and misunderstanding. All of these are creating public opinion. One day, however, calmness will return. Only then, right and fair judgment will fall onto me at the court of God."[3]

So, instead of being tried in court as a war criminal, Konoe chose death. In answering why, understandably Konoe's pride as one of the most respected court nobles did not allow him to go through the trial as a war criminal conducted by the enemy he had just fought. As mentioned earlier, there was, however, a more profound reason: his concern that his being at the court would surely put him into a situation in which he had to talk about the Supreme Command, suggesting the responsibility of the Emperor for the war. So to Konoe, choosing death was a far more dignified act. It was his last service in defense of the Emperor.

Konoe's death, however, hardly brought an end to the debate over his accountability for the calamitous experience that the nation had gone through. Agreeing to MacArthur's decision as the Supreme Commander for the Allied Powers (SCAP) to consider Konoe a war criminal, most of the Japanese press and the nation in general held him responsible for the war. They argued that the China Incident took place under Konoe's regime, and, to a great extent, it was Konoe's failure to solve it as Prime Minister that put the nation on its tragic path.

As we have seen, however, in Konoe's effort to settle the China Incident, which resulted in a series of policies such as the national mobilization bill, the National Service Association, the Wang Chiang-wei maneuver, the Tripartite Pact, and the U.S.-Japanese negotiations, nothing really suggests that it was Konoe who led Japan into disaster. On the contrary, Konoe devoted himself to keeping the nation from taking that path. All the policies and decisions Konoe agreed to enact were primarily for finding a way to end the quagmire of the China Incident, indicating that there is nothing to justify his stigmatization as a war criminal.

This was why MacArthur did not consider Konoe as a war criminal immediately after the war ended. Konoe was even given the task of taking part in writing a new constitution under the guidance of the Allied powers. As stated in Chapter 6, charging Konoe as a war criminal did not come until four months later in December, when the Allied powers realized that it would better serve their interest in rebuilding Japan to charge Konoe as a war criminal. This coincided with the growing demand from the Japanese public to hold him responsible for leading the nation to ruin.

So it is fair to say that Konoe was not accountable in terms of leading the nation to defeat, but the question of his failure to solve the China Incident still remains. Even here, one can hardly make a strong argument. Konoe himself admitted that he did not possess the qualities necessary to be an effective politician. In spite of this admission, it was the surrounding circumstances that created the false image of Konoe as someone who could be "a messiah" for a deeply troubled nation. Or one can look at it in a more cynical way: Konoe could have been chosen to lead because of his weak character. Each segment of society found him easy to manipulate because of his weak character, yet still found him beneficial to their interests because of his status and great popularity.

The argument that Konoe was brought against his will into something for which he was unfit does not mean, of course, he can be spared from his responsibility, if indeed he failed in settling the China Incident because of his character flaw. As we have seen, there is little room for anyone to make a justifiable argument. First of all, although the general perception that he was weak-minded and indecisive was correct, Konoe did not necessarily consistently prove himself to be so. For example, as Ikeda Seihin pointed out, in Konoe's third cabinet, particularly in dealing with the U.S.-Japanese negotiations, Konoe was far from being ineffective. Instead he was considerably persistent and compelling.[4] Although the negotiations failed, it was not because of Konoe's character flaw but because of the insoluble preconditions existing between the United States and Japan that made negotiations destined to fail from the outset. Moreover, one should note that, from the Manchurian Incident to the establishment of Konoe's first cabinet, there were six Prime Ministers. Unlike Konoe, some of them, such as Inukai Tsuyoshi or Hirota Koiki, were very experienced politicians and individuals with strength and decisiveness. Yet all failed in dealing with the China issues, indicating that Japan's involvement in China and the subsequent events were far too complex and dynamic for the mere nature of one individual's character to play any decisive role.

With regard to the right-wing ideology, one may argue that such ideology was one of the major factors that drove Japan down the path of aggression. Then it might be correct to say that Konoe, who wrote such an anti–Anglo-Saxon article as "Reject the Anglo-American–Centered Peace," had to carry some blame for fomenting such right-wing nationalist ideology. This is a weak argument also. Although it may have been a contributing factor, one has to admit that to argue that one article, no matter how sensational or provocative, could have a decisive effect in leading to the rise of right-wing nationalism is sheer nonsense. Moreover, ideology is one important element to generate nationalism but cannot be a "causing" factor for the rise of nationalism. What triggered it is something more tangible. Secondly, although Konoe shared the beliefs of the right-wing nationalists, one has to note, as discussed in Chapter 2, that Konoe as a right-wing nationalist belonged to the Kodo-ha, believing that the imminent threat Japan faced was from the north, the Communist intrusion. Accordingly, he opposed the military entanglement with China and the campaign for moving southward. Unfortunately, with the debacle of the Kodo-ha after the February Twenty-six Incident, Tosei-ha dominated the military, rendering the southward expansion and the subsequent military confrontation with the United States inevitable. It was the beginning of Konoe's long struggle against the Tosei-ha–controlled army, which Konoe was never able to put under his command.

It is undeniable that Konoe believed that the world was unequally structured. Such belief drove him to write the sensational and provocative article "Reject the Anglo-American–Centered Peace." Konoe never wavered from this belief. One may argue that such a firm belief of Konoe was one of the major factors leading to all the ensuing disasters. That argument, however, is also unconvincing. Konoe was considered a man of thought and lofty goals and never hesitated to express them, but when it came to how to achieve them, he was realistic and rational.

For example, Konoe rightly or wrongly had a firm belief that Japan's involvement in China was justifiable, and such involvement was a necessary step in achieving his goal of creating a truly fair and equal world structure. As is clear from his tenacious effort to solve the China Incident, Konoe understood, however, that to make China come along with Japan in creating a new world structure at gunpoint was countereffective. It was physically unfeasible and politically unwise. Thus, Konoe was against military expansion in China. To Konoe, the China Incident and the following military escalation was a war at the wrong place, at the wrong time, and against the wrong enemy.

It is not clear how Konoe wanted to achieve the establishment of the new world structure. Before he was able to have sufficient time to figure it out, surrounding circumstances brought him onto center stage despite his reluctance.

It has been sixty years since Konoe's death. Although peace and stability have replaced the devastation and tragedy of the war, the right and fair judgment that Konoe desired and believed would come has not yet come, still giving an opportunity for historians to write accounts on Konoe. The most recent one is *Konoe Fumimaro and Roosevelt*, by Nakagawa Yatsuhiro.[5] This is an unorthodox and extremely distorted account, portraying Konoe as a person with an almost completely different character from the one commonly accepted. Nakagawa argues that Konoe was not weak-minded but an extremely shrewd and calculating individual. Most astonishingly, Nakagawa claims that Konoe was a Communist as he deliberately led Japan to its southward expansion in order to destroy the Anglo-Saxon–oriented world structure and to establish a new order under Communist ideology. While it is encouraging to see that scholars eagerly continue to write on Konoe, seeing such a distorted account as that of Nakagawa, one cannot help but wonder when the conclusion to Konoe's tragedy will finally come.

Notes

INTRODUCTION

1. Mikiso Hane, *Modern Japan: A Historical Survey* (Boulder, Colo.: Westview Press, 1992), 198.

2. *Ibid.*

3. This great earthquake and the following major conflagration devastated Kanto region, particularly Tokyo, Kanagawa, and Chiba areas. The fire destroyed 120,000 houses and in all 450,000 houses were lost. The number of dead and missing was around 140,000. The economic and social impact of this earthquake was immeasurable. With the enormous frustration and confusion that came from the government's inability to deal with the situation, it became one of the major factors in the decline of party politics and the rise of militarism and right-wing nationalism. See Takayanagi Mitsukazu and Takeuchi Rizo, eds., *The Dictionary of Japanese History* (Tokyo: Kadokawa Shoten, 1966), 217.

4. A Genro was a senior politician who advised the Emperor and had a great influence on critical issues of governing. Prince Saionji was the last Genro.

5. As detailed in Chapter 4, Yabe Teiji as a professor of political science at Tokyo Imperial University and also as Konoe's personal acquaintance was directly involved in Konoe's endeavor to establish Taisei Yokusankai (the National Service Association). Such a personal relationship and his direct involvement in Konoe's governing as a prominent scholar made Yabe one of the most authoritative figures in the postwar writing on Konoe Fumimaro. Yabe's volume, *Konoe Fumimaro*, and also his diary are indispensable sources for anyone who wishes to understand Konoe Fumimaro as an individual and as a public servant.

6. This diary was published under the title *Prince Saionji and Political Situation* in 1951.

CHAPTER 1

1. See Konoe's family tree in Yabe Teiji, *Konoe Fumimaro* (Tokyo: Jiji Tsushinsha, 1958), 12.

2. Iwabuchi Tatsuo, "Prince Fumimaro Konoe," *Contemporary Japan* (December 1936), 372–3.

3. *Ibid.*, 373.

4. Yabe Teiji, *Konoe Fumimaro*, 19.

5. Konoe Fumimaro, *Seidanroku* (Tokyo: Chikura Shobo, 1936), 32.

6. *Ibid.*, 2.

7. Konoe Fumimaro, "Waga Henreki Jidai (Period of My Journey)," *Bungei Shunju* (September 1933), 193.

8. *Ibid.*, 193–4.

9. Oka Yoshitake, *Konoe Fumimaro: A Political Biography* (New York: Madison Books, 1992), 9.

10. Yabe Teiji, *Konoe Fumimaro*, 24–5.

11. Konoe Fumimaro, *Seidanroku*, 8–9.

12. Konoe Fumimaro, "Eibeihoni no Heiwashugi o Haisu" ("Reject the Anglo-American-Centered Peace"), in Konoe Fumimaro, *Seidanroku*, 231–41.

13. Yabe Teiji points out that, without the ideological background of this essay, it is difficult to understand Konoe's response to the theory of "International New Deal" by Colonel House, his use of the idea of "international justice and socialism" as an essence of his guidance in his first cabinet, his supportive thinking about the Manchurian Incident, his decision to have the Tripartite Pact, and his tragic death after Japan's surrender. See Yabe Teiji, *Konoe Fumimaro*, 31.

14. Konoe Fumimaro, *Seidanroku*, 233.

15. Yabe Teiji, *Konoe Fumimaro*, 31.

16. Konoe Fumimaro, *Seidanroku*, 10–11.

17. Konoe Fumimaro, *Seidanroku*, 252.

18. *Ibid.*

19. *Ibid.*, 253.

20. *Ibid.*

21. According to Konoe, this was particularly prominent in the case of how the Peace Conference was set up, as seen in the case of English violation of the principle of "One Nation One Vote." The principle was explicitly prescribed in the text of rules for the League of Nations. Yet England managed to have six votes by having each of its colonies as an independent nation at the conference. Another case is that the League's acceptance of the demand of the United States not to allow the League of Nations to interfere with the Monroe Doctrine and the rejection of Japan's submission of the bill for racial equality. To Konoe, this was absurd because, in terms of reasonability, racial equality had far more merit than the Monroe Doctrine. Konoe interpreted this absurdity as follows: "The acceptance of the Monroe Doctrine came because it was demanded by a mighty power, the United States. On the other hand, the rejection of racial equality came because it was submitted by a diminutive power, Japan." See Konoe Fumimaro, *Seidanroku*, 98.

22. Konoe Fumimaro, *Seidanroku*, 104.

23. Oka Yoshitake, *Konoe Fumimaro: A Political Biography*, 17–18.

24. Konoe Fumimaro, "Attitude Japanese House of Peers Should Take," in Konoe Fumimaro, *Seidanroku*, 151–69.

25. Yabe Teiji, *Konoe Fumimaro*, 36–7.

26. Right after Tokugawa Iesato succeeded Konoe's father, Atsumaro, in December 1903, he visited the ailing Atsumaro. Konoe happened to be there. Recalling this meeting with Tokugawa, Konoe thought who could have really imagined then that Konoe was going to succeed him three decades later. See Konoe Fumimaro, "Waga Henreki Jidai," 2.

CHAPTER 2

1. Namba Taisuke, the son of a member of the Diet, angered by the murder of his fellow anarchist Osugi Sakae, attempted to assassinate the regent on December 27, 1923. This incident further intensified an ideological crisis and brought down the Yamamoto Gonnohiyoe cabinet. Then, shortly before the passage of the bill of universal suffrage in March 1925 under the Kato Komei cabinet, the Peace Preservation Law was enforced in order to deal with the problem. See Mikiso Hane, *Modern Japan: A Historical Survey*, 232–4.

2. *Ibid.*, 243.

3. According to Ugaki, there was no such thing as changing one's mind; he never supported the coup attempt from the beginning. Ugaki remembered making some sympathetic and partisan remark to the right wing. To Ugaki, what happened was that the radicals misunderstood this remark. See Ugaki Kazushige, *Ugaki Diary* (Tokyo: Asahi Shinbunsha, 1954), 153–9.

4. Yabe Teiji, *Konoe Fumimoro*, 42

5. Shidehara was well known for his moderate and cooperative style of diplomacy, known as Shidehara Diplomacy. He particularly emphasized the importance of keeping on good terms with the British and the United States in the Sino-Japanese relationship. By the time of the Manchurian Incident, however, his style of diplomacy shared by pro–Western politicians such as Saionji was becoming increasingly outmoded in the eye of the right-wing nationalists in the political and social atmosphere of contemporary Japan.

6. This Manchurian Incident, leading to Japan's international isolation, turned out to be a prelude to the showdown between Japan and the United States and Japan's devastating defeat. As some historians call it, this was the beginning of the Fifteen Years' War from 1931 to 1945.

7. While the investigation of the Manchurian Incident led by the Earl of Lytton was going on, U.S. Secretary of State under Herbert Hoover, Henry Stimson, made the non-recognition statement, the so-called "Stimson Doctrine." In his statement, he declared that the United States would not recognize any encroachments on U.S. rights, the principle of the Open Door, or territorial integrity of China by force in violation of the Kellogg-Briand Pact. Nonetheless, the effect of the Stimson Doctrine on Japan's behavior was almost none. Disregarding the doctrine, Japan continued its aggression. Also despite these Western condemnations of Japan's action in Manchuria and Japan's defiance, overall response of the Western powers toward Japan's aggression remained rather conciliatory. See Jerald A. Combs, *The History of American Foreign Policy* (New York: Alfred A. Knopf, 1986), 260–1.

8. Konoe Fumimaro, *Seidanroku*, 242–55.

9. Such support from these people, however, often came along with dubious motivations such as the utilization of Konoe's high noble court status or his close relationship with Saionji for political gains or the enhancement of their causes.

10. Hashimoto, a leading jingoist, said after the Manchurian Incident, "We are like

a great crowd of people packed into a small and narrow room." According to him, there were three ways to solve the population problem: emigration, more trade in the world market, and territorial expansion. Hashimoto argued that the first two options were blocked by other powers, and so the only choice Japan had was expansion. He added that this expansion by Japan not only helped Japan to develop the undeveloped resources but also would be beneficiary to humankind. See Mikiso Hane, *Modern Japan: A Historical Survey*, 246–7.

11. Yabe Teiji, *Konoe Fumimaro*, 45.

12. Mikiso Hane, *Modern Japan: A Historical Survey*, 258.

13. When Konoe said "securing the Seiyukai cabinet," he perhaps had Mori Kaku in mind. In his article, "Genro, Jushin to Yo," Konoe writes that among party politicians, Mori Kaku was the only politician who correctly and earlier than anyone else predicted the stormy era of the 1930s. See Konoe Fumimaro, "Genro, Jushin to Yo," *Kaizo* (December 1949), 33.

14. Konoe Fumimaro, *Ushinawareshi Seiji: Konoe Fumimaro ko no shuki* (Lost Politics: Writings of Konoe Fumimaro) (Tokyo: Asahi Shinbunsha, 1946), 1–2.

15. *Ibid.*, 3.

16. Konoe Fumimaro, "Genro, Jushin to Yo," 34.

17. *Ibid.*

18. *Ibid.*

19. This incident was plotted by the political party members such as Suzuki Zenichi, Amano Tatsuo, and Army Reserve Lieutenant Colonel Yasuda Jonosuke. With mobilization of 3,600 people on July 11, this plan was to make the cabinet fall by attacking the Prime Minister and the elder statesmen and bombing Tokyo from the air, then establishing a "restoration government" that was to be more respectful to the Emperor. The incident was aborted because of the arrest of the plotters on the day before the plan's execution. See Yabe Teiji, *Konoe Fumimaro*, 48.

20. A Colonel Hashimoto Kingoro and a chairman of the seamen's association, Hamada Kunitaro, plotted this incident. In order to have national reform, they planned to cause a second Mukden incident in northern Manchuria and simultaneously disturb the military transportation with a general strike of the seamen's association. Their immediate aim was to bring down the existing cabinet by submitting three important demands to the gov-

ernment in order to set up a new one for national reform. See *ibid.*, 48.

21. This incident was plotted by army officers such as Muranaka Koji and Isobe Asaichi and a civilian, Nishida Etsu. Mobilizing military troops, they aimed to assassinate elder statesmen to establish a military government. Among their targets were Saito Makoto, Makino Nobuaki, Okada Keisuke, Suzuki Kantaro, Saionji Kinmochi, Takahashi Korekiyo, Kiyouira Keigo, Izawa Takio, and Shidehara Kijuro. See *ibid.*, 49.

22. This incident was a culmination of the conflict between two military factions: Tosei and Kodo. A fanatical Kodo faction officer, Aizawa Saburo, believed that the removal of the influential leaders of the Kodo faction, Araki Sadao and Mazaki Jinzaburo, from their positions was due to a conspiracy by Tosei faction general Hayashi Senjuro and a chief of the military affairs bureau, Nagata Tetsuzan. He took the matter into his own hands. On August 12, 1935, he walked into Nagata's office and killed Nagata with a sword. See Mikiso Hane, *Modern Japan: A Historical Survey*, 263.

23. Konoe Fumimaro, "Hobei Insho Ki" ("Impression of the U.S. Visit"), *Chuo Koron* (September 1934), 327–35.

24. Yabe Teiji, *Konoe Fumimaro*, 68–9.

25. Konoe Fumimaro, "Hobei Insho Ki," 331.

26. Hosoya Chihiro, "Nichibei Gaiko ni okeru Fushin no Tanjo" ("Birth of Distrust in U.S.-Japan Diplomacy"), *Chuo Koron* (November 1978), 76.

27. *Ibid.*, 78.

28. Choshu is one of the clans (Han) that existed before Meiji Restoration. The term clan was abolished after the Restoration and replaced with prefecture.

29. The Yamato spirit, called "Yamato Dmashii" in Japanese, is often seen as one of main characteristics of the Japanese.

30. Mikiso Hane, *Modern Japan: A Historical Survey*, 264.

31. It is difficult to justify Kita's death sentence. He did not have any direct involvement in the rebellion. The only responsibility he had was that the rebel officers were greatly influenced by his book, *A Plan for the Reorganization of Japan*. Along with Okawa Shumei, Kita was one of the most influential ideologists and right-wing nationalists. He devoted himself to the cause of establishing "Japanese Fascism."

32. Konoe Fumimaro, *Ushinawareshi Seiji*, 4.

33. *Ibid.*, 7.

34. *Ibid.*

35. Tatsuo Iwabuchi, "Prince Fumimaro Konoe," 367.

36. Konoe Fumimaro, *Ushinawareshi Seiji*, 8.

37. It is ironic to see that Saionji made a similar argument in 1918 when he was recommended to form a cabinet by Prince Yamagata, who strongly opposed the formation of a party government. Believing that by inducing Saionji to form a cabinet, he could prevent the formation of a party government, Yamagata said to Saionji, "You are on friendly terms with the parties. We are certain to support you. In short, you are surrounded by friends and without enemies." Saionji replied, however, "Friendship on all sides may easily mean enmity on all sides. The time is ripe for establishing a party government, and it is not wise to oppose it on the ground that the party movement is not enjoying amity all around." See Tatsuo Iwabuchi, "Prince Fumimaro Konoe," 367.

38. Yabe Teiji, *Konoe Fumimaro*, 76–7.

39. Konoe Fumimaro, *Ushinawareshi Seiji*, 8.

40. Mikiso Hane, *Modern Japan: A Historical Survey*, 267.

41. *Asahi Shinbun*, January 22, 1937, H2.

42. Mikiso Hane, *Modern Japan: A Historical Survey*, 268.

43. Ugaki Kazushige, *Ugaki Diary*, 278–9.

44. Yabe Teiji, *Konoe Fumimaro*, 83.

45. Harada Kumao, *Prince Saionji and Political Situation* (Tokyo: Iwanami Shoten, Vol. 5, 1951), 320–1.

46. Kido Koichi, *Kido Koichi Diary* (Tokyo: Tokyo University Press, Vol. 1, 1966), 565–6.

47. Harada Kumao, *Prince Saionji and Political Situation*, Vol. 5, 322–3.

CHAPTER 3

1. See Chapter 2, page 37.

2. Harada Kumao, *Prince Saionji and Political Situation*, Vol. 6, 4.

3. Yamaura Kanichi, "Konoe Naikaku wa Kakushite Umareta" ("This Is How the Konoe Cabinet Was Formed"), *Kaizo* (July 1937), 90.

4. Harada Kumao, *Prince Saionji and Political Situation*, Vol. 6, 9.

5. Okada Takeo, *Konoe Fumimaro: Emperor, Military, and Nation* (Tokyo: Shunjusha, 1959), 70.

6. Konoe Fumimaro, *Ushinawareshi Seiji*, 9.

7. Kido Koichi, *Kido Koichi Diary* (Tokyo: Tokyo University Press, Vol. 1, 1966), 565–66.

8. Harada Kumao, *Prince Saionji and Political Situation*, Vol. 6, 81.

9. *Ibid.*, 86.

10. Konoe Fumimaro, *Ushinawareshi Seiji*, 10.

11. *Ibid.*

12. Mikiso Hane, *Modern Japan: A Historical Survey*, 275–6.

13. Konoe Fumimaro, *Ushinawareshi Seiji*, 11.

14. *Ibid.*

15. Mikiso Hane, *Modern Japan: A Historical Survey*, 276.

16. Harada Kumao, *Prince Saionji and Political Situation*, Vol. 6, 30.

17. Mikiso Hane, *Modern Japan: A Historical Survey*, 277.

18. *Ibid.*

19. This idea of sending Miyazaki to China originally came from Ting Shao-jeng. Ting suggested that Konoe send Akiyama Sadao and Miyazaki Ryusuke when Chiang Kai-shek's definite plan was rejected because of the strong opposition from the army. See Konoe Fumimaro, *Ushinawareshi Seiji*, 12–13.

20. *Ibid.*, 15.

21. *Ibid.*

22. Yabe Teiji, *Koneo Fumimaro*, 91.

23. *Ibid.*

24. Konoe Fumimaro, *Ushinawareshi Seiji*, 15.

25. Oka Yoshitake, *Konoe Fumimaro: A Political Biography*, 66.

26. Konoe Fumimaro, *Ushinawareshi Seij*, 16.

27. Oka Yoshitake, *Konoe Fumimaro: A Political Biography*, 71.

28. Okada Takeo, *Konoe Fumimaro: Emperor, Military, and Nation*, 77.

29. *Ibid.*

30. *Ibid.*, 77–8.

31. Harada Kumao, *Prince Saionji and Political Situation*, Vol. 6, 143.

32. *Ibid.*

33. Kido Koichi, *Kido Koichi Diary*, Vol. 6, 603.

34. Harada Kumao, *Prince Saionji and Political Situation*, Vol. 6, 145.

35. *Ibid.*

36. Okada Takeo, *Konoe Fumimaro: Emperor, Military, and Nation*, 78.

37. *Ibid.*, 80.

38. Harada Kumao, *Prince Saionji and Political Situation*, Vol. 6, 208–19.

39. *Ibid.*, 193.

40. Okada Takeo, *Konoe Fumimaro: Emperor, Military, and Nation*, 81–2.

41. The Tokyo First Publishing Co., ed., *The Collection of the Speeches of Konoe Fumimaro* (Tokyo: The Tokyo First Publishing Co., 1938), 81.

42. Konoe Fumimaro, *Ushinawareshi Seiji*, 17–18.

43. Okada Takeo, *Konoe Fumimaro: Emperor, Military, and Nation*, 78–80.

44. John Hunter Boyle, *China and Japan at War, 1937–1945: The Politics of Collaboration* (Stanford, Calif.: Stanford University Press, 1972), 42–3.

45. Nakamura Takafusa and Hara Akira, eds., "The Introduction of Materials," *National Mobilization I — The Materials of Modern History* (Tokyo: Misuzu Shobo, Vol. 43, 1970), xv–xvi.

46. Togawa Isamu, *Konoe Fumimaro to Jushintachi (Konoe Fumimaro and Ministers)* (Tokyo: Kodansha, 1982), 257–8.

47. *Ibid.*, 258–9.

48. Yabe Teiji, *Konoe Fumimaro*, 96.

49. Togawa Isamu, *Konoe Fumimaro to Jushintachi*, 265–6.

50. *Ibid.*, 267.

51. Harada Kumao, *Prince Saionji and Political Situation*, Vol. 6, 250.

52. *Ibid.*, 276.

53. *Ibid.*, 283–4.

54. *Ibid.*, 271.

55. Togawa Isamu, *Konoe Fumimaro to Jushintachi*, 272.

56. Harada Kumao, *Prince Saionji and Political Situation*, Vol. 6, 328.

57. Konoe Fumimaro, *Ushinawareshi Seiji*, 22.

58. Yabe Teiji, *Konoe Fumimaro*, 102.

59. Ugaki Kazushige, *Ugaki Diary*, 311–5.

60. Kaga himself, realizing he was not capable enough to serve as Finance Minister, wanted to have Ikeda as his successor. Konoe also wanted to appoint Ikeda. Ikeda agreed to serve on the condition that Ikeda's close friend, Ugaki, would be in the cabinet. See Okada Takeo, *Konoe Fumimaro: Emperor, Military, and Nation*, 86.

61. Ugaki Kazushige, *Ugaki Diary*, 326–7.

62. *Ibid.*, 327.

63. *Ibid.*

64. *Ibid.*, 329.

65. *Ibid.*, 330.

66. *Ibid.*

67. *Ibid.*, 334–5.

68. *Ibid.*, 334.

69. *Ibid.*, 333–4.

70. The decision to set up the Five Minister Conference was made at the cabinet meeting on June 10, 1938. It was clearly designed to promote a unification in national policy making.

71. Yabe Teiji, *Konoe Fumimaro*, 105.

72. *Ibid.*, 104–5.

73. Harada Kumao, *Prince Saionji and Political Situation*, Vol. 7, 125.

74. *Ibid.*, 134.

75. Kido Koichi, *Kido Koichi Diary*, Vol. 2, 674.

76. Yabe Teiji, *Konoe Fumimaro*, 106.

77. Konoe Fumimaro, *Ushinawareshi Seiji*, 21.

78. A political critic, Togawa Isamu, writes that in order to provoke Japan, the Soviet Union sent these two telegrams with the expectation that Japan would decipher them and the army was completely taken in. See Togawa Isamu, *Konoe Fumimaro to Jushintachi*, 288.

79. *Ibid.*, 290.

80. Harada Kumao, *Prince Saionji and Political Situation*, Vol. 7, 51.

81. *Ibid.*, 50.

82. Yabe Teiji, *Konoe Fumimaro*, 109–10.

83. Togawa Isamu, *Konoe Fumimaro to Jushintachi*, 284–5.

84. *Ibid.*, 285.

85. Harada Kumao, *Prince Saionji and Political Situation*, Vol. 7, 233.

86. *Ibid.*

87. Ibid, 241.

88. Konoe Fumimaro, *Ushinawareshi Seiji*, 19–20.

89. *Ibid.*, 23.

90. Harada Kumao, *Prince Saionji and Political Situation*, Vol. 7, 238–3.

91. Togawa Isamu, *Konoe Fumimaro to Jushintachi*, 294.

92. Konoe Fumimaro, *The Collection of the Speeches of Konoe Fumimaro*, 143–44.

93. Harada Kumao, *Prince Saionji and Political Situation*, Vol. 7, 250.

CHAPTER 4

1. Harada Kumao, *Prince Saionji and Political Situation*, Vol. 7, 260.

2. *Ibid.*, 258.

3. Four assassins sent by the head of the secret police of the Nationalist government, Tai Ryu, broke into Wang's residence in Hanoi

on March 20, 1939. Assuming that Wang and his wife were in bed, they sneaked into the bedroom and fired shots at the person in the bed. It turned out to be, however, Wang's secretary, So Chu-mei. Anticipating an assassination attempt, Wang took the precaution of swapping bedrooms from time to time with So. It was pure luck that saved Wang's life. See Togawa Isamu, *Konoe Fumimaro and Jushin-tachi*, 305.

4. *Ibid.*, 306.

5. Yabe Teiji, *Konoe Fumimaro*, 117.

6. *Ibid.*, 152–3.

7. Harada Kumao, *Prince Saionji and Political Situation*, Vol. 7, 270–71.

8. *Ibid.*, 327.

9. *Ibid.*, 344.

10. *Ibid.*

11. *Ibid.*, 345.

12. John Hunter Boyle, *China and Japan at War*, 257.

13. Yabe Teiji, *Konoe Fumimaro*, 118.

14. Harada Kumao, *Prince Saionji and Political Situation*, Vol. 8, 155.

15. With regard to the formation of the Yonai cabinet, Konoe was not quite satisfied. He was quoted as saying, "The selection of Yonai has already been decided between Yuasa and Okada, and there is Harada's maneuvering behind the formation of the Yonai cabinet." See Yabe Teiji, *Konoe Fumimaro*, 119.

16. The treaty was signed on February 11, 1911. Under this treaty, Japan was able to fully restore its tariff autonomy, completing Japan's long effort to abolish the unequal treaty, which was imposed on Japan shortly after Japan was forced to end its isolation in the mid-nineteenth century.

17. Konoe Fumimaro, *Ushinawareshi Seiji*, 25.

18. *Ibid.*, 26.

19. Harada Kumao, *Prince Saionji and Political Situation*, Vol. 8, 270.

20. Akagi Suruki, *Konoe Shintaisei to Taisei Yokusankai (Konoe's New Structure and the National Service Association)* (Tokyo: Iwanami Shoten, 1984), 127.

21. Bakufu (the shogunate) usually refers to warrior-controlled political governing, which lasted from the beginning of the Era of Kamakura (1190) to the end of the Edo Period (1868). Under this system, the Emperor was supposedly still supreme, but in reality he was a figurehead.

22. Yabe Teiji, "Konoe Fumimaro and New Structure," *Chuo Koron* (January 1965), 433.

23. *Ibid.*

24. *Ibid.*

25. Harada Kumao, *Prince Saionji and Political Situation*, Vol. 8, 289.

26. *Ibid.*, 290.

27. *Ibid.*, 291.

28. Kido Koichi, *Kido Koichi Diary*, Vol. 2, 807.

29. *Ibid.*

30. Harada Kumao, *Prince Saionji and Political Situation*, Vol. 8, 293.

31. Yabe Teiji, *Konoe Fumimaro*, 135–6.

32. Yabe Teiji. "Konoe Fumimaro and New Structure," 434 .

33. *Ibid.*, 435.

34. *Ibid.*

35. Konoe Fumimaro, *Usinawarshi Seiji*, 26–7.

36. *Ibid.*

37. Konoe Fumimaro, *Ushinawareshi Seiji*, 30.

38. Toyoda Minoru, *Matsuoka Yosuke: Unmei no Gaikokan (Matsuoka Yosuke: A Destined Diplomat)* (Tokyo: Shinchosha, 1983), 325–6.

39. Konoe Fumimaro, *Ushinawareshi Seiji*, 30.

40. Toyoda Minoru, *Matsuoka Yosuke: Unmei no Gaikokan*, 349.

41. *Ibid.*, 350.

42. Harada said to Konoe, "As you know, I absolutely oppose the treaty with Germany. Although it has been said that the treaty was for the prevention of the war against the United States, in my opinion, it is rather opposite. It would rather increase chances of war with the United States. The letter from an officer in finance, Nishiyama Tsutomu, to the United States points out, 'The United States anticipates that the operation of a German landing in England would fail. If that happens, the British would be increasingly formidable. Meanwhile, a presidential election in the United States is approaching. There should not be any doubt that the United States will enter the war. Under this circumstance, it is very shameful that the Japanese press is acting like a German propaganda machine.' Accordingly I am convinced that the entry of the United States into the war is definite." See Harada Kumao, *Prince Saionji and Political Situation*, Vol. 8, 349–50.

43. *Ibid.*, 346–7.

44. *Ibid.*, 347.

45. *Ibid.*, 348.

46. *Ibid.*, 351.

47. Toyoda Minoru, *Matsuoka Yosuke: Unmei no Gaikokan*, 360.

48. Konoe Fumimaro, *Ushinawareshi Seiji*, 46.

49. *Ibid.*, 46–7.

50. *Ibid.*, 47.

51. *Ibid.*

52. *Ibid.*, 47–8.

53. *Ibid.*, 32–3.

54. *Ibid.*, 35.

55. *Ibid.*, 36.

56. In his testimony at the Far East Trial, Kido Koichi stated, "I was strongly concerned that an alliance between Germany and Japan would surely cause war between the United States and Japan. From this point of view, I gave a warning to Prince Konoe and Foreign Minister Matsuoka. To my surprise, they told me that the purpose of the alliance between Germany and Japan was to prevent the United States from coming into the war, and moreover, if Japan, without an alliance with Germany, was isolated in the Pacific, Japan could be attacked anytime by the United States. No matter what they said, however, to oppose my concern, I could not help but worry that an alliance between Japan and Germany would antagonize the United States against Japan and in the end Japan would have to fight against the United States and the British. On a few occasions, I expressed my opposition to the alliance to Konoe and Matsuoka. I was not, however, able to stop the government from ratifying the alliance." See Okada Takeo, *Konoe Fumimaro: Emperor, Military, and Nation*, 127–8.

57. Konoe Fumimaro, *Ushinawareshi Seiji*, 34.

58. *Ibid.*, 43–4.

59. Yabe Teiji, *Konoe Fumimaro*, 151–2.

60. Joseph C. Grew, *Turbulent Era: A Diplomatic Record of Forty Years, 1904–1945* (Cambridge, Mass.: The Riverside Press, 1952), 1223.

61. U.S. Congress, *Pearl Harbor Attack, Hearings before the Joint Committee on the Investigation of the Pearl Harbor Attack, 79th Congress, 1st Session* (Washington: Government Printing Office, 1946), 638.

62. Cordell Hull, *The Memoirs of Cordell Hull* (New York: The Macmillan Company, 1948), 909.

63. Oka Yoshitake, *Konoe Fumimaro: A Political Biography*, 136–7.

64. Iwanamikoza, History of Japan: Modern (Tokyo: Iwanamishoten, Vol. 23, 1963), 138.

65. Konoe Fumimaro, *Ushinawareshi Seiji*, 38.

66. As Toyoda Minoru points out, although Matsuoka's trip to Europe was officially to conclude the Four Power Treaty, Matsuoka had a hidden purpose: to conclude a neutrality treaty with the Soviet Union. Toyoda argues that there were only few people who were able to detect Matsuoka's concealed mission. See Toyoda Minoru, *Matsuoka Yosuke: Unmei no Gaikokan*, 393.

67. Konoe Fumimaro, *Ushinawareshi Seiji*, 39.

68. *Ibid.*, 40.

69. *Ibid.*

70. *Ibid.*, 41.

CHAPTER 5

1. Konoe Fumimaro, "Saigono Gozen-kaigi" ("The Last Imperial Conference"), *Jiyu Kokumin* (Tokyo: Jikyoku Geposha, Vol. 19, 1946), 6.

2. *Ibid.*

3. Cordell Hull, The Memoirs of Cordell Hull, Vol. 2, 995.

4. Okada Takeo, *Konoe Fumimaro: Emperor, Military, and Nation*, 177.

5. Konoe Fumimaro, "Saigono Gozen-kaigi," 11.

6. *Ibid.*

7. *Ibid.*

8. *Ibid.*, 12.

9. It is possible that some jealousy was involved in Konoe's decision not to ride with Matsuoka. See Okada Takeo, *Konoe Fumimaro: Emperor, Military, and Nation*, 178.

10. Okada Takeo states the following: "According to Tomita Kenji, when it became clear that the Pacific war was ending with the defeat of Japan, Konoe repeatedly regretted that he did not ride with Matsuoka to explain the situation to him precisely and gain his understanding. It is doubtful, however, that the U.S.-Japanese negotiations would have ended in the way Konoe hoped even if Konoe had ridden with Matsuoka and placated him. Nonetheless, it is absolutely true that Matsuoka's opposition toward the U.S.-Japan negotiations was one of the major factors in the failure of the negotiations. Then, it was fateful that Konoe and Matsuoka missed each other during the one-hour trip from Tachikawa Airport to the city of Tokyo." See Okada Takeo, *Konoe Fumimaro: Emperor, Military, and Nation*, 179.

11. Ohashi Tadaichi, *The Cause of the Pacific War: Truth of Matsuoka Diplomacy* (Tokyo: Kaname Shobo, 1952), 119.

12. Matsuoka was referring to the U.S.-

Japan Joint Declaration of November 1917 by Japan's special envoy, Ishi Kikujiro, and U.S. Secretary of State Robert Lansing. In the declaration, both nations recognized Japan's special interests in China, China's territorial sovereignty, the Open Door policy, and equal opportunity for commerce and industry in China.

13. Konoe Fumimaro, "Saigono Gozen-kaigi," 12–13.

14. *Ibid.*, 13.

15. Regarding why Matsuoka's amended draft was accepted without much objection, *The Road to Pacific War: The Outbreak of Japanese-American War* states the following: "The way Iwakura, Nomura, and the Ministry of the Army interpreted the Japanese-American Draft Understanding is unnatural in the context of the draft. On the other hand, Matsuoka's interpretation is more natural. Also, since Konoe and the Ministries of the Army and the Navy gave consent to the Tripartite Pact, they did not have much leverage nor were they in strong position to oppose Matsuoka's interpretation." See the Academy of Japan International Politics-Study Group on the Causes of the Pacific War, ed., *The Road to the Pacific War: The Outbreak of Japanese-American War* (Tokyo: Asahi Shinbunsha, Vol. 7, 1963), 189.

16. Konoe Fumimaro, "Saigono Gozen-kaigi," 13–14.

17. Konoe Fumimaro, *Ushinawareshi Seiji*, 69.

18. Yabe Teiji, *Konoe Fumimaro*, 161.

19. Konoe Fumimaro, "Saigono Gozen-kaigi," 14.

20. Cordell Hull, *The Memoirs of Cordell Hull*, 1000.

21. *Ibid.*, 1001.

22. Konoe Fumimaro, "Saigono Gozen-kaigi," 17–18.

23. *Ibid.*, 18.

24. *Ibid.*, 20.

25. *Ibid.*

26. Kido Koichi, *Kido Koichi Diary*, Vol. 2, 883.

27. *Ibid.*

28. Tsunoda Jun and Fukuda Shigeo, *The Road to the Pacific War: The Outbreak of the Japanese-American War* (Tokyo: Asahi Shinbunsha, Vol. 7, 1963), 197.

29. Konoe Fumimaro, "Saigono Gozen-kaigi," 23.

30. Okada Takeo argues that Konoe's thinking — avoiding the outbreak of war against the United States with the U.S.-Japanese negotiations while deciding to move southward to calm the military — is naive. At the same time, however, Okada points out that Konoe had no other choice. Unless he had made up his mind to move either northward or southward, he could have been either killed or forced to resign by the military. See Okada Tekeo, *Konoe Fumimaro: Emperor, Military, and Nation*, 185–6.

31. Konoe Fumimaro, "Saigono Gozen-kaigi," 24–5.

32. *Ibid.*, 25.

33. Joseph C. Grew, *Ten Years in Japan* (New York: Simon and Schuster, 1944), 399–400.

34. *Ibid.*, 400.

35. Konoe Fumimaro, "Saigono Gozen-kaigi," 25.

36. *Ibid.*, 26.

37. *Ibid.*, 27–8.

38. According to Konoe, Cordell Hull was shocked by the way Matsuoka interpreted his oral statement, and, afraid of misunderstanding, he took back his oral statement on July 17. See Konoe Fumimaro, "Saigono Gozenkaigi," 28.

39. *Ibid.*, 29.

40. Toyoda Minoru, *Matsuoka Yosuke: Unmei no G kokan*, 543.

41. Kido Koichi, *Kido Koichi Diary*, Vol. 2, 890.

42. Konoe Fumimaro, "Saigono Gozen-kaigi," 31.

43. *Ibid.*, 32.

44. *Ibid.*, 33–4.

45. *Ibid.*, 34–5.

46. *Ibid.*, 35.

47. Yabe Teiji, Konoe Fumimaro, 170–1.

48. *Ibid.*

49. *Ibid.*, 171.

50. Konoe Fumimaro, "Saigono Gozen-kaigi," 36.

51. Tsunoda Jun and Fukuda Shigeo, *The Road to the Pacific War: The Outbreak of the Japanese-American War*, Vol. 7, 263.

52. *Ibid.*, 263–4.

53. Konoe Fumimaro, "Saigono Gozen-kaigi," 37.

54. Cordell Hull, *The Memoirs of Cordell Hull*, 1021.

55. *Ibid.*, 1022.

56. *Ibid.*, 1022–3.

57. Konoe Fumimaro, "Saigono Gozen-kaigi," 41.

58. *Ibid.*

59. *Ibid.*, 42.

60. *Ibid.*

61. *Ibid.*
62. *Ibid.*, 43.
63. Joseph C. Grew, *Ten Years in Japan*, 426–8.
64. Konoe Fumimaro, "Saigono Gozen-kaigi," 41.
65. *Ibid.*, 45.
66. Tsunoda Jun and Fukuda Shigeo, *The Road to the Pacific War: The Outbreak of the Japanese-American War*, Vol. 7, 267.
67. *Ibid.*, 268.
68. Joseph C. Grew, *Turbulent Era: A Diplomatic Record of Forty Years, 1904–1945*, 1334.
69. Konoe Fumimaro, "Saigono Gozen-kaigi," 47.
70. *Ibid.*
71. *Ibid.*, 48.
72. *Ibid.*, 50.
73. Kiyomizu is the name of the temple located in Kyoto. It has a platform built over the very steep cliff and known as the place where people often commit suicide by jumping off from the platform.
74. Konoe Fumimaro, "Saigono Gozen-kaigi," 48–9.
75. *Ibid.*, 49.
76. *Ibid.*, 50.
77. Kido Koichi, *Kido Koichi Diary*, Vol. 2, 915.
78. Yabe Teiji, *Konoe Fumimaro*, 182.
79. Konoe Fumimaro, "Saigono Gozen-kaigi," 51.
80. Kido Koichi, *Kido Koichi Diary*, Vol. 2, 916.
81. *Ibid.*, 917.
82. Joseph C. Grew, *Ten Years in Japan*, 457.
83. *Ibid.*, 481–2. Sharing Grew's view on Konoe, Kazami Akira also made a similar remark that Konoe had no one to rely on; he was totally alone in his quest to have a successful end to the negotiation; yet he never gave in to such difficulty; it was nonsense to say that he was forced to resign because of his inability. See Yabe Teiji, *Konoe Fumimaro*, 184.
84. Konoe Fumimaro, *Ushinawareshi Seiji: Konoe Fumimaro-ko no Shuki*, 142.

CHAPTER 6

1. Yabe Teiji, *Konoe Fumimaro*, 189.
2. Nagao Kazuo, *Era of Konoe Fumimaro* (Tokyo: Koyo Publishing Inc., 1982), 204.
3. Yabe Teiji, *Konoe Fumimaro*, 471.
4. Kido Koichi, *Kido Koichi Diary*, Vol. 2, 967.
5. Yabe Teiji, *Konoe Fumimaro*, 475.
6. Kido Koichi, *Kido Koichi Diary*, Vol. 2, 1010.
7. Nagao Kazuro, *Era of Konoe Fumimaro*, 215.
8. See note 4 in Konoe Fumimaro, *Konoe Diary* (Tokyo: Kyodo Tsushinsha, 1968) 39–40.
9. Kido Koichi, *Kido Koichi Diary*, Vol. 2, 1078–1079.
10. Yabe Teiji, *Konoe Fumimaro*, 490.
11. Konoe Fumimaro, *Konoe Diary*, 10–11.
12. Yabe Teiji, *Konoe Fumimaro*, 500.
13. Konoe Fumimaro, *Konoe Diary*, 15.
14. Yabe Teiji, *Konoe Fumimaro*, 500.
15. Konoe Fumimaro, *Konoe Diary*, 36–37.
16. *Ibid.*, 48–53.
17. *Ibid.*, 51.
18. *Ibid.*, 65.
19. *Ibid.*, 73.
20. *Ibid.*, 83.
21. *Ibid.*, 105
22. Yabe Teiji, *Konoe Fumimaro*, 518.
23. *Ibid.*, 529–33.
24. *Ibid.*, 533.
25. *Ibid.*
26. Kido Koichi, *Kido Koichi Diary*, Vol. 2, 1192.
27. *Ibid.*, 1193.
28. *Ibid.*
29. *Ibid.*, 1194.
30. *Ibid.*
31. Yabe Teiji, *Konoe Fumimaro*, 542.
32. *Ibid.*, 544.
33. Kido Koichi, *Kido Koichi Diary*, Vol. 2, 1208–9.
34. Yabe Teiji, *Konoe Fumimaro*, 552.
35. *Ibid.*, 556–7.
36. The declaration says the following: "After the defeat of Germany, Japan was the only remaining major nation continuing the war. Japan rejected the demand of unconditional surrender from the United States, Great Britain, and China. Therefore, the request from Japan asking the Soviet Union to take a role as a mediator has no foundation. Under this Japanese defiance to the declaration, the Allied powers have proposed participation of the Soviet Union in the war for ending the aggression, thus promoting termination of the war, reducing war casualties, and allowing quick restoration of peace. According to the duty of the Soviet Union toward the Allied powers, the Soviet government has accepted the above proposal and joined in the Allied Declaration. The Soviet government believes that is the only means to promote peace, save

each nation from sacrifice and suffering, and prevent Japan from such danger and destruction as Germany had to go through. Accordingly, the Soviet Union declares war against Japan, effective on August 9." See Yabe Teiji, *Konoe Fumimaro*, 565–6.

37. *Ibid.*, 566.

38. Kido Koichi, *Kido Koichi Diary*, Vol. 2, 1224.

39. The Emperor was referring to the Allied powers' August 13 response to Japan's telegram indicating Japan's acceptance of the Potsdam Declaration with a condition that the declaration did not alter the sovereign power of the Emperor.

40. Yabe Teiji, *Konoe Fumimaro*, 575.

41. Mikiso Hane, *Modern Japan: A Historical Survey*, 338.

42. Yabe Teiji, *Konoe Fumimaro*, 577.

43. Kido Koichi, *Kido Koichi Diary*, Vol. 2, 1226–7.

44. Tojo survived but he was bitterly ridiculed later by the public who thought his suicide attempt was a fake to save his own life.

45. Kido Koichi, *Kido Koichi Diary*, Vol. 2, 1234.

46. Yabe Teiji, *Konoe Fumimaro*, 586–7.

47. Although speculative, it is interesting to note how much influence this meeting with Konoe had on MacArthur's decision to reverse his position on Japan's right-wing nationalism and the financial clique. At the outset of the occupation, believing that Japan's extreme view of ultranationalism combined with corporate greed of the financial clique was a key factor for driving Japan into aggression, MacArthur was determined to purge the right-wing nationalists and dismantle the financial clique in order to make sure that Japan would not repeat the same mistake. This determination of MacArthur, however, only resulted in his realization that, as Konoe pointed out, these two elements were indispensable for speedy political stabilization and economic recovery. Today Japan is considered to be one of the most stable nations politically and economically and one of the most pacifist nations on this earth. Few can dispute that, behind such successes of Japan, there were the conservative elements of right-wing nationalism and the financial clique as the economic backbone, proving the correctness of Konoe's argument in his statement to MacArthur. Although there is no proof that MacArthur was actually influenced by his meeting with Konoe in his decision to reverse his position on Japan's right-wing nationalism, it is equally difficult to prove otherwise.

48. Yabe Teiji, *Konoe Fumimaro*, 589.

49. Prince Higashikuni was replaced by Shidehara after the fall of his cabinet on October 5, due to the political conflict caused by the direct order from GHQ of the Allied powers, asking for resignation of some of the members of Higashikuni's cabinet.

50. Nishi Toshio, *Unconditional Democracy: Education and Politics in Occupied Japan, 1945–1952* (Stanford, Calif.: Hoover Institution Press, 1982), 112–13.

51. See *New York Herald Tribune*, Wednesday, Oct. 31, 1945, 30.

52. Yabe Teiji, *Konoe Fumimaro*, 593–4.

CONCLUSION

1. Goto Ryunosuke, "Konoe Fumimaro o Kataru (Talk on Konoe Fumimaro)," *Koen*, no. 137 (Dec. 15, 1968), 28–9.

2. Goto was referring to Tojo's suicide attempt when he was charged as a war criminal. Tojo survived but was bitterly ridiculed by the public, who thought Tojo's suicide attempt was a fake to save his own life.

3. Goto Ryunosuke, "Konoe Fumimaro o Kataru," 30–1.

4. See Chapter 5, page 120.

5. Nakagawa Yatsuhiro, *Konoe Fumimaro to Ruzuverto: Dai Toa Senso no Shinjitsu (Konoe Fumimaro and Roosevelt: The Truth of the Great East Asian War)* (Tokyo: PHP Kenkyujo, 1995).

Bibliography

PRIMARY SOURCES (BOOKS AND OTHER MATERIALS)

Asahi Shinbun, ed. *Kaisoroku (The Memoirs of Cordell Hull)*. Tokyo: Asahi Shinbun-sha, 1949.

_____, ed. *Showa 15-nen Asahi Nenkan (1939 Asahi Yerabook)*. Tokyo: Asahi Shinbun-sha, 1939.

_____, ed. *Showa 16-nen Asahi Nenkan (1940 Asahi Yearbook)*. Tokyo: Asahi Shinbun-sha, 1940.

_____, ed. *Showa 17-nen Asahi Nenkan (1941 Asahi Yearbook)*. Tokyo: Asahi Shinbun-sha, 1941.

_____, ed. *Showa 18-nen Asahi Nenkan (1942 Asahi Year Book*. Tokyo: Asahi Shinbun-sha, 1942.

Asahi Shinbunsha Hotie Kishadan. *Tokyo Saiban (Tokyo Trial)*. 3 Vols. Tokyo: Asahi Shinbunsha, 1962.

Association of Historical Study. *A Chronological Table of Japanese History*. Tokyo: Iwanami Shoten, 1966.

Bungei Shunju. "Konoe Fumimaro-ko Kondan Kai (Konoe Fumimaro Conference)." *Bungei Shunju* (July, 1936): 78–100.

Chiang Kai-shek. *Generalissimo Chiang Assails Konoye's Statement*. Chungking: The China Information Committee, 1939.

_____. *The War and Human Freedom: Address by Cordell Hull, Secretary of State Over the National Radio Network, July 23, 1942*. Washington D.C.: United States, Dept. of State, 1942.

Gaimusho. *Gaimusho no Hyaku-nen (One Hundred Years of Foreign Ministry)*. Tokyo: Hara Shobo, 1966.

_____. *Nihon Gaiko Nenpyo Narabi Shuyo Monjo (Chronology of Japanese Diplomacy and Primary Issues)*. Tokyo: Hara Shobo, 1969.

Grew, Joseph C. *Ten Years in Japan*. New York: Simon and Schuster, 1944.

_____. *Turbulent Era: A Diplomatic Record of Forty Years, 1904–1945*. Ed. Walker Johnson. Cambridge: The Riverside Press, 1952

Harada, Kumao. *Gaionji ko to Seikyoku (Primce Saionji and Political Situations)*. 8 Vols. Tokyo: Iwanami Shoten, 1951.

Hull, Cordell. *The Memoirs of Cordell Hull*. 2 Vols. New York: The Macmillan Company, 1948.

Kaizo. "Stama-Yamamoto Torahiko Kaidan (Stahmer-Yamamoto Torahiko Meeting)." *Kaizo* (November, 1940): 130–137.

Kido, Koichi. *Kido Koichi Kankei Bunsho (Documents Regarding Kido Koichi)*. Tokyo: University of Tokyo, 1966.

_____. *Kido Koichi Nikki (Kido Koichi Diary)*. 2 Vols. Tokyo: University of Tokyo Press, 1966.

Konoe, Fumimaro. "Genro, Jushin to Yo (Genro, An Elder Statesman and I)." *Kaizo* (December, 1949): 32–36.

_____. "Hobei Insho Ki (Impression of the U.S. Visit)." *Chuo Koron* (September, 1934): 327–335.

_____. *Jinchu Hokoku no Seishin: Konoe Fumimaro-ko Enzetsu Kunwashu (Spirit of Being Outspoken: The Collection of Prince Konoe's Speeches)*. Tokyo: Daiichi Shuppansha, 1938.

_____. *Join to Seiji (The Upper House and Politics)*. Tokyo: Nipon Tokusho Kyokai, 1924.

_____. "Kokushi ni Arawaretaru Nippon Seishin (Japanese Spirit Seen in the National History)." *Nippon Seishin Koza, XII*. Edited by Sato Yoshisuke (Tokyo: Shinchosha, 1935): 1–14.

_____. *Konoe Fumimaro kao no Shuki Heiwa e no Doryoku. Struggle for Peace: Writings of Konoe Fumimaro*. Tokyo: Japan Telephone and Telegram, 1946.

_____. "Konoe Fumimaro-ko Shuki: Saigono Gozenkaigi (Writings of Prince Konoe: The Last Council in the Imperial Presence)." *Jiyu Kokumin* (February 15, 1946): 1–55.

_____. *Konoe Nikki (Diary of Konoe)*. Tokyo: Kyodo Tsushinsha, 1968.

_____. *Konoe Shusho Enjutsu Shu (The Collection of Prime Minister Konoe Fumimaro's Speeches)*. Tokyo: Tokyo First, 1939.

_____. *The Memoir of Prince Fumimaro Konoe*. Tokyo: Asahi Shinbunsha, 1945.

_____. *Nihonni Yobikakeru / Konoe Fumimaro (Appealing to Japan / Konoe Fumimaro)*. Tokyo: Konnichino Modaisha, 1937.

_____. "Pariyori (From Paris) Part I." *Taiyo* (August, 1919): 164–170.

_____. "Pariyori (From Paris) Part II." *Taiyo* (September, 1919): 142–147.

_____. "Saigo no Gozenkaigi" (The Last Imperial Conference). *Juyo Kokumin*, Vol. 19 (February 15, 1946): 1–55.

_____. *Seidanroku (The Talks on Politics)*. Tokyo: Chikura Shobo, 1936.

_____. "Shin Nihon no Sugata o Shimese (Show What New Japan Is)." *Bungei Shunju* (September, 1934): 118–123.

_____. "Toyo Teki Honno (Oriental Instinct)." *Nihon Hyoron* (August, 1939): 16–19.

_____. *Ushinawareshi Seiji: Konoe Fumimaro kao no Shuki (Lost Politics: Writings of Konoe Fumimaro)*. Tokyo: Asahi Shinbunsha, 1946.

_____. "Waga Henreki Jidai (Period of My Journey)." *Bungei Shunju* (September, 1933): 193–195.

Koo, V. K. Wellington. *The Manchurian Question: China's Case Against Japan: The Geneva Debates Between Dr. K. V. Wellington and Mr. Yosuke Matsuoka*. Peiping: The Northeastern Affairs Research Institutes, 1933.

League of Nations— Delegation from Japan. *Japanese Case as Presented Before the Special Session of the Assembly of the League of Nations*. Geneva: League of Nations, 1933.

Matsuoka, Yosuke. *An Address on Manchuria, Its Past and Present*. Westport, CT: Greenwood, 1969. (Reprint from Matsuoka address titled "Problems of the Pacific" in the Proceedings of the Third Conference of the Institute of Pacific Relations held at Nara and Kyoto, Japan, from October 29 to November 9, 1929.)

_____. "Dissolve the Political Parties." *Contemporary Japan* (March, 1934): 661–667.

_____. *Hijojini Saishi Zenkokumin ni Uuttaeru: Ikkoku Ittoron, Seito Kaishuron (In a Time of Crisis, Appealing to a Nation: A Theory of One Nation/One Party and a Theory of Improvement of Party Politics)*. Tokyo: Bunmeisha, 1934.

_____. *Japan's Case in the Sino-Japanese Dispute, as Presented Before the Assembly of the League of Nations, at the Final Meeting on the Subject by His Excellency*. New York: Japan's Chamber of Commerce of New York, 1933.

Misuzu Shobo. *Gendaishi Shiryo: Nichu Senso (Documents on Contemporary History: Sino–Japanese War)*. 3 Vols. Tokyo: Misuzu Shobo, 1964.

_____. *Gendaishi Shiryo: Koka Sodoin (Documents on Contemporary History: National Mobilization).* Tokyo: Misuzu Shobo, 1970.

_____. *Gendaishi Shiryo: Taiheiyo Senso (Documents on Contemporary History: War in the Pacific).* 3 Vols. Tokyo: Misuzu Shobo, 1968.

Takayanagi Mitsuyoshi and Takeuchi Rizo, eds. *Dictionary of Japanese History.* Tokyo: Kadokawa Shoten, 1966.

Ugaki Kazushige. *Ugaki Nikki (Ugaki Diary).* Tokyo: Asahi Shinbunsha, 1954.

U.S. Department of State. *Far Eastern Series* (Doc. S1.38: 17–20). Washington, D.C.: U.S. Department of State, 1981.

Yomei Bunko. *Konoe Fumimaro-ko Kankei Shiryo Mokuroku (A List of Documents Related to Prince Konoe Fumimaro).* Kyoto: Yomei Bunko, 1961.

SECONDARY SOURCES (BOOKS)

Akagi, Suruki. *Konoe Shintaisei to Taisei Yokusankai (Konoe's New Structure and the National Service Association).* Tokyo: Iwanami Shoten, 1984.

Arima, Yoritake. *Yujin Konoe.* Tokyo: Kobundo, 1949.

Beard, Charles A. *President Roosevelt and the Coming of the War, 1941: A Study in Appearances and Realities.* New Haven, Conn.: Yale University Press, 1948.

Berger, Gordon M. *The Search for a New Political Order: Konoe Fumimaro, the Political Parties, and Japanese politics During the Early Showa Era.* Indiana: Bloomington: University, 1972.

Berger, Marie-Claire. *Sun Yat-sen.* Stanford, Calif.: Stanford University Press, 1994.

Boyle, John Hunter. *China and Japan at War, 1937–1945: The Politics of Collaboration.* Stanford, Calif.: Stanford University Press, 1972.

Brown, Allan Robert. *The Figurehead Role of the Japanese Emperor: Perception and Reality.* Ann Arbor, Mich.: University Microfilms, 1972.

Browne, Courtney. *Tojo: The Last Banzai.* New York: Holt, Rinehart and Winston, 1967.

Bunker, Gerald E. *The Peace Conspiracy: Wang Ching-wei and the China War, 1937–1941.* Cambridge, Mass.: Harvard University Press, 1972.

Ch'i, Hsi-sheng. *Nationalist China at War: Military Defeats and Political Collapse, 1939–1945.* Ann Arbor: The University of Michigan Press, 1982.

Connors, Lesley. *The Emperor's Adviser: Saionji Kinmochi and Prewar Japanese Politics.* London: Croom Helm, 1987.

Doemecke, Justus D. *When the Wicked Rise: American Opinion-Makers and the Manchurian Crisis of 1931–1933.* Lewisburg, Pa.: Bucknell University Press, 1984.

Esthus, Raymond A. *American Policies Toward Japan: 1937–1941 with Particular Reference to the Diplomacy of Ambassador Joseph C. Grew.* Durham, N.C.: Duke University Press, 1951.

Finn, Richard B. *Winners in Peace: MacArthur, Yoshida, and Postwar Japan.* Berkeley: University of California Press, 1992.

Fletcher, William Miles, III. *The Search for a New Order: Intellectuals and Fascism in Prewar Japan.* Chapel Hill: The University of North Carolina Press, 1982.

Hashimoto, Tetsuo. *Nichibei Kosho Hiwa (Secret of U.S.-Japan Negotiations).* Tokyo: Shiunso Press, 1946.

Hattori, Nobuaki. *Historical Background of Tojo Regime.* Tokyo: Hakuyosha, 1949.

Heinrichs, Jr., Waldo H. *American Ambassador Joseph C. Grew and the Development of the United States Diplomatic Tradition.* Boston: Little, Brown and Company, 1966.

Hinton, Harold B. *Cordell Hull: A Biography.* New York: Doubleday, Doran, 1942.

Hosoya, Chihiro, and Oohata Tokushiro. *Taiheiyo Senso e no Michi (The Road to the Pacific War).* Tokyo: Asahi Shinbunsha, Vol. 5, 1963.

Hoyt, Edwin P. *Warlord: Tojo Against the World*. Lanham, Md.: Scarborough House, 1993.

Iriye, Akira. *After Imperialism: The Search for a New Order in the Far East, 1921–1931*. Chicago: Imprint, 1990.

_____. *The Origins of the Second World War in Asia and the Pacific*. London and New York: Longman, 1987.

Ireye, Akira, and Warren Cohen, eds. *American, Chinese and Japanese: Perspectives on Wartime Asia, 1931–1949*. Wilmington, Del.: Scholarly Resources, 1990.

Kiya, Ikusaburo. *Konoe-ko Hibun (The Secret Story of Prince Konoe)*. Wakayama-ken: Kyosan Shuppankai, 1950.

Kutakov, Leonid N. *Japanese Foreign Policy on the Eve of the Pacific War: A Soviet View*. Tallahassee, Fla.: The Diplomatic Press, 1972.

Hane, Mikiso. *Modern Japan: A Historical Survey*. San Francisco: Westview Press, 1992.

Large, Stephen S., ed. *Showa Japan: Political, Economic and Social History, 1926–1989*. London: Routledge, Vol. 1, 1998.

Matsuura, Masataka. *Nichu Sensoki ni Okeru Keizai to Seiji: Konoe Fumimaro to Ikeda Seihin (Economy and Politics in the Sino–Japanese War: Konoe Fumimaro and Ikeda Seihin)*. Tokyo: Tokyo Daigaku Shuppankai, 1995.

Meador, Prentice. *War-time Speeches of Cordell Hull, Secretary of State*. Urbana: University of Illinois Press, 1964.

Morley, James William, ed. *Deterrent Diplomacy: Japan, Germany, and the USSR, 1935–1940*. New York: Columbia University Press, 1970.

Nagao, Kazuro. *Konoe Fumimaro no Jidai (Era of Konoe Fumimaro)*. Tokyo: Tokyo Shuppan, 1982.

Nakagawa, Yatsuhiro. *Konoe Fumimaro to Ruzuveruto: Dai Toa Senso no Shinjitsu (Konoe Fumimaro and Roosevelt: The Truth of the Great East Asian War)*. Tokyo: PHP Kenkyujo, 1995.

Nakamura, Kikuo. *Showa Seijishi (Political History of Showa)*. Tokyo: Keio Tsushin, 1958.

Nakamura, Masanori. *The Japanese Monarchy, 1931–1991 Ambassador Joseph Grew and the Making of the "Symbol Emperor System."* New York: M. E. Sharpe, 1992.

Nakamura, Takafusa. *A History of Showa Japan, 1926–1989*. Tokyo: University of Tokyo Press, 1998.

Nihon, Seiji Gakkai. *Konoe Shintaisei no Kenkyu (Study of Konoe's New Structure)*. Tokyo: Iwanami Shoten, 1973.

Nishi, Toshio. *Unconditional Democracy: Education and Politics in Occupied Japan, 1945–1952*. Stanford, Calif.: Hoover Institution Press, 1982.

Noyori, Hideichi. *Konoe Naikaku Shutsugen ni Atarite (Regarding the Birth of the Konoe Cabinet)*. Tokyo: Nichi Nichi Shinbunsha, 1937.

Ohashi, Tadaichi. *The Cause of the Pacific War: Truth of Matsuoka Diplomacy*. Tokyo: Kaname Shobo, 1952.

Oka, Yoshitake. *Konoe Fumimaro: A Political Biography*. New York: Madison Books, 1992.

_____. *Konoe Fumimaro: "Unmei no Seijika" (Konoe Fumimaro: "A Destined Politician")*. Tokyo: Iwanami Shoten, 1994.

Okada, Takeo. *Konoe Fumimaro: Tenno to Gunbi to Kokumin (Konoe Fumimaro: Emperor, Military and Nation)*. Tokyo: Shunjusha, 1959.

Pratt, Julius W. *The American Secretaries of State and Their Diplomacy: Cordell Hull 1933–1944*. Vols. 12 and 13. New York: Cooper Square, 1964.

Saito, Ryoe. *Azamukareta Rekishi: Matsuoka to Sangoku Domei no Rinen (Deceived History: Matsuoka and Reasoning of the Tripartite Alliance)*. Tokyo: Yomiuri Shinbunsha, 1955.

Scholarly Resources Inc. *Guide to the Microfilm Edition of the Supreme Commander for The Allied Powers: Historical Monographs, 1945–1951.* Wilmington, Del.: Scholarly Resources, 1989.

Shima, Yasuhiko, and Arai Shinichi. *History of Japan: Modern.* Tokyo: Iwanami Koza, Vol. 21, 1965.

Shinchosha. *Matsuoka Yosuke: Higekino Gaikokan (Matsuoka Yosuke: A Tragic Diplomat).* Tokyo: Shinchosha, 1979.

Togawa, Isamu. *Konoe Fumimaro to Jushintachi (Konoe Fumimaro and Ministers).* Tokyo: Kodansha, 1982.

Towell, William P. *Cognitive Complexity of a Foreign Decision-Maker Under Conditions of Rising Threat: Joseph C. Grew and U.S.–Japan Relations, 1938–1941.* Urbana: University of Illinois Press, 1975.

Toyoda, Minoru. *Matsuoka Yosuke: Unmei no Gaikokan (Matsuoka Yosuke: A Destined Diplomat).* Tokyo: Shinchosha, 1983.

Tsunoda, Jun, and Fukuda Shigeo. *Taiheiyo Senso e no Michi: Nichibei Kaisen (The Road to the Pacific War: The Outbreak of the Japanese-American War).* Tokyo: Asahi Shinbunsha, Vol. 7, 1963.

Utley, Jonathan G. *Going to War with Japan, 1937–1941.* Knoxville: The University of Tennessee Press, 1985.

Yabe, Teiji. *Konoe Fumimaro.* Tokyo: Jiji Tsushinsha, 1958.

Yamaura, Kanichi, ed. *Mori Kaku.* Tokyo: Editorial Committee of Mori Kaku Biography, 1941.

Yatsugi, Kazuo. *Tojo Hideki and His Era.* Tokyo: Santen Shobo, 1981.

Newspapers

Japan Times. 1937–1945   *New York Times.* 1937–1945   *Asahi Shinbun.* 1937–1945

Articles in Japanese

Abe, Kenichi. "Torai no Shin Seiji Taisei to Sono Ninmu (This New Political Structure and Its Task)." *Kaizo* (July, 1940): 45–53.

Abe, Shinnosuke. "Baba Naiso no Ichi (Position of Home Minister Baba)." *Kaizo* (July, 1937): 54–61.

_____. "Konoe Fumimaro Ron (A View on Konoe Fumimaro)." *Bungei Shunju* (July, 1937): 172–178.

Adachi, Gan. "Kokumin Saihensei Undo no Sobyo (Assessment of the Movement for Regrouping a Nation)." *Nihon Hyoron* (December, 1938): 183–191.

Arima, Yoriyasu, and Kiyoshi Miki. "Taidan: Shin Seiji Taisei (Talk: New Political Structure)." *Kaizo* (August 20, 1940): 62–90.

Ayusawa, Iwao. "Beikoku no Sekai Seisaku (U.S. World Policy)." *Kaizo* (August, 1941): 291–303.

Baba, Tsunego. "Kanryo Seiji Ron (A View on Bureaucratic Politics)." *Chuo Koron* (January, 1937): 155–162.

_____. "Konoe Fumimaro Ron (A View on Konoe Fumimaro)." *Chuo Koron* (December, 1933): 162–168.

_____. "Konoe Fumimaro Ron (A View on Konoe Fumimaro)." *Kaizo* (July, 1940): 70–78.

_____. "Konoe-ko to Kizokuin (Prince Konoe and the House of Peers)." *Kaizo* (February, 1931): 152–157.

_____. "Konoe-ko to Shinto (Prince Konoe and Shinto)." *Chuo Koron* (December, 1938): 228–235.

_____. "Konoe Naikaku no Shorai (Future of Konoe Cabinet)." *Chuo Koron* (November, 1938): 38–45.

_____. "Konoe Naikaku Ron (A View on Konoe Cabinet)." *Kaizo* (July, 1937): 100–107.

Fujimura, Toru. "Showa Kenkyukai no Keizai Seisaku (The Economic Policies of Showa Study Association)." *Showa Dojin* (November–December, 1967): 14–19.

Fujita, Shozo. "Tennosei to Fuashizumu (The Emperor System and Fascism)." Iwanami Yujiro, ed. *Iwanami Kozo: Gendai Shiso.* V. Tokyo: Iwanami Shoten, 1957: 153–187.

Goto, Isamu. "Naikaku Kaizo to Konoe-ko no Seijika Seishin (Restructure of Cabinet and Prince Konoe's Political Spirit)." *Kaizo* (January 2, 1941): 216–220.

_____. "Shintaisei to Taisei Yokusankai (New Structure and Taisei Yokusankai)." *Kaizo* (December, 1940): 251–255.

_____. "Shintaisei Undo no Doko (Direction of New Structure Movement)." *Kaizo* (July, 1940): 79–83.

Goto, Ryunosuke. "Konoe Fumimaro o Kataru (Talk on Konoe Fumimaro)." *Koen* (December 15, 1968): 1–34.

_____, and Goto Fumio. "Taisei Yokusankai." *Keizai Orai* (November, 1967): 166–179.

_____, and G. Richard Storry. "Konoe-ko ni tsuite Kataru (Talk on Prince Konoe)." *Showa Dojin* (1959): 5–12.

Hara, Katsu. "Nishi o Meguru Rekyo no Shin Gaiko Sen (New Diplomatic Battles Among the Posers Over Japan and China)." *Chuo Koron* (August, 1937): 60–69.

Hara, Yuzo. "Konoe Naikaku no Kihon Seiko (Fundamental Policy of Konoe Cabinet)." *Daiyamondo* (August, 1940): 9–10.

Hayashi, Shigeru. "Nihon Fusashizumu no Seiji Katei, I (Political Process of Japanese Fascism, I)." *Shiso* (August, 1953): 919–932.

_____. "Nihon Fusashizumu no Seiji Katei, II (Political Process of Japanese Fascism, II)." *Shiso* (September, 1953): 1085–1102.

_____. "Seito wa dokoe iku yo? (Where Are Political Parties Going?)." *Jiyu* (February, 1938): 44–50.

Hayashi, Hirokichi. "Shin Seiji Taisei no Koso (An Idea of New Political Structure)." *Kaizo* (September, 1940): 14–21.

Hisayama, Yoshio. "Konoe-Hiranuma Sujiku (Essence of Konoe and Hiranuma)." *Nihon Hyoron* (May, 1939): 154–159.

Horie, Tomoichi. "Hoku Shi Jihen no Keizai teki Haikei (Economic Background of North China Incident)." *Chuo Koron* (September, 1937): 37–50.

Hosoya, Chihiro. "Nichibei Gaiko ni okeru Fushin no Tanjo (Birth of Distrust in U.S.-Japan Diplomacy)." *Chuo Koron* (November, 1978): 66–79.

Imanaka, Tsugimaro. "O Seiken no Seiritsu to Jihen Shori no Shin Dankai (Establishment of Chiang Regime and New Level of China Incident Settlement)." *Chuo Koron* (April, 1940): 134–142.

Inahara, Katsuji. "Sangoku Joyaku to Beikoku no Ugoki (The Tripartite Pact and U.S. Reaction)." *Kaizo* (November, 1940): 224–231.

Ishi, Kinichiro. "Kita Ikki to Seinen Shoko (Kita Ikki and Young Officers)." *Shiso* (February, 1958): 59–74.

Ishida, Takeshi. "Fashizumu-ki ni okeru Kanryo-teki Shihai no Tokushitsu (Merit of Structure of Bureaucracy in Era of Fascism)." *Shiso* (December, 1953): 1446–1466.

Ishihara, Koichiro. "Sangoku Domei to Towa Kyowa Ken (The Tripartite Pact and East Asia Co-Prosperity)." *Kaizo* (November, 1940): 96–107.

Ishimitsu, Tomoyuki. "Fasho Sensen no Hajo (Break of Fascist Front Line)." *Nihon Hyoron* (January, 1937): 34–41.

Iwabuchi, Tatsuo. "Konoe and Kido." *Sekai Bunka* (January, 1946): 37–46.

_____. "Konoe-ko to Nichibei Kosho (Prince Konoe and U.S.-Japan Negotiation)." *Genron* (January, 1946): 31–39.

_____. "Konoe Naikaku to Gikai (Konoe Cabinet and the Diet)." *Kaizo* (February, 1941): 146–151.

_____. "Seiji to Gunbu (Politics and Military)." *Chuo Koron* (February, 1941): 97–108.

_____, and Mitsugu Saito. "Seikai Yowa (5): Konoe Fumimaro to Kido Koichi (Konoe Fumimaro and Kido Koichi)." *Nonso* (July, 1962): 170–181.

Kajima, Noboru. "Seijika Konoe no Shuso Shintai (A Course of Action of Politician Konoe as Prime Minister)." *Chuo Koron* (November, 1970): 112–119.

Kawakami, Jotaro. "Konoe Naikaku to Shinto Mondai (Konoe Cabinet and New Party Question)." *Kaizo* (May, 1938): 133–139.

Kazami, Akira. "Konoe Fumimaro-shi o Megute (A View on Konoe Fumimaro)." *Bungei Shunju* (November, 1949): 56–67.

Kitagawa, Kazuo. "Shintaisei, Shinnaikaku to Zaikai (New Structure, New Cabinet, and the Financial World)." *Kaizo* (September, 1940): 184–191.

Kiyosawa, Retsu. "Nichi Doku Kyotei no Kikensei (Risk of the Japan-Germany Alliance)." *Nihon Hyoron* (January, 1937): 52–64.

Kuroda, Kaku. "Taisei Yokusan Undo no Goken Hosei (Legality of the Movement of the National Service Association)." *Kaizo* (January, 1941): 55–70.

Kushima, Kensabro. "Sangoku Domei to Ni So Kankei (The Tripartite Pact and the Russo-Japanese Relationship)." *Kaizo* (November, 1940): 288–295.

Kusuyama, Yoshitaro. "Sangoku Domei to Ei-Bei Gasaku (The Tripartite Pact and the U.S.-British Alliance)." *Kaizo* (November, 1940): 114–121.

Minobe, Tatsukichi. "Waga Gikai Seido no Zento (Future of Our Diet Politics)." *Chuo Koron* (January, 1934): 2–14.

Mitani, Taichiro. "Kyutei Seijika no Ronri to Kodo (Thoughts and Behavior of Royal Court Politicians)." *Sekai* (October, 1966): 190–195.

Miyazawa, Toshiyoshi. "Taisei Yokusankai Undo no Horiteki Seikaku (Legal Character of Taisei Yokusankai)." *Kaizo*, XXIII. 1 (January 1, 1941): 112 – 128.

Mori, Tohei. "Konoe Naikaku no Jinbutsu (Personalities of Konoe Cabinet)." *Kaizo* (September, 1940): 178–183.

Muroto, Kenzo. "Kyokoku Shintaisei no Koso (A Plan of New National Structure)." *Chuo Koron* (August, 1940): 80–93.

Nakamura, Tetsu. "Nipon teki Keitai ni okeru Koka to To (Japanese-Style Nation and Political Party)." *Kaizo* (July, 1941): 42–56.

Nakano, Tomio. "Nippon Yokusan Taisei (The Yokusan Structure of Japan)." *Kaizo* (January 14, 1941): 12–16.

Oota, Unosuke. "Hokuchi Jihen ga Okoru made (Until the North China Incident)." *Chuo Koron* (August, 1937): 48–50.

Ozaki, Hidemi. "Hoku Shi Jihen (North China Incident)." *Kaizo* (August, 1937): 94–101.

_____. "Nanjin Seif Ron (A View on the Nanjin Government)." *Chuo Koron* (September, 1937): 23–35.

Sakanishi, Rihachiro. "Shin Seifu Juritsu no Igi (Significance of Establishment of New Government)." *Chuo Koron* (April, 1940): 129–133.

Sasaki, Soichi. "Seiji Taisei no Seibi to Shin Seito Undo (Consolidation of Political Structure and Movement of New Political Party)." *Kaizo* (August, 1940): 102–119.

_____. "Taisei Yokusankai to Kenpo-jo no Ronten (Issues of Taisei Yokusankai and the Constitution)." *Kaizo* (February, 1941): 8–48.

_____. "Waga Gikai Seiji no Sai-ginmi (Re-examination of Our Diet Politics)." *Kaizo* (January, 1932): 2–37.

Sato, Kenryo. "Atarashi Kokumin Undo e no Taibo (Expectations for New National Movement)." *Kakushin* (November, 1938): 44–52.

Sekiguchi, Tai. "Nikaku Kaizo to Yokusankai Kaiso (Restructuring Cabinet and Remolding Yokusankai)." *Kaizo* (May, 1941): 114–121.

Sugiyama, Heisuke. "Konoe-ko no Seijisei (Political Nature of Prince Konoe)." *Chuo Koron* (August, 1940): 102–110.

_____. "Matsuoka Gaiso Ron (A View on Foreign Minister Matsuoka)." *Kaizo* (November, 1940): 232–250.

Sugimura, Kojiro. "Konoe-ko ni Nozomu (Expectations of Prince Konoe)." *Nihon Hyoron* (August, 1940): 12–17.

Suzuki, Yasuzo. "Yokusan Gikai to wa nani ka? (What Is the Yokusan Diet?)." *Kaizo* (February, 1941): 72–82.

Suzuki, Yosabro. "Hoku Shi no Kenaku ka (Deterioration of North China)." *Kaizo* (August, 1937): 102–110.

Takami, Hiroshi. "Matsuoka-Starin Kaiken (Matsuoka-Stalin Conference)." *International Academic Association Report* (April, 1941): 117–122.

Takemura, Tadao. "Do So Kaisen to Nichi Bei Kankei (Outbreak of the Russo-German War and the U.S.-Japan Relationship)." *Kaizo* (Jikyoku Ban) (July, 1941): 266–279.

Tanaka, Sogoro. "Konoe Fumimaro." *Kaizo* (January, 1941): 89–101.

_____. "Taisei Yokusankai: Nihon-teki Fuashizumu no Shocho to Shite (Taisei Yokusankai: As a Symbol of Japanese Fascism)." *Rekishigaku Kenkyu* (October, 1957): 1–14.

Teraike, Kiyoshi. "Konoe Naikaku to Gunbu to Seito (Konoe Cabinet, Military, and Political Party)." *Kaizo* (July, 1937): 93–99.

_____. "Shin-seito Undo no Tenbo (Expectations for New Party Movement)." *Kaizo* (March, 1937): 259–267.

Tsukui, Tatsuo. "Shintaisei o Habamumono (Obstruction to New Structure)." *Chuo Koron* (August, 1940): 94–101.

Tsumura, Hedematsu. "Gaiko no Shisaku (Diplomatic Failure)." *Nihon Hyoron* (January, 1937): 215–219.

Uchida, Shigetaka. "Nippon Seiji no Shin-tenkai (New Turn of Japanese Politics)." *Kaizo* (May, 1941): 34–43.

Yabe, Teiji. "Atarashi Seiji Taisei to wa (What the New Political Structure Is)." *Shukan Asahi* (July 14, 1940).

_____. "Konoe Fumimaro Iko Kaisetsu (Interpretating Konoe's View)." *Kaizo* (December, 1949): 37–38.

_____. "Konoe Fumimaro to Kido Koichi (Konoe Fumimaro and Kido Koichi)." *Chuo Koron* (January, 1940): 62–68.

_____. "Konoe Fumimaro to Shintaisei (Konoe Fumimaro and New Structure)." *Chuo Koron* (January, 1965): 429–435.

Yamakawa, Hitoshi. "Konoe Naikaku no Meirosei (Clarity of Konoe Cabinet)." *Bungei Shunju* (July, 1937): 52–59.

_____. "Konoe Naikaku Shutsugen no Igi (Meaning of Forming Konoe Cabinet)." *Kaizo* (July, 1937): 76–84.

_____. "Nichi Doku Kyotei to Sono Hajo (Japan-Germany Alliance and Its Consequence)." *Nihon Hyoron* (January, 1937): 65–74.

Yamaura, Kanichi. "Konoe, Arima, Kazami, to Shin To (Konoe, Arima, Kazami and New Party)." *Kaizo* (July, 1940): 54–61.

_____. "Konoe Fumimaro Jikyoku Dan (Talk on Konoe's Situation)." *Kaizo* (May, 1936): 60–69.

_____. "Konoe-ko wa Naze Shutsuba Shinakataka (Why Did Not Konoe Run for Election?)." Chuo Koron (February, 1940): 38–41.

_____. "Konoe Naikaku wa Kakushite Umareta (This is How the Konoe Cabinet Was Formed)." *Kaizo* (July, 1937): 85–92.

_____. "Konoe Shui no Hentai (Changes in Konoe's Surroundings)." *Kaizo* (November, 1938): 116–120.

Yoshioka, Bunroku. "Konoe Naikaku to Tai Shi Gaiko (Konoe Cabinet and Foreign Diplomacy Toward China)." *Gaikojiho* (July, 1937): 40–48.

ARTICLES IN ENGLISH

Adams, Frederick C. "The Road to Pearl Harbor: A Reexamination of American Far Eastern Policy, July 1937–December 1938," *JAH* 58 (1971): 73–92.

Anderson, Irvine H., Jr. "The 1941 De facto Embargo on Oil to Japan: A Bureaucratic Reflex." *PHR* 44 (1975): 201–31.

Baba, Tsunego. "Hirota's Renovation Plans." *Contemporary Japan* (September, 1936): 166–177.

_____. "Reconstruction of Political Parties." *Contemporary Japan* (May, 1940): 618–620.

Board of Planning. "On the National Mobilization Law." *Tokyo Gazette* (May, 1938): 1–9.

Butow, Robert J. C. "Hull–Nomura Conversation: A Fundamental Misconception." *American Historical Review* 55 (1960): 822–36.

Cho, Yukio. "From the Showa Economic Crisis to Military Economy." *The Developing Economies* (December, 1967): 568–596.

Clauss, Errol MacGregor. "The Roosevelt Administration and Manchukuo, 1933–1941." *The Historian* 32 (1970): 595–611.

Conroy, Hilary. "Nomura Kichisaburo: The Diplomacy of Frama and Desperation." In *Diplomats in Crisis United States-Chinese-Japanese Relations, 1919–1941.* Edited by Richard and Dean Burns and Edward M. Bennett. Santa Barbara, Calif.: ABC-Clio, 1974: 297–316.

Crowley, James B. "Japanese Army Factionalism in the Early 1930s." *Journal of Asian Studies* (May, 1962): 309–326.

Duus, Peter. "Nagai Ryutaro and the White Peril, 1905–1944." *Journal of Asian Studies* (November, 1971): 41–48.

_____. "Nagai Ryutaro: The Tactical Dilemmas of Reform." *In Personality in Japanese History.* Edited by Albert M. Craig and Donald H. Shively. Berkeley: University of California Press, 1970: 399–424.

Esthus, Raymond A. "President Roosevelt's Commitment to Britain to Intervene in a Pacific War." *MVHR* 50 (1963): 28–38.

Fisher, Galen M. "The Cooperative Movement in Japan." *Pacific Affairs* (December, 1983): 478–491.

Fujii, Shinichi. "The Cabinet, the Diet, and the Taisei Yokusankai." *Contemporary Japan* (April, 1941): 487–498.

Funata, Chu. "Outlines of the New Political Party," *Contemporary Japan* (August, 1940): 994–1003.

Furusawa, Isojiro. "The Wartime Non-Party Diet." *Contemporary Japan* (April, 1941): 461–476.

Furuta, Tokujiro. "The Late Prince Saionji and the Genro System." *Contemporary Japan*, (January, 1941): 64–70.

Hara, Yuzo. "More Is Expected of Konoe Cabinet than Preceding Regime." *Contemporary Japan* (August, 1940): 1–3.

Herzog, James H. "Influence of the United States Navy in the Embargo of Oil to Japan, 1940–1941." *PHR* 35 (1966): 317–328.

Hoshi, Yama. "Konoe Pins Much Hope to Future of Throne." *Contemporary Japan* (October 31, 1940).

Hoshino, Masao. "General Election Next Year and the New Political Order." *Contemporary Opinion* (November, 1940): 12–14.

Hosoya, Chihiro. "Miscalculations in Deterrent Policy: Japanese-U.S. Relations, 1938–1941." *Journal of Peace Research* 5 (1968): 97–115.

_____. "The Tripartite Pact, 1939–1940." In *Deterrent Diplomacy: Japan, Germany and the USSR, 1935–1940.*" Edited by James W. Morely. New York: Columbia University Press, 1976: 191–257.

Iriye, Akira. "The Role of the United States Embassy in Tokyo." In *Pearl Harbor as History: Japanese-American Relations, 1931–1941.* Edited by Dorothy Borg and Shumpei Okamoto. New York: Columbia University Press, 1973: 107–126.

Iwabuchi, Tatsuo. "Prince Fumimaro Konoe." *Contemporary Japan* (December, 1936): 365–376).

Kada, Tetsuji. "The Theory of an East Asiatic Unity." *Contemporary Japan* (July, 1939): 574–581.

Koellreutter, Otto. "National Socialism and Japan." *Contemporary Japan* (April, 1939): 194–202.

Kuhara, Fusanosuke. "The Basis for a New Party." *Contemporary Japan* (July, 1940): 811–817.

Nagata, Tetsuji. "New Political Party Still Object of Many Leaders." *Contemporary Opinion* (February 25, 1937): 19–20.

Narita, Tetsuo. "Inukai Tsuyochi: Some Dilemmas in Party Development in Pre–World War II Japan." *American Historical Review* (December, 1968): 492–510.

Ogata, Taketora. "Behind Japan's Greater Cabinet." *Contemporary Japan* (December, 1937): 378–388.

_____. "Whither the Political Parties?" *Contemporary Japan* (June, 1937): 8–17.

Ozaki, Hotsumi. "The New National Structure." *Contemporary Japan* (October, 1940): 1284–1292.

Pratt, Julius W. "The Ordeal of Cordell Hull, *Review of Politics* 28 (1966): 76–98.

Welles, Sumner. "Roosevelt and the Far East." *Harpers* (Feb.–Mar., 1951): 27–38 and 70–80.

Index